Scope and Aim
The Naked Philosopher
as
The Intuitive Self

Balkrishna Naipaul's aim in *The Naked Philosopher as The Intuitive Self* is to clear up muddled confusion about how philosophers arrive at philosophy; philosophers should not concern themselves so much with what is actually happening; their proper concern is with what is possible, or conceivable, which comes together after long contemplation, from where arises the Intuitive Self. Once this emergence is grasped, it is then examined against concepts and the manner in which they fit together as seen in the rules of language and of grammar. However, the rules of language from the Western viewpoint is limited because its ongoing misunderstanding of uses of words based on forms of expression. For this reason, emphasis is put on the origins of language pertaining to Hindu linguistics, which has much to do with sound, and spontaneous recognition of vowels that give meaning to words that flow into sentences. From this angle, Western philosophy is examined, and a gradual understanding is shown how much western philosophy owes both its origins and ongoing quest to Hindu philosophy.

The Naked Philosopher
As
The Intuitive Self

The Naked Philosopher

The Intuitive Self

The Naked Philosopher
As
The Intuitive Self

By

Balkrishna Naipaul

The Naked Philosopher as The Intuitive Self
Copyright © 2015 by Balkrishna Naipaul.
All Rights Reserved
Cover design by Global Publications
National Library of Canada Cataloguing in Publications
ISBN 978-0-9878000-3-9
Naipaul, Balkrishna Maharagh, 1940.

A work of nonfiction: based on scholarly works on epistemology, etymology, ontology, linguistics, Hindu philosophy, philosophy of language, Vedanta, Advaita Vedanta.

All rights reserved. No part of this book may be reproduced or transmitted in any form or by any means, electronic or mechanical, including photocopying, recording, or by any information storage and retrieval system, without permission in writing from the copyright owner.
 This is a work of nonfiction. Names, characters, places and incidents either are the product of the author's travels, incidental meetings or in conversations or are used in a historical context, and any resemblance to any actual persons, living or dead, events, or locales is entirely coincidental.
Published in Canada by Global Publications and in USA by CreateSpace.

.

Also by Balkrishna Naipaul

FICTION:

SANGAM: The Jhansi Legacy

Dancing Moon Under The Peepal Tree

The Mansion

The Other Side of The House

Suwan and The Circle of Seven

The Yoga of Love

Legends of The Emperor's Ring

Arc On The Horizon

POETRY:
Finding the Voice

Dedication

For my adopted Son, Sachin

Whose penetrating questions always seem prompted by The Intuitive Self

Also for my grandchildren:
Prince Pascal and Princess Saffron,

CONTENTS

1
The European Theatre of Philosophy
In Search for Meaning, Page 13

2
The Essence of Sat and Existence as they relate to Consciousness, Page 99

3
The Advaitin's Way:
Ganesha Chaturthi As
The Gateway to Consciousness, Page 157

4
Śabda, Page 219

5
Philosophy of Language
Within a Hindu Context, Page 281

6
Glossary, Page 351

The European Theatre
In
Search of Meaning

The European Philosophical Theatre In Search of Meaning

I believe that the first time philosophy came to me happened in my thirteenth year while defending an essay I had written for my form two junior college master: I was challenged to prove a point I had raised in my essay that the Catholic Church was corrupt from its very inception. It was a minor point stated in parenthesis, but the master took me up to the principal of the college, who was a Catholic priest. The priest demanded that I either remove the parenthesis or prove it without a doubt. All I had at my disposal in my small Indian village community in Trinidad was my personal copy of A History of Europe by H.A.L. Fisher, which was also the required history text book used by the entire school. However, there was a reference to Spinoza's Political Treatise in the book, which gave me some hope. Baruch Spinoza's philosophy was dear to one of my uncles who was the Island's only Indian journalist at the time; and, after reading through my essay he took down a worn volume from among his collection of favourite books and showed me Spinoza's Theological–Political Treatise.

Among other things, I was struck by what Spinoza referred to as "bibliolatria", the idolatry of the book, or an image contained in the book. This struck hard against what I was told by Church authority that governed my school, or what we were urged to accept vis-à-vis Hindu and JudoChristian belief system: that, while Hindus worshipped a plurality of gods, there was no idol worship among either Jews or Christians. Spinoza's idea of Bibliolatry was not just a wild strike against Christianity, but for me it had struck directly into the heart of Biblical inerrancy; the belief that the Bible is perfect, "without error or fault in all its teachings" (1).

To begin with, Spinoza denounced the belief that Moses was the author of the first five books of the Bible, which Christians call the Pentateuch and what Jews call the Torah; moreover, his analysis proved that the Bible was a compilation of texts written by many different authors and not revealed as one single continuous stream. The contention in my essay had to do with the kind of falsehood that Spinoza had condemned the Catholic Church. It also had to do with the zeal with which the Roman Catholic clergy proceeded in their mission to convert Heathens to their cause of creating Jesus Christ as God in order to establish Catholicism as the one and only true religion. In this sense, a crusade started from the inner chambers of the Papacy, which in time would reach everywhere. And, with Bible in hand that claimed the authority of God, it prompted the new adherents to group together in a zealous force, capable of taking the new Church even further than the former Roman Empire had gone, using "paganist" ideas to trap minds and souls of the unsuspecting converts (2).

It was an easy ride for the new missionaries, perhaps the first since the dawn of history to create out an army of zealous believers for the sole purpose of capturing nonbelievers of the new faith to bring all and sundry into the ironclad net into the Catholic Church. Indeed, these zealots had learnt much from the Buddhist monks, six centuries before, how to preach; but whereas the Buddhist monks preached and allowed their listeners to decide for themselves what they intend to do with the teachings of the Buddha, the Christian missionaries moved with their sword in the shape of the Cross (3).

Later, the Church, with its reformed imperial Roman army now fitted out to serve Catholicism, would first turn its attention to the expansion of Christendom and then against the Mohammedans in the Holy land, while aiming to convert or contain them even in their homelands. Of course, all of this culminated in the two-hundred year Crusade, which was achieved through what Spinoza called bibliolatry and inerrancy. Indeed, Spinoza was very clear about this, for in his *Tractatus Theologico-Politicus*, he clearly showed that where scriptures are properly understood, it 'gave no authority for the militant intolerance of the clergy who sought to stifle all dissent by the use of force.' Indeed, this use of force became the hallmark of the Church in dealing with all questions that challenged its interpretation of the Bible. In fact, any dissent became intolerable and sacrilegious, which resulted in torture and the most painful form of death. There is little doubt that it was this intolerable use of force by the clergy that caused Spinoza to condemn the Church, and all organized religions that depended on "institutionalized interpretation of scriptures", which he said in Chapter 12, "is in parts imperfect, corrupt, erroneous, and inconsistent with itself, and that we possess but fragments of it".

Stumbling upon Spinoza did not only prove useful in arguing my case at junior college but also served as a beacon of light in making sense about my own religious background: that while scriptures ought to be understood before they can claim obedience to faith, they should also be separated from the independence of philosophy. Indeed, it was here where I learnt the true meaning of Vedanta, traditionally referred to as the end of the Vedas. After all, as it were, I had been brought up with the Vedas, and although I was an ordained pundit at the age of twelve, I knew very little about Vedanta, other than the meagre idea that there was a body of knowledge appended at the end of each of the Vedas. This separate body of works called the Vedanta milked the Vedas to produce a different kind of knowledge that stands between the Vedas and the Upanishads. It is the real division between religion and philosophy, or religion and science, or religion based on faith, rather than philosophy based on enquiry by virtue of intuitive knowledge.

Another major perspective derived from reading Spinoza's *Tractatus Theologico-Politicus*, was the undisputed understanding that, unlike Christians, Jews, and Muslims, Hindus have no central scriptural text that could put them in the category of "bibliolatry". They accept all scriptures equal in value but follow that one that is equitable to their soul's calling. Which also explained for me the reason why there are so many religious sects among Hindus: each is free to worship according to the scriptures from which they give their obedience or faith. Indeed, they may follow different paths but, intuitively, they know that they would eventually arrive at the feet of the one supreme Reality: that which is above Prakriti or Nature (similar to Spinoza's cosmology of God and Nature), and known by the wise, the knower of the Vedanta, as Brahman.

At the end of each of the Vedanta, there is that collective body of knowledge known as the Upanishads. This is filtered knowledge from the raw stuff of the Vedas, derived from the wellspring of Hindu philosophy. Unlike Christian belief, it is above anything associated with pantheism or panentheism or having any likeness to what Spinoza called "bibliolatry". Here it takes the brightest of minds, with a commitment to truth to seek true knowledge that comes, not from pure reason but, from the deepest of trust in the Intuitive Self. Similar to Spinoza's critique of the Bible, it is here where Hindus come to understand that the real "word of God", or true religion, is not something written in books but "inscribed on the heart and mind of man" (4).

Of course, Spinoza's inscription had something for me with regard to separating religion from philosophy: it had the power to move religion away from blind faith and push the individual in this higher plane of consciousness to unite him with the ultimate Reality in order to make him one with God, and not subservient to God. This idea is akin to what Sri Krishna says in the Bhagavad Gita Ch. 7: 4-5: all of humanity is part of his lower nature, known as Prakriti and comprising of earth, water, fire, air, ether, mind, the intellect called buddhi, and the I-sense or ego called ahamkara. This lower nature contrasts with Krishna's higher nature known as the Purusha, which sustains the entire universe. At first, there may seem to be an artificial divide between the higher and lower, and for some it might give credence for subservience of the lower to the higher. But, on closer reading of the text, we understand that Krishna wants just the opposite. The lower, inert side is meant to be enjoyed by all as a play of consciousness, in the same way of the Rasa when Krishna dances with the cowherds to an uplifting fulfilment. Even so, just as the cowherds reach a state of bliss, in the Rasa dance with Krishna, they learn about their own higher nature in that sublime climax of discovery. In that moment, they are made new: the uniting of the lower with the higher by the unique and "exclusive sentient principle", just as souls are being created, activated and energised by an infinitesimal portion of the Supreme Lord, all creation is sustained by its own effort. As such, man is part of Sri Krishna's lower nature, not doomed to serve the absolute God but to serve man and nature in God. In this service, which comes with rising of consciousness and knowledge of the Self, man can rise up and unite with the Divine only by realization of his true self.

Indeed, there is a formula for coming to terms with the idea of Self Realization, which has nothing to do with belief, or religious rites; it is experienced in the inner working of the heart, which is the wellspring of Consciousness from where real philosophy springs forth. In this regard, reason is the enemy of philosophy; it only plays a post-prescriptive role after the Intuitive Self has grasped the "I" aspect of the inner Self, while experiencing the true nature of the individual person and its relationship with Reality. Thus, it is only when the soul or Self that realises it is part and parcel of the Reality, that Reason enters the fray of philosophy (5).

From this point onwards, philosophy becomes one of reflection and contemplation, but reason takes on the role of grammar; its purpose is to ensure that thoughts, ideas, thesis, antithesis, and synthesis, flow smoothly without corrupting the wisdom experientially gained from the knowledge obtained through the intervention of the
Intuitive Self.

From the foregoing, it is significant to observe that enlightened Hindus will say that philosophy is the highest wisdom, which is the medium between man and the Highest Reality. It is the crux or kernel of truth that comes between mundane knowledge and insights garnered from the knowledge of the Self. The corollary to this is the notion that esoteric knowledge like Advaita Vedanta cannot come purely from reason, largely because the source of this knowledge "is obtained" from neither the mind nor the intellect. Perhaps this is why Socrates always claimed that the only thing he knew with certitude is that he knows nothing; it was a popular saying among the ancient Rishis of India, too; the earliest of philosophers whose works make up the bulk of the Upanishads, within this context, as extolled in the Keno Upanishad that enquired in the existence of Brahman.

Is it possible to live without knowing anything? Obviously, India's ancient Rishis and even Socrates had something else in mind: living in that space of what Buddhists call *Śūnyatā* or emptiness, and which Hindus interpret as "Reality that ultimately transcends existence" had little to do with what western philosophers refer to as, the certainty of the void.

Within the Buddhist framework of understanding Śūnyatā it had to do with the emptiness of the world without Self and not the absolute void that western thinking attributes to Maya. In fact, Ananda, the Buddha's brother asked, "Lord, in what respect it is said that the world is empty?" The Buddha replied, "Insofar as it is empty of a self or of anything pertaining to a self." The reply falls squarely on the Buddhist notion of Pali anatta or Sanskrit "anatma", the absence of atma or soul in Buddhist cosmology as it pertains to emptiness, as a quality of Dharma (6). Even so, there still seems to be that unavoidable paradox with western interpretation of Śūnyatā, even when carried over to Hindu thought in the stark linkage to Maya or illusion. It seems to matter less that Hindus have quite another interpretation of Śūnyatā, which first arrived in Hindu mathematics when the zero (śūnya) was invented to solve complicated formulae. It is a compound word: *śūnya + ta*, which literally means "zero-ness" but which the Buddhists interpreted as "nothing-ness". However, the word has a magical potency to it as it relates to Hindu spirituality: The early sages and seers, commonly referred to as munis and rishis, used the root *svi + ta* of *śūnya + ta* to refer to a death-like state in meditation before the word for this mentally inactive state was termed *Samadhi*. From this rudimentary state, a form of meditation called Sahaja developed, long before the advent of the Vedic Age, or even before the very first Rig Veda was even heard of; its objective was to kill the mind in order for consciousness to flourish. It became the objective of Śaivism, which not only predates the Vedas but remains the most dynamic force in Hinduism today. In this sense, Śūnyatā is not a noun but a verb; it corresponds to emptying the mind in order to know the Self or the inner infinite being, known in Hindu philosophy as Brahman.

Perhaps the idea of "knowing nothing" might be another way of saying, 'to know all outside the realm of nature', which might correlate to knowing the ultimate reality. In a manner of speaking this might lead to an understanding of Spinoza's Parmenides assertion that "everything in the universe is One", which is one of the major precepts in both Saivism and Advaita Vedanta. Indeed, Spinoza held this notion very close to his knowing self: "that there is only one substance and that substance is either God or nature." Remarkably, this is a borrowed statement almost word for word from the Bhagavad Gita where Krishna says:

Etad yonini bhutani sarvani 'ty upadharaya
Aham krisnasya jagatah prabhavah pralayas tatha

'Know that my higher and lower nature are the womb of all beings; as such, while everything resides in me, few know that I am the origin and dissolution of the whole universe.' After all, like so many of the early Greek philosophers, Parmenides was no stranger to Hindu thought; he would have, at least, been exposed to Buddhist monks who were in great demand from the Ganges to Rome by the upper crust of society as unrivalled able teachers. These upper echelons of society needed their children to know more than just bread and butter issues; they wanted their children to know how things work in the universe, both intellectually and scientifically; but even more so, they wanted to know the nature of reality and the link between nature and God that is responsible for making man wise. They wanted to know the secret that frees man from his finite state and that, which makes him infinite. In effect, they were asking deep philosophical questions that Spinoza later contemplated: how to get away from the continuum of mind and body to arrive at the conclusion that "Nature or God is wholly selfcontained, self-causing, and self-sufficient". This approach to knowledge was beyond the western mind; it is the cornerstone of Advaita philosophy: that everything in the universe is not just part of God but is the aggregate whole of what Advaita Vedanta calls Brahman.

The idea of the need to know of that, which started so very early in my life, the aggregate whole of the universe is Brahman, is in itself the dividing line, between religion and philosophy. However, the evidence for this does not come from belief or reason but a natural intelligence and propensity in the human person to experience the highest reality. Indeed, the inscription that Spinoza to which related earlier in this part of this book also alluded to the idea of the importance of experiential knowledge as a necessity when separating religion from philosophy. For, if everything in the universe is the expression of the Divine or Nature – or by whatever name we choose to call it – then the upshot of this would seem to be the removal of free will from the realm of human actions. This might seem particularly relevant, especially within the purview of the western mind-set that nothing can be solved without the sharpest of logical reasoning. The significance of this can be seen within the Cartesian belief that mind and body are two different kinds of things, but which Spinoza vigorously refuted: "mind and body are just different ways of conceiving the same reality." Of course, mind has everything to do with intellect, and once the body dies everything goes. Intelligence however exists beyond mind and intellect; it is the link between the elements, as a collective, that binds the sum of nature in that order of existence, which the ancient Hindus called Cit (pronounced chit) or Consciousness. For this reason, experiential knowledge can only come from the Intuitive Self, which has nothing to do with either the mind or body but which relates to the soul; it is the gateway to the essence of life, perennially existing in the wellspring of creation. However, how one arrives at this experiential knowledge has to do with the ancient Hindu practice of Yoga, which completely nullifies the western preoccupation of either belief or logical reasoning.

I believe that Spinoza's thinking on freedom had something to do with the power of the Intuitive Self. From a Hindu point of view, it certainly has much to do with *Moksha* or Liberation. However, Spinoza's idea of freedom is flawed when compared with moksha: 'Experience tells us clearly that men believe themselves to be free simply because they are conscious of their actions and unconscious of the causes whereby these actions are determined.' The intent is there but a kind of false freedom tripped up by faulty reasoning primarily driven by ideology embedded in a politically motivated belief system. However, he would later say, "The dictates of the mind are simply another name for the appetites that vary according to the varying state of the body" (7). Within the context of Hindu thought, this exposition of Spinoza's freethinking would hardly be considered relevant to any philosophical model. Still, it is important for one particular reason, which has to do with the extent that reason remains on the far side of intuitive "inquiry". Indeed, totally feeling inadequate about what he had to say about freedom, from a philosophical point of view, he later suggested, 'Each individual is a localised concentration of the attributes of reality, a quasi-individual, since the only true individual is the universe in totality' (ibid,7).

The idea that "true individual is the universe in totality" has a qualified agreement with Advaita Vedanta, insofar as in keeping abreast of the ancient Rishis who claimed that everything in the universe is part of Brahman. But, then the Vedantic goal of Moksha or Freedom slips out of Spinoza's mind when he said, "to become free, the individual must, by means of rational reflection, understand the extended causal chain that links everything as one"(8). The error is the emphasis put on "rational reflection", which is the antithesis to the Hindu approach to inquiry. However, to grasp the significance of this, it is important to understand the pivotal role of Yoga that brings the individual or philosopher to the Intuitive Self.

 According to Patanjali, when the enquirer is in a state of yoga over a long period engaging in deep meditation and reflection, misconceptions that exist in "the mutable aspect of human beings" easily disappear (9). Under such circumstances, the mind no longer has the power over will and the Intuitive Self subtly takes over in a guiding fashion in order to create intelligence. Indeed, it is from here where the Self emerges to entail insight into our very own nature. Moreover, it is from here where misconceptions are dispelled, and from where perceptions arrive, without recourse to logical reasoning. In this regard, Patanjali outlines five types of misconceptions that the practitioner will discover in his quest to know reality. These are insight, error, imagining, deep sleep and recollection.
 Insight arises from the depths of the inner being and surfaces as "guided perceptions" through the Intuitive Self; here conclusions are "given" rather than reasoned from the intellect, which is the most reliable system of learning. By

contrast, error arises from inferior knowledge based on false mental construct due to emphasis placed solely on logical reasoning. Likewise, imagining brought about by "word knowledge" usually conveys hypothetical stuff that does not exist in real life situations. Deep sleep contrasts well with the other two states of consciousness: the waking and the dreaming states in which there is no true experiences of Reality. However, in the deep-sleep state, because the underlying ground is "undistracted", here the enquirer is enabled to know all, through the inner controller known as the Self. After all, this is the real objective of meditation, for after the practitioner has reached a certain plane of mastery, the steadfast mind, through steady tempering, slowly gives up its hold on the intellect until it dissolves in what is called Sahaja Samadhi, a state where the mind no longer exists and the Self shines supreme in Oneness with Brahman. Sahaja meditation or Sahaja Yoga is an ancient discipline in yoga that predates the Vedas; and since the oldest of the Vedas, the Rig, dates back 7000 years, Sahaja Yoga stands out as one of the oldest yoga systems known in the ancient world. However, over the millennia different names have been ascribed to Sahaja, three of which have been popularised within the last two hundred years: Laya, Kriya, and Kundalini. In fact Sahaja is associated with Śaivism, and when the meditation session culminates in Samadhi, which is a death-like state to the untrained person, the practitioner appears to be either in deep sleep or a corpse. Surprisingly however, it is from here, in this deep sleep, where the practitioner transcends the world of appearances and is enabled to recollect real Existence, so long as the rising consciousness were not eclipsed by previously learnt methods: those life experiences that are germane to all who are conditioned by traditional learning.

The immensity of awe experienced in deep sleep cannot be fully grasped from a simple narrative, and perhaps this is the reason why so many philosophers shy away from contemplating its promise as a serious philosophical construct. Indeed, Spinoza came very close to alluding to it in this thought, there is another, third kind, which we shall call intuitive knowledge. And this kind of knowing proceeds from an adequate idea of certain attributes of God to the adequate knowledge of the essence of things (10). Even so, doubt got the better of him, which caused him to say, 'we lack the understanding to see the bigger picture, the chain of causes that make all events a necessary part of divine reality' (11). True, the vision of wholeness cannot come from the limited checks and balances ingrained in pure logical thinking, except where a new language like mathematics makes use of symbols like that of the very alphabet of Sanskrit to weave a philosophy of Existence. In Sanskrit, every letter has symbolical weight largely because words only give approximate meanings. Thus mathematical-like calculations must be employed in putting together letters to form words as well as arriving at approximate meaning of both the formation of words and how they impact on other words in a sentence. For this reason, Sanskrit sentences are short, especially in treatises that relate to philosophical expressions, conveyed through aphorisms. This choice of expression has nothing to do with style; the rishis of the ancient world usually saw their thoughts and ideas floating before their very eyes even before they had any comprehension of what they intended to say, first as a chain of individual letters, during deep sleep. And, it was only after long periods of contemplation on what had appeared before them in cryptic form, did they seek to express this revealed knowledge in aphorisms. To the uninitiated, these ideas may seem encrypted and impossible to break the code that would allow others to find meaning, which is why there are so many commentaries on even the shortest of the Upanishads.

The "bigger picture" that Spinoza had alluded to in his *Tractatus Theologico-Politicus* had everything do with the structure of thought processes in Hindu philosophy, even though he may have known nothing about Hindu thought; after all, his writings came much before Arthur Schopenhauer, the man responsible for introducing the Vedas and the Upanishads into Western culture; although, as a Latin scholar he could have had seepages of Hindu influence on the Greek, which influenced Western thought. The importance of this has to do with the emphasis placed on the Upanishads by Schopenhauer without investigating the significance of language on the thought processes of the Rishis, especially as it relates to mantras.

Interestingly enough, the evolution of mantras belong to the Tantric period, which predates even the oldest of the Vedas known as the Rig. In fact most of the Rig deals with poems and hymns, while the Tantras deal with mantras, which later go on to influence much of the philosophical attributes found in the Upanishads. On the surface, this might appear contradictory, since the Upanishads were supposed to reflect the deeper teachings of the Vedas. However, the truth of the matter suggests the enormity of the influence the Tantras had on those Vedas that convey the ritualistic side of Hinduism. Indeed, this is the side Western intellectual culture confuses with Hindu philosophy, without having a clue about the significance of the evolution of ideas in the same vein as George Wilhelm Friedrich Hegel so ably made in his views on the development of ideas. Within this context of Hegel's idea that absolute truth is not propositional truth but conceptual, rises to an approximation of Tantric thought that underlines both the evolution and significance of mantra.

Indeed, mantra is germane to the idea of absolute truth in that it is the first principle of Tantric esotericism. Even so, it did not happen overnight; it took centuries to arrive at a stage where it could affect a shift in ideas that could be absorbed with the advent of the Vedic period. At first there were just monosyllables, just a single sound captured from the rhythm of breathing during deep sleep. Gradually these were reoriented in pictographs, using a single triangle with a dot or bindu in the middle of the triangle. In time, this transference became the accepted symbol of the Śiva-Śakti glyph known in the ancient world as the first yantra: a symbolical drawing found in caves in the Himalayas that represented creation and dissolution, which the practitioner could concentrate on for enormously long periods of time in the quest to dissolve the mind. Gradually, however, as the practitioner deepened the experience, the image of the triangle, which represented Śiva, would multiply while the dot or bindu, representative of Śakti, would remain seated in the middle of the original triangle. Gradually, the experience obtained from the explosive multiplication of the triangles would move the practitioner to find words to construct complicated mantras. This was the next most important evolutionary step in the rising of consciousness, for by repeating the mantras created from within the inner recesses of the soul, represented by the bindu or Śakti, the practitioner could now free himself of the shackles of nature and commune directly with Śakti, which is representative of cosmic energy.

According to Lalan Prasad Singh, mantra, "is the most potent weapon to cut asunder the trammels of Maya" (12); even so, it is not an intellectual process. Compared with Vedic hymns, which create a psychological climate for spiritual practices, Tantric mantras create an acoustic vibration necessary for the awakening of the Kula Kundalini that would propel the practitioner into that higher state of consciousness necessary for knowing Reality. This knowledge of Tantra, which predates the Vedas, was eclipsed by the advent of the Vedas although its evolutionary influences remained in the background of the ritualistic workings of that portion of the Vedas, the Karma Kanda, which has to do with religion. In this regard, Tantra slowly emerged to influence much of Hindu philosophy, even though a much more refined Sanskriti culture overshadowed the primary language, which had the effect of keeping Tantra in the background. For instance Kula is the equivalent of Śakti, which depicts an element of free spirit, especially as seen in Kundalini Consciousness.

The counterpart of Kula or Śakti is Śiva; Śiva is the equivalent of Brahman, both of which correspond to Consciousness in Advaita Vedanta, which is the crux of Hindu philosophy. Śaivism claims that Śiva resides on the Sahasrara Chakra located on the crown of the head, while Kula Kundalini remains dormant at the base of the spine above the yoni, the female generative organ used primarily for procreation. Interestingly, yoni in Sanskrit means source and refers to the source of everything. Its home is triangular and corresponds to the creative element situated just below the Muladhara Chakra: the first of seven psychic centres that are approximately located in areas corresponding to the following: below the navel, the spleen, the heart, the throat, between the eyebrows, and at the crown of the head. Kundalini or Śakti, which is smaller than the size of the atom, remains coiled as a sleeping serpent at the base of the Muladhara Chakra with its head sealing the hub from where three nadis or psychic rivers traverse the length of the spinal cord to reach the Sahasrara Chakra at the crown of the head. Two of the three "rivers", the Ida and Pingala, flank the right and left sides of the spinal column, while Śusumna, the larger of the tree, which Kundalini traverses to reach the Sahasrara when awakened by the individual aspirant or Sadhak through persistent chanting of mantras or prolonged periods of meditation. Indeed, the rising of Kundalini depicts the rise in consciousness, but in order for Kundalini to rise, the practitioner has to engage in a combination of exercises according to one's disposition. These include, hatha yoga (exercises involving asanas), pranayama (alternating rhythmic breathing exercises), mudra (skilled yoga movements), bandha (muscular movements that lock, seal, and bind movements of breathing), or persistently engage in pranayama and long periods of meditation. Obviously, the objective of this is enlightenment, which comes with the union of Kundalini or Śakti with Śiva.

Indeed, although physically apart, union between Kundalini and Śiva occurs when Consciousness rises in the practitioner to the point where harmony within the practitioner becomes evident, for therein lays the representation of cosmic balance.

From the Hegelian point of view, nothing in the above is propositional but absolutely conceptual from its very inception. One can also go so far as to say that there had been some sort of method at play in the evolution of the idea from the experience of the very first vibrational sound, experienced in deep sleep and which created the first Tantric one-word mantra, Soham.

Soham is a Sanskrit word formed from two words, Sah and Aham, by grammatical rules known as sandhi. Sah means "he", and Aham means "I". Sah and Aham represent the sound caused by the incoming and outgoing breath. The Rishi who observed this from deep sleep seemed to have asked the question, "Koham?", 'Who am I?' However, from a deeper perspective and perhaps in a dialectical sort of way, Soham is not just the sound of the incoming and outgoing breath, but the answer to one of the great philosophical questions "Who am I?" (In modern Hindi it is, Mē kŏna hūm). Initially, the question might have addressed the individual self, but seen from the Hegelian dialectic, then comes the next question, 'Who is *He*? Might it be that *He* is none other than Śiva, or Brahman, the Universal Self? Therefore, making this link, the individual self now becomes One with the Universal Self or Brahman, the greatest force that controls everything in the universe (13).

Prior to the utterance of Soham as mantra, there emerged in the individual consciousness the bindu, a mere speck of a dot, enclosed within the triangle. Soon, thereafter, came the awareness that there existed a definite connection between these two phenomena, which resulted in the creation of the first yantra with the bindu in the middle of the triangle as a pictorial mantra. Then emerged the big bang with the spontaneous duplication of the triangle within a mandala, the outer limits of our planetary world; this not only suggest the push by Śakti to cause Śiva to expand, but a cosmological phenomenon tied to the ongoing expansion of the universe (14). Philosophically speaking this represents the causal will of Śakti to unite with Śiva, triggered by the vibratory force of mantra. In a manner of speaking, all of this suggests the existence of a dialectic, not much different from the Hegelian dialectic that kept the Rishis examining the real from the unreal, not through logical sequencing but what kept surfacing on the Self from the great depths of the sea of consciousness. From this pool also came the concept of nondual awareness or Advaita, as expounded by many of the Rishis in the Upanishads, which is also part of the unfolding dialectic in the same manner by which so many philosophical schools emerged from the core beliefs in Hindu philosophy.

The outgrowth of the six systems of Hindu philosophy from Tantra and the Vedas in some respect represents the ongoing dialectic that accounts for the great mix observed in Hindu thought. Sāṃkhya, for instance, happens to be atheistic and theoretically dualistic, especially in its treatment of consciousness and matter as two separate objects; likewise, Nyaya, which takes its name from the Nyaya Sutras, and Vaisheshika, both employ logic to arrive at the source of knowledge. However, while Nyaya rigidly sticks to logic to espouse its views about the universe, Vaisheshika holds tightly to its atomistic perspective that "all objects in the physical universe are reducible to a finite number of atoms" (15), which tallies well with our present-day composition of the periodic table. This in itself may tacitly allude to the creative, generative and dissolutionary forces implicit in Hindu cosmology known as the Triad, and represented in the Hindu Pantheon by Brahma, Vishnu and Mahesh. However, there is no reason to believe that Nyaya philosophers would ever agree to this. These three systems of later Hindu philosophy have no real connections with the three earlier philosophical systems, the one associated with Yoga and which is the first direct ascendant from Tantra; the other two, Mimāmsā and Vedanta have direct roots in the Vedas that went on to influence Vedanta and the Upaniṣhadic philosophies. In fact, by its very name, Mimāmsā, which means exegesis, is concerned with arriving at truths from its enquiry into the use of language, especially about textual interpretation, and criticism pertaining to history, grammar and syntaxes.

Actually, there are three Mimāmsās carrying the prefixes of "Purva", "Uttara" and "Brahma"; the earlier or Purva Mimāmsā categorises in a systematic manner the ritualistic and sacrificial portions of the Vedas classified as Karma Kanda; these comprise the Samhitas and the Brahmanas. The latter, or Uttara Mimāmsā, however includes the Āraṇyakas (the forest books) portion of the Brahmanas and the Upanishads, which deal with Jnana. By comparison, the Brahma-Mimāmsā Shastra, also known as the Brahma Sutra, is that body of knowledge that comprises the entire Vedanta. Here the authoritative works of the Bhagavad Gita, the Itihasas, the Puranas, the Vedas, and the Upanishads are summarised in aphorisms by Veda Vyasa as instructed by the leading Rishis of the day. Indeed, the purpose of this was to "determine the purport of the entire Vedic literature in order to give the Vedanta Shastras the voice of authority" (16). Moreover, categorized as "Mimāmsā", this exegetically body of knowledge carries the status of an authorised "Bible".

But, unlike Spinoza's 'bibliolatry', the ambitiously but thoroughly scrutinised Veda Vyas text is thought to reveal the correct meaning of the Vedanta Shastra. Even so, as revealed scriptures, nothing was allowed to pass down to Hindu civilization without scrutiny, even though there has never been a central authority in the form of an institutional organization of human beings, such as a Church. For this reason, there has never been a schism among the vast number of religious sects organized under one of the four major Hindu groups known as Vaishnava, Śaiva, Shakta, or Smarta. Under the Vaishnava sect there are subgroups that are loyal to one of the ten incarnates of Vishnu. According to the Linga Purana, there are twenty eight avatars of Śiva; however, the Svetasvatara Upanishad mentions only four: the Ardhanārīśvara (the lord who is half woman and half man), Rudras, of whom Rama is also claimed by Śaivas (although claimed by the Vaishnavas), Hanuman, the sage Agastya, the sage and philosopher Adi Shankara, and Ashwatthama, are all accepted as bona fide avataras of Śiva.

By contrast, the followers of Śaktism are of two completely different persuasions: there are those who focus on the several consorts of Śiva as Devi or Goddess in the role of Divine Mother, or even as Mother of God, while others look upon her as cosmic energy. In the later aspect, as Śakti, she is equated as Brahman, the formless entity that comprises every single aspect of the universe (17). In this respect, she is not just the power that underlies the male principle; as Devamata, she is the creatrix from whom everything in the universe flows. And as such she is the absolute Godhead. She predates the Vedas but is mentioned at least eighty times in the Rig Veda as Aditi, both as mother of the gods, such as Indra, Surya, and Vamana, but more pertinently as the Limitless One. Indeed, in the Valmiki Ramayana, Rama had to "supplicate" Aditi to get her blessings before embarking on his all-important fight with the most powerful earthly demon king, Ravana.

The act of supplication by one God before another may seem superfluous to anyone who understands the importance of Rama in that he was not only regarded as an incarnate of Śiva but also considered to be the tenth incarnate of Vishnu; from Vaishnava understanding, he was God on earth. However a close reading of either the Tulsidas or Valmiki Ramayana, clearly indicates that before man can rise to the status of God, he must demonstrate all the attributes of the perfect man. In this sense, Rama's supplication is the demonstration of Advaita virtue of karmic duty, in the same way that Arjuna had to do his duty, as instructed by Sri Krishna in the Bhagavad Gita. In this sense, there is no contradiction in

either the idea of one God supplicating before another God or in the idea of
Advaita Vedanta, where there is no duality between man and God, especially in the sense that Aditi, like Brahman, is formless and not an object of worship.

The idea of supplication brought to Rama by Agastya Muni, one among the great sages at the time, is that Rama should recognise his lower nature, wrapped up in that bundle of matter, and merge in that state of divine Consciousness known as Brahman or Aditi. Indeed, in the Valmiki Ramayana, Rama manifests here as Maryada Purushotama, the ideal man who rises to that of a Divine being and does not bow down to supplicate Aditi. After all, Aditi is formless; he stands on one foot with his chosen arrow mounted on his bow, as he recites from his heart a hymn praising Aditi given to him by the all-powerful Agastya Muni, the sage also sometimes accorded the title of avatar of Śiva.

At the point where Rama should release his most powerful arrow, however – the arrow formally gifted to him by the Archer of all archers, Śiva – Rama becomes frozen, at which time he becomes the mere observer. In a manner of speaking, Rama suddenly remembers himself and yields to the all-important Vedic directive: as God of all things, become silent and allow man embroiled in Prakriti to work out his own problems. This idea is reminiscent of Krishna taking birth at a time when the affairs of man seemed mindless of good conduct and the laws governing Dharma is waning. Here Krishna's mission is to remove the recalcitrant spoilers and re-establish Dharma but he cannot act on his own; he must observe the old Vedic directive, to which he later said in the Gita that were earlier established by him. Indeed, this was the reason why Krishna chose Arjuna, whom he must school before embarking in battle to restore Dharma. Thus, while Rama remains frozen and cannot act by virtue of the old Dharmic law of laws, Sita, his consort, takes possession of her husband and manifests as the Dharmic Warrior against corruption in the combined form of Durga as spoken of in this mantra:

> Om Jayanti Mangala Kali Bhadra Kali Kapalini Durga Kshama Śiva Dhatri Svaha Svadha namo-astu-te.

The meaning of which is: 'O, Omnipotent, Omnipresent, Omniscient One. She Who Conquers Over All, AllAuspicious, the remover of Darkness, the Excellent One Beyond Time, the bearer of the Skulls of Impure thought, the reliever of difficulties, loving, forgiveness, supporter of the Universe, etc...' However, flanked at the sides of this composite Sita – the consort of Śiva – that now bears six arms and the marks of the most powerful Goddess in the Hindu Devi Pantheon, are Vishnu and Surya to the right, and Śiva and Ganesha to the left. And behind them is the larger than life, Rama, frozen in time while gazing upon the entire battlefield that is about to consume almost all of the southern subcontinent in the fight against Ravana and his army that is recruited from as far away as Iran and Syria. (To show how wide a sweep the war with Ravana had engulfed the world, some Biblical scholars claim that the Germans have descended from the Ancient Assyrians) (18). Indeed this was supposed to be Rama's battle, to cleanse the subcontinent of adharma and reinstate Dharma. But such a battle could not be done by one man alone, regardless how righteously divine that person might have been. As a problem that transcended the humble mind of individuals in societal setting, it required the cosmic energy of the Devi to penetrate all of Prakriti, the lower nature of the Divine, to lift up and imprint on the individual souls the essence of that consciousness, which is part and parcel of the Divine. In this way, the wholeness of Dharma would again be established, which would allow all of humanity to arrive at that state where Rama had arrived: the man who discovers his divinity as the upholder of Dharma and who thus rose up to be *Maryada Purushotama*, a perfect human being.

Interestingly, the deities that flank Sita as Dharmic Warrior – Vishnu, Surya, Devi or Durga, Śiva and Ganesha – happen to be the principle deities worshipped by the sect known as the Smarta Sampradaya. Depending on the tradition followed by Smarta households, one of these deities is kept in the centre of the altar surrounded by the remaining four.

Worship is offered to all the deities, represented by small Murthis called the Panchayatana Puja set, bearing likeness of human, made from five types of stone. Alternatively these murthis could be supplanted by five representative marks drawn on the floor of the altar. The chosen murthi placed in the centre is indicative of the devotee's Ishta Devata, or personal deity.

While, as a movement, Smarta is relatively new, as a tradition (Sampradaya) it has its roots in Vedic practice that goes back to the time of the Rig Veda. Indeed, the word Smarta is derived from the Sanskrit, "smriti", which has two meanings; the first has its origins in "what is remembered from tradition". It is from this memory that we get the major texts of the Itihasas of the Ramayana and the Mahabharata, plus the six Vedangas, and the eighteen Puranas. In this regard, smriti carries the voice of authority, but not with the same force compared with Sruti, which is the counterpart of Smriti. Indeed, Sruti gets its authority from having the status of revealed knowledge, while smriti is empowered from remembering the practice ordained in tradition, and thus regarded as the first "source of Dharma" (19). From this point of view, the distinction is made between "movement" and "practice" when speaking about Smarta.

During the early days of the Vedas, stretching back to at least seven thousand years ago, especially as seen in the Rig Veda, the tradition of worshipping a host of gods and goddesses were standard practice. Perhaps these elevated men and women were model leaders who upheld the Dharma and commanded the respect of the seers and sages to the extent that these elevated souls were regarded as gods and goddesses. Thus although Smarta is considered to be a relatively new development as a sect, the practice has its origins in the days of the Rig Veda. These gods, commonly referred to as the Vishvadevas, has nothing to do with Vishnu, one of the principal gods of the Hindu Pantheon; "Vishva" carries the meaning of "whole" or "universe" and "Deva", God. Thus the Vishvadevas connote to universal gods. The major deities belonging to this group are, Agni, representative of energy and who receives the oblations on behalf of all the gods, such as Aditya, Brhaspati, Indra, Mithra, Soma, Varuna, Vayu, Vishnu, etc. Indeed, there are at least fifty gods propitiated by hymns in the Rig Veda, some of whom later migrated to Iran, Iraq and Assyria, and from where they occupy a slightly different role, as seen in the system of worship observed by the Mitanni in Hittite cuneiform.

Smarta certainly has an interesting history, especially in how it influenced Indo-Iranian belief systems such as Zoroastrianism, which had its roots in Agni, the fire god that distributes the received oblations to the principal god. Or Rita, that cosmic principle that holds the universe together; then there is also Asha, the goddess of the dawn; Soma, the generative principle controlled by the Moon God, who until the advent of Islam was also central to Arabic belief. Of course, there is also Mithra, who not only graduated to Maitriya – the friendly or benevolent one – in Buddhism, but who went on to influence early Roman theology and even Christian belief during the reign of Constantine. However, the importance of this sect, which became a powerful movement by the time Adi Shankaracharya endorsed it in the 8th century CE, is noted in his following verse:

Guru Brahma, Guru Vishnu, Guru Deva Maheshwara.
Guru Sakshath Parambrahma, Tasmai Shri Gurave
Namaha.

Which is translated thus: "Guru is Brahma the creator, Guru is Vishnu the preserver, Guru is Śiva the destroyer. Guru is directly the supreme spirit — I offer my salutations to this Guru." In other words the Guru, especially the manner in which Shankaracharya accepts him in the proper noun form, is given the same status as that given to Sri Krishna, who is known in the Bhagavad Gita as Jagat Guru, the World Guru in a non-personalized rendition. This statement was strategic to the idea of Advaita Vedanta in that, while some could reconcile the idea of Brahma, Vishnu and Śiva – the three main Deities of the Hindu Pantheon – as the Three in One, it nevertheless allowed his critics for a modified form of Dvaita or duality in the practice of Hinduism. Strategically speaking, by polemically presenting his argument in this manner, Shankaracharya could easily defeat his critics that came from Buddhists and Sāṃkhya philosophers who believed neither in God nor in the existence of the soul. Indeed, by approaching the Divine as the formless Jagat Guru, Shankaracharya had managed to unite all of the different strains of Advaita Vedanta that the Rishis and Munis had variously presented in the Upanishads.

Philosophically speaking, by embracing Smarta, Shankaracharya was able to silence his Dvaita critics by compelling them to see Dvaita in Advaita, as "equal reflections" of the One Saguna (formless) Brahman, expressed as unity in plurality. In other words, he managed to give a "modified form" to the "formless" as a means of granting "gravitas" to that, which is unknown, but which can be known by reaching into the Self of all, according to their peculiar state of Consciousness. This took care of the idea of "personal God", missing in Advaita Vedanta, rather than "distinct beings".

Which brings me to the central question in this paper: what does philosophy means to me, within the context of the European theatre of philosophy in search for meaning? The thread that connects the different philosophical renderings touched thus far has to do with the epistemology of the Hindus in comparison with western thought: how does one arrive at an understanding of knowledge outside the realm of pure reason or logical candour. Outside of Nyaya philosophy, none of the rishis who contributed to the major bulwark of the Upanishads saw any contradictions in their expositions concerned with the nature and scope of how they arrived at their understanding of knowledge of the universe or the nature of the Divine commonly referred to as Brahman. The reason for this had to do with their methodology of enquiry: by observation, over a very long time, sometimes sitting alone in caves deep into the Himalayas or while roaming through dark forests surrounded by all sorts of danger. This sadhana or discipline took them into a journey of the undivided Self experiencing the deepest of consciousness that, after years of enquiry at the point where "mind" became non-existent, they were able to see, feel, listen, and even taste the raw elements of life, which they expressed as the Maruts. In western parlance this indivisibility of the five elements seem to have anticipated John Dalton's atomic theory, so long after Krishna had said in the Bhagavad Gita that, to know him, one must understand the indivisible composition of Prakriti as his lower nature. Indeed, the exposition we have from the Upanishads could not be disputed even either by the "atheistic" Sāṃkhya or Nyaya philosophers.

This idea of the elements, which is a pointer to the extent that western science owes to the Hindus, with regard to astronomy, is illustrated in a discussion of the subject with Apollonius in the 3rd century BCE, who had journeyed to India to learn the essential platform of Hindu philosophy based on the secrets of Advaita Vedanta. In this regard, one of the first questions Apollonius asked of Iarchas, his Indian host, of what the Indians thought the cosmos to be composed.

Iarchas thus replied, "Of elements."
"Are there then four?" he asked.

"Not four," said Iarchas, "but five."

"And how can there be a fifth," said Apollonius, "alongside of water and air and earth and fire?" "There is the ether", replied the other, "which we must regard as the stuff of which gods are made; for just as all mortal creatures inhale the air, so do immortal and
divine natures inhale the ether."

Apollonius again asked, which was the first of the elements, and Iarchas answered: "All are simultaneous, for a living creature is not born bit by bit."

"Am I," said Apollonius, "to regard the universe as a living creature?"

"Yes," said the other, "if you have a sound knowledge of it, for it engenders all living things."

"Shall I then," said Apollonius, "call the universe female, or of both the male and the opposite gender?" "Of both genders," said the other, "for by commerce with itself it fulfils the role both of mother and father in bringing forth living creatures; and it is possessed by a love for itself more intense than any separate being has for its fellow, a passion which knits it together into harmony. And it is not illogical to suppose that it cleaves unto itself; for as the movement of an animal is obtained by use of its hands and feet, and as there is a soul in it by which it is set in motion, so we must regard the parts of the universe also as adapting themselves through its inherent soul to all creatures which are brought forth or conceived.

"For example, the sufferings so often caused by drought are visited on us in accordance with the soul of the universe, whenever justice has fallen into disrepute and is disowned by men; and this animal shepherds itself not with a single hand only, but with many mysterious ones, which it has at its disposal; and though from its immense size it is controlled by no others yet it moves obediently to the rein and is easily guided.

"And the subject is so vast and so far transcends our mental powers, that I do not know any example adequate to illustrate it…"

The Last two paragraphs are reminiscent of what Krishna said in the Eleventh Chapter of the Bhagavad Gita, and as far as the account of the composition of the universe, particularly pertaining to the five elements, this too can be said to be a paraphrase of what Krishna said about his "lower nature" in the Bhagavad Gita. What is interesting about this clever narrative, which is excerpted from *The Life of Apollonius of Tyana* by Pbilostratus 220 AD (in Mountain Man Graphics, Australia, Southern Spring 1995), is the controversy that not only surrounds the age of Hindu astronomy, but the question of who learnt from whom? Indeed, even as a student, I was often told by my professors that there is no such thing as Hindu astronomy; that the Hindus incorporated much of their knowledge of astronomy from the Arabs, who in turn learnt their science from the Greeks. The significance about bringing Apollonius into this discussion has to do with the enormity of Apollonius' presence in both Greek society and the ancient world: in some respects, he wielded influence as that of a wise man with the same grandeur of Socrates and Jesus Christ. Not only that, because Apollonius travelled far into Africa, West Asia, and India, the enormous influence he left behind, especially of his knowledge of Hindu culture, language, mathematics, science and philosophy, those who knew him either loved him or hated him. Indeed, the hatred of his teachings based on Hindu spirituality and philosophy, mounted a campaign to destroy much of his legacy in his writings; consequently, much of his writings and that of historians who wrote about him has been deliberately destroyed. However, the purpose of bringing Apollonius into this discussion should not be lost: it has to do with the extent that Greek mathematics, science and philosophy owes so much to the Hindus. After all, could it be possible that a man like Apollonius, so well informed and so well known to the ancient world, not know the existence of the fifth element that is such an integral part of physics and astronomy? Likewise, relating to the concept of Gaia, the Greek idea of Earth as a pulsating entity with a personality of a Living Being, is there any relationship to the Hindu idea of the Universe "as a living creature?" Is it possible that a man, so well informed as Apollonius, would not know that ether, as the fifth element, had been in currency in Greece, sufficiently to enquire, "which we must regard as the stuff of what gods are made?"

Indeed, long before Alexander's conquest of the lands west of the Sind, the Hindus and the Buddhists were trading more than durable goods with the Persians, the Greeks, the Romans, the Assyrians, the Chaldeans and the Egyptians, and even with the Ethiopians, and Somalians (together with the Djibouti known as the land of the Punts). The Bhagavad Gita, along with many of India's ancient philosophical and religious texts were known to them, largely because Hindu and Buddhist teachers were recruited to teach the secrets of the Hindus and Buddhists to the upper echelons of those societies. Indeed, much of Plato's or Socrates' ideas about the nature of the soul, or the Pythagorean Theorem, were not just dreamt up in Greece; much of these were learnt from Hindu masters by visiting travellers in pursuit of knowledge, in the same manner that Apollonius had visited India.

So, what accounted for this apparent vacancy of Indian science and the broad spectrum of Indian philosophy in ancient Greece? Could there have been a Conspiracy of History as suggested by British historian, Arnold Toynbee in his twelve- volume Study of History? Or, was the conspiracy levied against Hindu knowledge in every sphere of life, so well established in the Grecian and Roman world that, it had become taboo to utter publicly, for fear of corrupting the architects of society, in the same way that Socrates' brand of philosophy was held in contempt for corrupting the youth of

Athens, and which eventually led to his execution? Or could it be that the gems of Hindu thought, found in Sāṃkhya concerning number theory, or theories of Hindu science and mathematics, were stolen and renamed and hoped never to be discovered by the foreigners of the east. Such was the case of Pythagoras, one of the biggest thieves in the history of civilization who had absconded with the mathematical works of Baudhayana, which Pythagoras named after himself and came down through the ages as Pythagoras Theorem. There is no need to go into what the theory proves since every schoolchild is thought this at least in middle school. But what the student does not know is the source of the theorem which is found in the Śulbha Sutra:

dirghasyaksanaya rajjuh parsvamani, tiryadam mani cha yatprthagbhuta kurutastadubhayan karoti

The verse, which every educated schoolchild also sees in India, is simply put: a rope stretched along the length of the diagonal (hypotenuse) produces an area that the vertical and horizontal sides (the two legs) make together. Apart from the fact that Baudhayana is credited with deriving the approximate value of the square root of two by finding a circle the same area of the square, or transforming the rectangle into a square of the same area, the purpose of which had to do with the Hindu practice of being meticulously precise in building altars. Baudhayana took note of this Vedic practice that were in use for thousands of years and realized that there was a distinct mathematical equation involved in the construction of the Vedic altars and thus authored the Baudhayana Sutras (c800 BCE), which offered insights into Dharma from daily rituals, as well as mathematics.

From the Shatapatha Brahmana, it is learned that the earth was represented by a circular altar, and the heavens were represented by a square altar; the ritual consisted of converting the circle into a square of an identical area from which is observed the beginnings of geometry! However, the rectangular altars were of special length and breadth in which a mandatory square or rectangle, comprising of two triangles, were joined at their hypotenuse. In other words, imagine Baudhayana employing Yajur Veda enumerates to construct a perfect square, then cutting the square in half along the diagonal line, thus creating two hypotenuse triangles. Later, Baudhayana, and Apastamba in his Dharma and Grihya Sutras, would furnish the Hindu world with mathematical details about his methodology used in the construction of the Vedic altars. Thus, this practical application, while helping Baudhayana to prove his theorem, was of little help to Pythagoras, who was left in the dark, even though Euclid later solved the puzzle and helped popularize it in the ancient Greek world, especially in his work dealing with trigonometric identity. Indeed, Baudhayana was able to prove his theorem because of the decimal based value system that was current in India for centuries prior to even Baudhayana's time, while the number system in the West lacked completion without zero. Indeed,

even during the Buddhist period, the zero was referred to as Śunya, which the Greeks foolishly misinterpreted as "void". Hence, according to Abraham Seidenberg, Author of a paper entitled, "The origin of Mathematics: *"India is thus the cradle of the knowledge of geometry and mathematics."* Still, this knowledge is not just to illustrate India's glory; the purpose here is to offer an important clue that shed light into the mind of the Hindu and his method of knowing. After all, this is the major theme of this book, and the reason for raising the question of the place of science in the Hindu world is to contrast how real knowledge is gained, which is not so much from reason but from paying attention to the nominative behaviour of the
Intuitive Self.

From a philosophical point of view, perhaps what is even more significant than what Pythagoras obtained from the Hindus by way of mathematics is the depth of his natural and moral philosophy, rather what has traditionally assumed to have come from the Egyptians. Indeed, there is little doubt that the Egyptians had learnt much from the Indians (see notes at the end of this section), especially in their contacts with Buddhist and Hindu monks who were imported into Alexandra, long before Lycurgus had even dreamt of travelling into India. Here he had encountered the ponderous Laws of Manu from which he culled the chief principles of his laws – as affirmed by Sir William Temple:

"The care of education from the birth of children, the austere temperance of diet, the patient endurance of toil and pain...the temples, the defense of commerce with strangers, and several others, by him established by the Spartans, seem all to be wholly Indian, and different from any race or vein of thought or imagination, that have ever appeared in Greece, either in that age or any other since. (20)

Furthermore, Temple goes on to say, "From these famous Indians, it seems most probable that Pythagoras learned, and transported into Greece and Italy, the greatest part of his natural and moral philosophy, rather than from the Egyptians...Nor does it seem unlikely that the *Egyptians themselves might have drawn much of their learning from the Indians*. Long before Lycurgus, who likewise travelled to India, brought from thence also the chief principles of his laws." (20).

In addition to what Sir William Temple said in the above, it is interesting to note that, in the same vein of speaking about the Hindus and their contribution to Greek science, especially in the field of astronomy, algebra, geometry, he also mentioned the seven sages, heretofore regarded as Greek Masters of great mind and intellect. However, if one reads Sir William carefully there might be a very subtle suggestion that the seven "Greek" Masters might indeed be the celebrated Seven Rishis found in most Sanskrit texts as the Saptarishis. These wise men who have contributed to the Vedas, the Vedangas, and the Upanishads were so prominent in the ancient Hindu world that they are accorded permanent seats in the arrangement of the most prominent constellation known as Kṛttikā in Sanskrit, or Ursa Major in Latin.

The point of view here is that the enquirer should learn to identify himself with the source of manifestation; then, it would be easy for those who wish to know, to grasp the knowledge of Sāṃkhya and that which is in the Bhagavad Gita, as well as all that is manifest in the literature of the Upanishads.

It would seem that knowledge of the great elements as delineated in the above and derived from the Bhagavad Gita and Sāṃkhya, is paramount for anyone who intends to pursue a philosophical understanding of the nature of man and the universe. To recap, it is important for the knower to have sufficient knowledge of the nature of his body, the senses, mind, intellect, and ego, as well as the source of the universe, in order to obtain knowledge, directly. When the student of philosophy identifies with his essential nature in the process of expanding the perpetual faculty of the mind (*cetanā*) from awareness to consciousness in the perfect state of being, he no longer identifies with the material objects of the world. Such a state of perfection is the goal of the student of philosophy, which leads the true enquirer from *cetanā* to *prajnana*, from individual consciousness to universal consciousness. This style of study (sadhana) leads one from the gross self to the subtlest aspect of being, which eventually comes with the realization that the real Self as the Self of the Universe, and from which the Intuitive Self emerges.

Indeed, there is a clear parallel with what functions in the universe and that which functions in the human being: The Bhagavata Gita tells us that *sattva* is the harmonious quality; *rajas* the active and passionate; and *tamas* the slothful. All of the forms and means of the universe come out of these three gunas, and the gunas themselves come out from the one single source: the Lord of life and the universe. The sun, moon, the constellations, and the elements of earth come into existence from the Lord of life, who is the source of the universe. As Krishna says in the Bhagavad Gita, they exist because of Him, but as Krishna reminds us in Chapter IX: 4 in the Bhagavad Gita, he does not exist because of the existence of these objects:

*Mayā tatam idaṁ sarvaṁ jagad avyakta-mūrtinā
mat-sthāni sarva bhūtāni na cāhaṁ tesv avasthitah*

By Me, in My Unmanifested form, this entire universe is pervaded. All beings are in Me, but I am not in them.

The thrust of Sir William's subtlest of meaning comes thus:

"...Allow me to say for the giving some Idea of what those Sages or Learned Men were or may have been, is more asie and obvious. The most Ancient Grecian that we are at all acquainted with, after Lycurgus, who was certainly a great philosopher as well as Law-giver, were the seven Sages: though the Court of Crocus is said to have been much resorted to, by the Sophists of Greece, in the happy beginnings of his Reign. And some of these seven seem to have brought most of those Sciences out of Egypt and Phoenicia, into Greece; particularly those of Astronomy, Geometry, and Arithmetick. These were soon followed by Pythagoras (who seems to have introduced Natural and Moral Philosophy) and by several of his Followers, both in Greece and Italy. But of all these, there remains nothing in writing now among us; for that Hypocrates, Plato, and Xenophon, are the first philosophers, whose works have escaped the injuries of Time. But that we may not conclude, the first writers we have of the Grecians were the first learned or Wise among them; we shall find upon enquiry, that the more Ancient Sages of Greece appear, by the Characters remaining of them, to have been much Greater Men. They were generally Princes or Law-givers of their countries, or at least offered and invited to be so, either of their own or of others that desired them to frame or reform their several Institutions of Civil Government. They were commonly excellent Poets, and great physicians: They were learned in Natural Philosophy, that they foretold, not only Eclipses in the Heavens, but Earthquakes at land, and storms at Sea, Great Drowths and great Plagues, much plenty, or much scarcity of certain Sorts of Fruits or Grains..." (21: Miscellanea, Part II. p 158)

As suggested earlier, Pythagoras did not only lean heavily on the Baudhayana's algebraic theorem of the hypotenuse but most of his social and moral philosophy was wholly borrowed from Sāṃkhya philosophy. Morally he viewed philosophy as how it is practiced among the Hindus: as a way of life in which the chief goal is to know the Highest Reality, which he paraphrased as "those who spend their time in the contemplation of nature, and as lovers of wisdom." In this regard, he linked the Hindu idea of the immortality of the soul to the Divine, from which he saw the soul as an eternal spark. And, concerning the "cosmos" he totally accepted the Hindu idea of *Rita* as that which serves as the inherent order to the Universe, or which holds the cosmos in balance. Thus, in his pursuit of philosophy, he accepted the Hindu idea that real knowledge was something more than being a lover of wisdom; philosophy had to conform to the essence of knowing the Divine dictated by a manner of knowing, which the Hindus believe came from the Intuitive Self. Nevertheless, there were constraints in his understanding of Sāṃkhya: he totally misconstrued Sāṃkhya theory of number, which also had an idiotic effect on later philosophers such as Aristotle. Indeed, Pythagoras understood Sāṃkhya to mean that all things consist of numbers, to the extent that he saw all "physical bodies themselves are made of numbers, or since numbers themselves are not ultimate, the elements of numbers are the elements of everything." And like Aristotle, he saw "units possessing magnitude" as if numbers were the "actual matter of which things were composed." In many ways this interpretation of Sāṃkhya number system contradicts Pythagoras' claim to his understanding of the Divine, and to some extent even betrays his misapprehension of the divine law in nature, or the Divinity of Nature as Krishna explained it the Bhagavad Gita. There is no doubt that Pythagorean mathematics of nature, as understood by Aristotle, stems from Pythagoras' attempts at making sense of Sāṃkhya's delineation of numbers as related to the unity and limit of substances forming the basic elements of everything in the universe. However, unless this is put in proper perspective, like Pythagoras' lack of essential proof of how Baudhayana's hypotenuse worked, there is no limit to the chaos that follows, which is why much of Aristotle's metaphysics makes little sense to the essential flow of Hindu philosophy. The crux of Pythagoras' foolishness is particularly seen in what is assumed to be Aristotle's summary of Pythagoras' ten principles: the opposite of the following: limit, odd, one, right, male, at rest, straight, light, good, and square. Pushing these opposites to the limit, he claimed that the monad was God and the good, "the true nature of the One, Mind itself"; but the indefinite Dyad is a *"daimon"* and evil, concerned with "material plurality." From a Hindu perspective, everything here is laughable, largely because even when viewed from a distance, these views further betray not only his lack of knowledge, but the inherent idea that Pythagoras did not spend enough time among the Great Masters to get an insight into Hindu cosmology, which is essential for an understanding of the nature of Brahman. Indeed, had he studied even the first of the Mahavakyas, *Prajñānam Brahman*, "Brahman is Consciousness", he would not have fallen into the mousetrap of Sophistic bigotry; he would have avoided the pitfall of equating mind with God or attempting to find the opposite of God in demons. Symbolically, it would have been plausible to equate God with One, but Mind does not exist in either Hindu cosmology or with the idea of God; mind operates at a lower level: according to Krishna in the Bhagavad Gita, Chapter XIII, verse 3, mind is part of his lower nature, or Prakriti. At this level of understanding, the word for God in Sanskrit is either Isha or Purusha (the personified higher nature of the Divine), or Brahman, which is Consciousness. At the lower level of being in the material body, or in nature designated as Prakriti, Mind operates as the substratum pervading physical existence. Thus the Purusha or Brahman is spiritual existence and Prakriti physical existence. Hence mind can only exist at the physical level of existence. In this way mind emanates from physical existence, where such things as demons and goblins operate, which arise from the soul's attachment to the body and the lack of discernment and discrimination between Prakriti and Purusha, which further causes disillusionment. Sri Krishna clinched this important lesson in Chapter XIII: 2, with the statement, "Prakriti is related to the kshetra or the field and Purusha is related to the kshetrajnam or knower of the field," or knowing the body.

Perhaps the greatest betrayal came with Pythagoras' supposed understanding of the elements. Or, the devising of his theory of the elements and how they came into being. There is little doubt that these were extrapolated from his reasoning mind and not the Intuitive Self, according to the Hindu method of knowing. Thus, Pythagoras claimed Earth

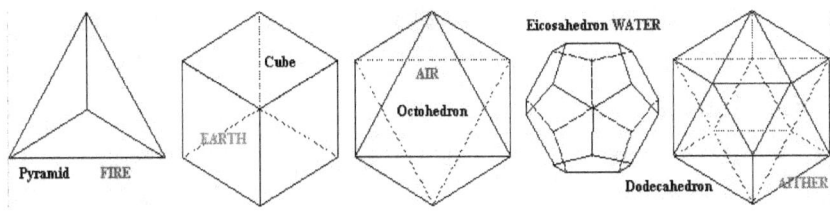

is made from the "cube"; air from the octahedron; fire from the pyramid; water, from the eicosahedron (a solid equilateral triangular with twenty plane faces); and the ether, which he calls "the sphere as the whole", is the mathematical sold derived from the dodecahedron, a regular solid figure with twelve equal pentagonal faces.

There is little doubt that Pythagoras intended to project something of a graphic representation of the elements to prove his scientific fortitude to the ancient world. However, while the cube, pyramid, and dodecahedron, belong to Pythagoras, the octahedron and icosahedron belong to Theaetetus who lived between c.415-369 B.C; so, this moderately late date naturally calls into question the real origins of the co-called elemental solids. It would seem to have a considerable advantage, although seemingly unlikely to prove anything in Pythagoras' favour, especially if one pays close attention to the discovery of the details in a scholium found in the Vatican library in 1808 by François Peyrard, entitled Euclid's Elements (22). This discovery was thought to have descended through the 4th century AD Greek mathematician, Theon of Alexandria, but that proved incorrect: while there are various lines of copies of Euclid's Elements, this one was noted by Robert Lawlor in his book, *Sacred Geometry: Philosophy and Practice,* as not belonging to Theon. However, this scholium is key to the unravelling of some of the mysteries pertaining to the authenticity of works attributed to Pythagoras, particularly the suggestion that directly contradicts the tradition that ascribes to Pythagoras "anything that came along."

To put these solids in their proper perspective, although they are also termed Platonic solids, it should be stated that they existed at least 1000 BC and were known among the Neolithic people of Scotland, as shown below in the stone

models of the cube, tetrahedron, dodecahedron, icosahedron and octahedron, which date from about 2000 BC and are kept in the Ashmolean Museum in Oxford (24). Even so, there is controversy surrounding the existence of these stones:

because they are found randomly in different parts of Britain and Scotland, as well as in parts of Eastern Europe and Asia Minor, their shapes are not uniform; and because some are small enough to fit into the hands, they are thought to be amulets.

Among other things, outside the controversies surrounding works claimed to belong to Pythagoras, he was a traveller; He certainly did travel to India and conversed with many of the then Rishis associated with some of the major Hindu works concerned with the Shastras. There is no doubt that he would have also been familiar with the Upanishads and the Bhagavad Gita, in which he was exposed to know both the scientific and philosophical aspects of the *great* elements, which is thus expressed in Chapter XIII: 5-6 in the Bhagavad Gita:

mahā-bhūtāni ahaṅkāro buddhir avyaktam eva ca
indriyāṇi daśai'kam ca pañca ce'ndriyagocarāḥ

icchā dveṣaḥ sukhaṁ duḥkhaṁ saṅghātaś cetanā dhṛtiḥ
etat kṣetram samāsena savikāram udāhṛtam

On the face value of these two verses the ideas expressed would seem very basic. They simply say that the five great elements, the *mahā-bhūtāni*, represent false ego (*ahaṅkāro*), spiritual intelligence (*buddhiḥ*), and the unmanifested stage of the three modes of nature (*avyaktam eva ca)*, which are: sattva, rajas, and tamas. The unmanifested modes of "material nature" is called *pradhana*, a term in Sāṃkhya

philosophy evolved from two root words in Sanskrit: *pra*, which means before, and *dha*, to place; hence, that which is first placed, or the applied meaning of the primal position in a philosophical sequence of cosmic emanations. According to Sāṃkhya philosophy, pradhana is "the original root of matter defined as the state of equilibrium of the three gunas": sattva, rajas and tamas. From these come the ten senses *Indriyāṇi daśai*), five of which are for the purpose of acquiring knowledge: eyes, ears, nose, tongue and skin, and the other five are followed by the "working senses": voice, legs, hands, anus, and genitals. However, above the senses is the mind within, which is also considered a sense; taken together these bring the total number of senses to eleven. However, from the point of view of Sāṃkhya, these represent a significant part of this branch of Hindu philosophy, which is basic to the numbering system; and, consequently came the five objects of the senses
(*pañcace'ndriyagocarāḥ*) expressed as smell, taste, form, touch, and sound. Thus, the aggregate of these amounts to twenty-four elements referred to in Vedanta as the true representation of the integrated Maha Bhutani, and called by Sri Krishna *kshetram*, the field of activity. But this is not the end of delineation: the object is to know "the field of activity, from which one can understand the obstacles of knowing the perpetual activity of the mind (*saṅghātaś cetanā dhṛtih*); it is what stems from desire, hatred, happiness, and distress (*icchā dveṣaḥ sukhaṃ duḥkham*), which come from interactions represented by the five great elements in the human body

and everything in nature. This is the difference between the object of determining raw science, such as Pythagoras' geometrical expression of the elements, as opposed to finding a method of knowing the living symptoms of those very elements (represented by the enquiring mind, cetanā), which has the potential to move one to a higher state of conviction, and thence in which to climb towards Consciousness. This conviction manifests in the subtle body known in Sāṃkhya as the composite of mind, ego, and spiritual intelligence.

What is significant about the elements, from a philosophical viewpoint, is the extent to which Western philosophers wedded to logic considered the elements a masterpiece in the application of logic to mathematics. This idea bears witness to the fact that the *elements*, as a single idea, was the most attractive principle to scientists such as Nicolaus Copernicus, Johannes Kepler, Galileo Galilei, and Sir Isaac Newton. It also lends argument why such mathematician philosophers such as my friend Bertrand Russell and Alfred North Whitehead – so influenced by Baruch Spinoza – have attempted to create their own Foundational Elements for their respective disciplines by adopting the axiomatized deductive structures that Euclid's work introduced.

Philosophically speaking, for the Hindu mind, the five great elements do not just carry meaning into tangible physical elements that we can perceive through our senses. They refer to the qualities of the physical elements in a derivative manner. For example, water here refers to the quality of liquids that enable them to flow. Fire refers to the quality of a flame to generate light and heat. When these elements combine with each other, they have the potential to create every object in this universe. It is with regard to this that Sri Krishna says that the building blocks of the universe are nothing but his manifestation. Interestingly, early Indian scientists, such as Baudhayana and Brihaspati, claimed that, the other elements such as we have in the Periodic Table as we know it today, owe their origins to thermal fusion during their course of other heavier elements coming together from collapsing stars to form lighter elements under extremely high temperatures; this in turn makes other elements. However, if they only stayed in stars there would not be any changes in their structure, but as these stars explode, the elements get scattered as new elements across the galaxy as carbon, oxygen, silicon, etc., as did all the elements in gas clouds, until they too again collapse to form new generations of stars, such as ours. These are the very ingredients that comprise life that are not only traceable to stars; they indeed gave their lives billions of years before we arrived in the form in which we are now recognised.

Thus, an element is defined in one way by the modern scientist and another way by the Indian systems of philosophy. According to the latter the five senses of perception are the means to take cognisance of the elements. The ear perceives sound that is characteristic of ether or Akash. The skin is endowed with the sense of touch, which is peculiar to air. The eye cognizes form revealed by light or fire. The tongue experiences tastes of things, dissolved in water; but for the aid and agency of water nothing can be tasted. The nose contacts smell produced by earth. These five instruments of knowledge are thus recognized as the revealers of the five elements, of which the world is constituted. Furthermore, the faculty of feeling is designated as the mind. The intellect is that which distinguishes the good from the bad, the agreeable from the disagreeable. That which creates the sense of agency is the egoism, without which action is impossible. The individuality of one is based on the peculiarities of these three internal organs.

It nevertheless seems that the authors of the Upanishad had anticipated Spinoza's quest to know, and which he sincerely believed the real "word of God", or true religion, is not something written in books but "inscribed on the heart and mind of man", and which can only arrive through exploring the nature of the self in the deepest of Consciousness. Benedictus Spinoza, who was called by Renan "the greatest Jew of modern times" main doctrine has been ably condensed and set forth by Lewes in the History of Philosophy as follows:

"The great reality of all existence is sub-stance. Not substance in the gross and popular sense of body or matter, but that which is substans—which is standing under all phenomena supporting and giving them reality." Descartes had assumed a duality, a God and a real world created by God. Spinoza reduced this duality to an all-embracing unity. *"The absolute existence—this substance (call it what you will) is God. From Him all individual concrete existences arise. All that exists, exists in and by God; and can only thus be conceived. . . . He recognizes God as the fountain of Life; he sees in the Universe nothing but the manifestation of God; the Finite rests upon the bosom of the Infinite; the inconceivable variety resolves itself into unity. There is but one reality, and that is God."*

Interestingly, during the next century the celebrated Herbert Spencer, the ardent protagonist of the evolutionary philosophy, described the universe, in his classic book First Principles, as being a mode of manifestation of what he called *"an Actuality lying behind Appearances,"* and also as *"the unknown Reality underlying matter and force."* G. W. F. Hegel, gave voice to similar ideas: *"Nature is the extreme self-alienation of spirit, in which it yet remains one with itself."* And again: *"The reality is the universal, which goes out of itself, particularises itself, and opposes itself to itself"* (interestingly, Krishna predicted this line of reason in the Bhagavad Gita: the self is the enemy of the Self). First Principles, as being a mode of manifestation of what he called *"an Actuality lying behind Appearances,"* and also as *"the unknown Reality underlying matter and force."*

Bertrand Russell, in his *Outlines of Philosophy*, has lucidly explained how the problem of perception has become more obscure than ever:

"What passes for knowledge suffers from three defects: cocksureness, vagueness, and self-contradiction. Naive common-sense supposes that common objects, such as chairs, trees, etc. are what they appear to be, but that is impossible since they do not appear exactly alike to any two simultaneous observers. If we are going to admit that the object is not what we see, we can no longer feel the same assurance that there is an object. . . . Now physics says that a table or a chair is 'really' an incredibly vast system of electrons and protons in rapid motion with empty space in between. But the scientist being but a man cannot more than anybody else see these electrons and protons. He sees only certain patches of colour; but he has a learned explanation 'Light-waves start from the electrons (or, more probably, are reflected by them from a source of light), reach the eye, have a series of effects upon the rods and cones, the optic nerve and the brain, and finally produce a sensation.' But he has never seen anything more than the patches of colour; and the physical and physiological processes leading to sensation, on his own showing, lie essentially and for ever outside experience."

Russel further entertains with his observations 'In waking life we are critical of the interpretative hypotheses that occur to us, and therefore do not make such wild mistakes as in dreams. But the creative as opposed to the critical mechanism is the same in waking life as it is in dreams. . . . All adaptation to environment acquired during the life of an individual might be regarded as learning to dream, dreams that succeed rather than dreams that fail. The dreams we have when we are asleep usually end in a surprise; the dreams we have in waking life are less apt to do so . . . one might say that a person properly adapted to his environment is one whose dreams never end in the sort of surprise that would wake him up. In that case he will think that his dreams are objective reality. But if modern physics is to be believed, the dreams we call waking perceptions have only a very little more resemblance to objective reality than the fantastic dreams of sleep. They have some truth, but only just so much as is required to make them useful.'

Russell's work forms a natural link between that of the philosophers and that of the scientists, and thus we may now fitly ascertain what the latter have to say of the points under examination. One of the greatest nineteenth-century scientists was Thomas Henry Huxley, and the following quotations from Vol. VI, of his Collected Essays serve to show how much ancient Indian philosophy anticipated modern Western thought.

To sum up. "If the materialist affirms that the universe and all its phenomena are resolvable into matter and motion, Berkeley replied, True; but what you call matter and motion are known to us only as forms of consciousness; their being is to be conceived or known; and the existence of a state of consciousness, apart from a thinking mind, is a contradiction in terms. I conceive that this reasoning is irrefragable. And therefore, if I were obliged to choose between absolute materialism and absolute idealism, I should feel compelled to accept the latter alternative. Indeed, upon this point Locke does, practically, go as far in the direction of idealism as

Berkeley, when he admits that 'the simple ideas we receive from sensation and reflection are the boundaries of our thoughts, beyond which the mind, whatever efforts it would make, is not able to advance one jot."

Huxley continues, "For example, I get the ideas of coexistence, of number, of distance, and of relative place or direction. But all these ideas are ideas of relations, and may be said to imply the existence of something which perceives those relations. If a tactile sensation is a state of the mind, and if the localization of that sensation is an act of the mind, how is it conceivable that a relation between two localized sensations should exist apart from the mind? Thus it seems clear that the existence of some, at any rate, of Locke's primary qualities of matter, such as number and extension, apart from mind, is as utterly unthinkable as the existence of colour and sound under like circumstances. Will the others—namely, figure, motion and rest, and solidity—withstand a similar criticism? I think not. For all these, like the foregoing, are perceptions by the mind of the relations of two or more sensations to one another. If distance and place are inconceivable, in the absence of the mind of which they are ideas, the independent existence of figure, which is the limitation of distance, and of motion, which is change of place, must be equally inconceivable."

Huxley tells us that the key to all philosophy lies in the clear apprehension of Berkeley's problem—which is neither more nor less than one of the shapes of the greatest of all questions, 'What are the limits of our faculties?' And it is worth any amount of trouble to comprehend the exact nature of the argument by which Berkeley arrived at his results, and to know by one's own knowledge the great truth which he discovered—that the honest and rigorous following up of the argument which leads us to 'materialism,' inevitably carries us beyond it.

And so, Huxley goes on to prove his argument with an analogy of ordinary sensation. "Let the point of the pin be gently rested upon the skin, and I become aware of a feeling, or condition of consciousness, quite different from the former—the sensation of what I call 'touch.' Nevertheless this touch is plainly just as much in myself as the pain was. I cannot for a moment conceive this something which I call touch as existing apart from myself, or a being capable of the same feelings as myself. And the same reasoning applies to all the other simple sensations. A moment's reflection is sufficient to convince one that the smell, and the taste, and the yellowness, of which we become aware when an orange is smelt, tasted, and seen, are as completely states of our consciousness as is the pain which arises if the orange happens to be too sour. Nor is it less clear that every sound is a state of the consciousness of him who hears it. If the universe contained only blind and deaf beings, it is impossible for us to imagine but that darkness and silence should reign everywhere. It is undoubtedly true, then, of all the simple sensations that, as Berkeley says, their 'esse is percipi'—their being is to be 'perceived or known.' But that which perceives, or knows, is termed mind or spirit; and therefore the knowledge which the senses give us is, after all, a knowledge of spiritual phenomena."

We may continue the foregoing with what a great physicist in the last century has written: All through the physical world runs that unknown content, which must surely be the stuff of our consciousness. Here is a hint of aspects deep within the world of physics, and yet unattainable by the methods of physics. And, moreover, we have found that, where science has progressed the furthest, the mind has but regained from Nature that which the mind has put into Nature." (Sir Arthur Eddington: Time, Space and Gravitation.)

Undoubtedly, there is an element of muteness in certain western philosophers, too, especially in their understanding of how we might perceive the world: for some, the nature of the world is outside one's perception, and although interconnected and especially dynamic, "it is therefore contradictory." Indeed, we have Hegel with his dialectic as a method by which 'human history unfolds', which he claims that, "history progresses as a dialectical process" (25). Indeed, this dialectic is precisely how the Rishis approached their method of knowing: the premise comes from the Intuitive Self and explored in the thesis, then tested in the antithesis, which often result in synthesis and thereafter rolls into other Upanishadic writings.

Or, in parenthesis, we could concur with the Lankavatara Sutra, which states: "Mind exists; not the objects perceptible by sight. Through objects visually cognised, mind manifests itself in the body in one's objects of enjoyment, residence, and so on." Furthermore, we are also informed in the Sutra: "By appearance is meant that which reveals itself to the senses and to the discriminating-mind and is perceived as form, sound, odour, taste, and touch. Out of these appearances ideas are formed, such as clay, water, jar, etc., by which one says, this is such and such a thing and is not other—this is name. When appearances are contrasted and names compared, as when we say: this is an elephant, this is a horse, a cart, a pedestrian, a man, a woman, or, this is mind and what belongs to it—the things thus named are said to be discriminated. As these discriminations come to be seen as mutually conditioning, as empty of self-substance, as unborn, and thus come to be seen as they truly are, that is, as manifestations of the mind itself—this is right-knowledge. By it the wise cease to regard appearances and names as realities. . . Appearance-knowledge belongs to the ignorant and simple-minded ... who are frightened at the thought of being unborn. . . Perfect-knowledge belongs to the world of the Buddhas who recognize that all things are but manifestations of mind; who clearly understand the emptiness, the "unbornness", the egolessness of all things. . . . When appearances and names are put away and all discrimination cease that which remains is the true and essential nature of things and, as nothing can be predicated as to the nature of essence, it is called the 'Suchness' of reality. This universal, undifferentiated, inscrutable, 'Suchness' is the only reality." Then, the Buddha clinches for us in a statement in the Lankavatara Sutra addressed to Mahamati: "...the error in these erroneous teachings that are generally held by the philosophers lies in this: they do not recognize that the objective world rises from the mind itself; they do not understand that the whole mind-system also rises from the mind itself ; but depending upon these manifestations of the mind as being real they go on discriminating them, like the simple-minded ones that they are, cherishing the dualism of this and that, of being and non-being, ignorant of the fact that there is but one common Essence. On the contrary, my teaching is based upon the recognition that the objective world, like a vision, is a manifestation of the mind itself. "

The Upanishads have their origin in the Vedanta that in turn are nourished by that portion of the Vedas known as the Jnana Kanda (as opposed to the Karma Kanda that variously deals with religious ceremonial sacrifices) embodying spiritual teachings, from which these are further milked to produce an understanding of existence, reality, and being, pervaded in the universe. It is from here where Dvaita or duality is called into question and from where the idea of Advaita or Oness is brought into synthesis. However, the methodology employed to arrive at this synthesis is paramount: it has everything to do with the knowledge of the object and the knower. Knowledge of the object has to do with categories, as outlined by Shankaracharya in his Vivekachudamani that expounds the sense of Advaita Vedanta philosophy, while the knower is distinctly different from the individual self.

Epistemologically speaking, the Rishis spoke about correct knowledge that employs a trilateral approach, which includes a triune of differentiation. The first is Pramatir: the subject, the knower and the knowledge; the second, Pramana: the cause or the means of the knowledge; and thirdly, Prameya: the object of the knowledge. Taken together, these are known in Sanskrit as Pramanas; however, distinction is made between knowledge gained by means of perception (Pratyaksha) and knowledge gained by means of inference known as Anumana. But perhaps even more important is that body of knowledge gained from Sruti or revealed scriptures through the medium of sound known as Śabda.

Śabda or sound, sometimes referred to in Hindu philosophy as the first cause, occupies an exalted position in the hierarchy of pramana: in any dispute encountered in knowing, Śabda always wins over perception and inference, which pushes logic and reasoning outside the realm of knowing. The reason for this is that Śabda is experienced in the Self, in the same manner in which Brahma had experienced Om after one thousand days of meditation on the Self. Indeed, perception and inference are starting points when one opens the portals of enquiry in any attempt to know but, at the threshold of knowing, when the object of knowledge and the knower converge, perception and inference drop off to reveal ultimate reality.

In my world of philosophy, there can hardly be any room for consideration of inputs from such giants as either Hume or Leibniz, the two of whom featured highly in Kant's philosophy. Nevertheless, had Hume not been so thoroughly wedded to inductive reasoning, he could have been a likely candidate on my list of useful philosophers in the same way that I include Bertrand Russel as being on the fringe of an Advaita Vedantist. Indeed, I had a long association with Bertrand Russel during my university days at London, and during which time we often discussed mysticism, poetry, beauty, language and linguistics (within the context of one of his very early essays, *Denoting*), from which he would often say that without having to choose, his larger self had a natural inclination for Advaita Vedanta. He once said to me it was Advaita that had prompted him to explore possibilities about *Denoting*: 'a phrase may be denoting and yet not denote anything', in the same way that whether one experiences the Self or do not experience the self, this only has meaning for the experiencer. *Denoting* had come to him four years after he had his mystical illumination while watching his best friend's wife suffer a heart attack. That experience had changed his life, and although he had already put aside Christianity as not having any meaning for him, he began reading the Brahma Sutras. He said that Shankaracharya's commentary on the Brahma Sutra had a mathematical quality about it; it is a unique body of work written in a language as symbolical as mathematics. He also said that it is something that needs a determined discipline, and an almost "devotional quality of time", not just to read and understand but on which to meditate in order to be transported into that abode of knowing. By extension, it is possible to say with certainty that, Bertrand Russel's work on Logical Atomism is a direct result of his encounter with Advaita Vedanta: the theory is based on the notion that the world consists of "ultimate logical facts that cannot be broken down any further"(26). Furthermore, the world operates in such a way that no 'part can be known without the whole being known first.' This statement squares off Advaita in such a profound way that it begs the question about the real meaning of Monism, without the slightest attempt to either infer or speculate on perceptions: everything is derived from the One, without even trying to give it a name; however, what matters is the "essence". Bertrand Russell's mathematics as a symbolical language and his use of linguistics in his philosophy is nothing new. Way back during the days of the Rig Veda, there was Brihaspati, the noted Guru of the Gods, but also a fearless wizard of a physicist and mathematician, who had mastered the art of splitting the atom and even fusing the elements to create vehicles that are now comparable to what we have as science fiction (27).

Indeed, between Brihaspati's time and that of Panini, most of what had been passed off as Greek mathematics or Greek systems of logic, came through Panini as important developments in the history of Indian science. This in turn did not only have a significant impact on all mathematical treatises that followed Panini's pioneering work, but it also had an influence on Sanskrit, grammar, and linguistics from the 6th BC onwards. G. G. Joseph, in *The Crest of the Peacock* argues, "The algebraic nature of Indian mathematics arises as a consequence of the structure of the Sanskrit language. Likewise, P.Z. Ingerman, in his paper titled *Panini-Backus Forms* (28) posits that Panini's work provided an example of scientific notational model that could have propelled later mathematicians to use abstract notations in characterizing algebraic equations and presenting algebraic theorems and results in a scientific format. The point about this is that mathematical philosophers like Ludwig Wittgenstein, Alfred North Whitehead, and Bertrand Russell were more than familiar with Panini's abstract notations; they even had the opportunity to teach them as breakthroughs in their professorial careers at Cambridge.

For many, this development meant mastering new skills to strengthen the mind and widen the intellect; however, for Panini and his followers, even like latter-day Bertrand Russell, it had little to do with developing razor-sharp reasoning powers. The *real* challenge had to do with how to gain access to the Self in order to see the world with a greater sense of clarity, from which tools like symbolic logic and linguistics could help to transport them into the inner working of the Self. For the sceptics this would seem farfetched, but the greatest push of Vedic education had to do with working with mathematical models and linguistic drills that would push students at a very tender age on how to sidestep the mind and gain access to the Self. After all, Vedanta always vented the belief (garnered from the life-experiences of the rishis) that the Self was the storehouse of real knowledge and once the student had access to "It", everything that were worthy of knowing just flowed into the intellect to create divine intelligence.

Which takes us back to Emanuel Kant who, in his first *Critique*, was very much concerned about justifying metaphysics as a legitimate subject of enquiry, which he thought had been blocked by the philosophical impasse between empiricist Hume and the ultra-rationalist, Leibniz. The fundamental principle here was Hume's refutation of Leibniz's metaphysical judgments, which he claimed were the basis of all knowledge that are "known and justified purely by the intellect". Hume countered with his analogy of the mind as *tabula rasa*, a blank sheet "waiting to be written into by the world of experience". This undoubtedly had some appeal for Kant, which prompted him to ask, "What are the necessary preconditions for having any experience at all?" It was a strategic move on the part of Kant with the intention of synthesizing the Hume-Leibniz conundrum thereby breaking the impasse. Unfortunately, Kant surrendered with his quasi solution: in order to interpret the world of the human mind, there is the need to "impose certain structures on the flux of incoming sense-data", which is his doctrine that the world is something perceived and hence an appearance to the perceiving mind. It was acutely and laboriously developed in his Critique of Pure Reason.

Kant made the problem of the possibility of knowledge a primal one in the realm of metaphysical inquiry, and attempted to solve the question of the conditions of knowledge by the critical rather than the empirical method. In this procedure he acted exactly like Shankaracharya, who anticipated him on other points. Both, however, agree that the critical intellect ought not to set itself up as the container of reality and that, when it does so, it loses its power to perceive truth and becomes instead, in Kant's words, "a faculty of illusion."

Kant revolutionized Western complacency about the character of our experience, for he revealed the creative character of the mind's contribution and showed that experience is a synthetic knowledge a priori fashioned from integration bounds derived from the mind itself. His great analysis of the structure of the human cognitive mechanism resulted in a demonstration of its limitations inasmuch as whatever becomes an object of knowledge is subjectively enveloped in the forms of space, time, and causality. "But what originates these perceptions—what changes the mind from its prior to its present state? Something, external and extrinsic, changes it. What is this something? What it is, in itself, we can never know: because to know it would bring it under the forms and conditions of the mind, i.e., would constitute it a phenomenon—unknown, therefore, but not denied—this ens—this something is; and this Kant calls Noumenon." (Lewes: History of Philosophy.)

The world which runs on time, extends in space, and is governed by causation, is a world of mental appearance only, not a world of real being. Reality is forever hidden to us because of the ever-presence of these mental limitations. Hence Kant's twelve 'Fundamental Judgements', which he called the *Categories*. For me, these categories have a close resemblance to Panini's *four padas* and eight limbs of yoga. However, the biggest breakthrough for me, as far as western philosophy goes, is Kant's *forms of intuition*, which he immediately spoiled by calling it his *Copernican Revolution*.

According to Arthur Schopenhauer, Kant's most distinguished follower, Kant's greatest merit is "his distinction of the phenomenon from the ultimate reality". Unfortunately, Schopenhauer felt that Kant chose to overlook this as an important breakthrough. However, what Schopenhauer meant by a breakthrough had to do with the conditional proposition of the Advaita "reversal of experience" to bring the *tabular rasa* clean of any writing; that, only after the student had intentionally reversed the imprinted mind back to the former state of "a blank sheet", could real progress be made. Schopenhauer believed that Kant's attempt in trying to synthesize the opposite views of Leibniz the rationalist (who had put all his trust on the intellect) and Hume, had been one of the greatest missed opportunities, which could have ushered in progress with the preferred values of Advaita philosophy.

Writing one hundred years after Emanuel Kant, Schopenhauer superficially accepted Kant's *noumenal* world as "unknowable to the subjective self". Indeed, the "subjective" self is fickle and constantly changing with changes in the body, expectations, and flights of the imagination. But the real Self, which has to do with Consciousness is, indeed, knowable. Schopenhauer more or less admitted this in a sort of parable in his writing by utilizing what he called the "subterranean passage"; it is found by realizing "we ourselves are also among those entities we require to know"; that we are the "thing in itself" (29). The riddle here is, what constitutes the "I"? He is certain about the answer, "it is only revealed to us in the world of phenomena", so it cannot be our real essence, which is "the thing in itself", Kant's *noumena* that is theoretically possible to know, if we have the means of knowing. Indeed, this answer is taken directly from the Mandukya Upanishad. Even so, he obfuscates, "The will is not something that belongs to the individual, but a universal striving force, manifest, trapped, in the individual being by its insatiable desire to reveal itself in the world of appearance" (30).

Although Schopenhauer is credited to be an Upanishad scholar, it is obvious from the answer to his question that he never quite understood the philosophical differences between the "individual being" and the Self. This might be so because he got his knowledge of Hindu philosophy through Anquetil du Perron's Latin translation of some of the Upanishad from a Persian copy that was previously rendered from a Mughal version in 1775. Indeed, while he is correct in saying that "the will is not something that belongs to the individual", he does not say whether it belongs to the First Cause, the Self, the Creator, Brahman, or Ultimate Reality expressed in the Divine. Moreover, he implies that the "universal striving force" can be trapped in the individual being with "insatiable desire". From the point of view of Advaita Vedanta, this is the grossest of misunderstandings: the universal force is neither striving, nor can it ever be trapped; it is without desire, for as Krishna says in Chapter Seven of the Bhagavad Gita, He possesses everything, and is never in need nor desirous of anything. However it is only that, belonging to his lower nature and expressed as Prakriti, which displays afflictions observed in the individual. The greater part of these afflictions, known as *Kleshas*, are: ignorance or ávidyā, ego or asmitā, attachment to pleasure or raga, aversion to pain or dveṣa, and fear of death or Abhinivesha.

In Vedanta, however, the individual is not entirely stuck with these afflictions as punishment or retributions for past Karmas. Patañjali shows the way out of these afflictions in his Yoga Sutras, which is the path that many of the ancient rishis embraced in their sadhana or daily practices (akin to Kant's Categories), which ultimately channelled them to reach their goal of uniting with Brahman. In this regard Schopenhauer's "will" is found in the higher Self, that element of consciousness, which is in all; it is not outside of us but is found deep, within our inner beings that ultimately integrates us in Consciousness known by the ancients as Sat or Existence.

Thus, on the question of what philosophy means to me, I conclude with this quotation from the Vashista Yoga Sara: "Liberation is not on the other side of the sky, nor is it in the nether world, nor on the earth; the extinction of the mind resulting from the eradication of all desires is regarded as liberation. O Rama, there is no intellect, no nescience, no mind and no individual soul (Jiva). They are all imagined in Brahman. To one who is established in what is infinite, pure consciousness, bliss and unqualified non-duality, where is the question of bondage or liberation, seeing that there is no second entity? The mind has, by its own activity, bound itself; when it is calm [and reaches that state of a blank slate] it is free."

REFERENCES

References

1. Benedict de Spinoza: A Theologico-Political Treatise / A Political Treatise (v. 1), Translated from Latin by R.H.M. Elwes , George Bell and Sons, Covent Garden, 1887.
2. Rhodes, Ron: Reasoning from the Scriptures with Catholics, Harvest House Publishers, 2000. Paperback.
3. Andrea Bistrich: "Discovering the common grounds of World Religions. pp. 19-22; For a critique of Karen Armstrong's work, see "Karen Armstrong," in Andrew Holt, ed. *Crusades-Encyclopedia*, Apr. 2005, accessed Apr. 6, 2009.
4. *The correspondence of Spinoza*, G. Allen & Unwin ltd., 1928, p. 289. See also John Laird, Journal of Philosophical Studies, Vol. 3, No. 12 (Oct., 1928), pp. 544–545.
5. Roy, Sumita: (2003), *Aldous Huxley And Indian Thought*, Sterling Publishers Pvt. Ltd.

6. Garfield, Jay L: Nagarjuna: Mūlamadhyamaka kārika 24:8-10. in *The Fundamental Wisdom of the Middle Way: Nagarjuna's Mulamadhyamakakarika*, Oxford University Press. (1995).
7. Benedict Spinoza: (as 1, above) The chief works of Benedict de Spinoza, Volume 2, Part Three, p.134.
8. Younkins, Edward, E: Spinoza on Freedom, Ethics, and Politics. *Questions Libre*, . Montreal, May 7, 2006. No 178
9. Patanjali: Ashtanga (Yoga. yogaś-citta-vṛttinirodhaḥ ||2||)
10. Curley, Edwin M: *The Collected Works of Spinoza*. Princeton University Press. (1985).
11. Bennett, Jonathan: *A Study of Spinoza's Ethics*. Hackett. (1984). pg. 276.
12. Singh, Lalab Prashad: Tantra, Its Mystic and Scientific Basis. Pg. 97.
13. Goodman, David, Ed: Be as You Are: The Teachings of Sri Ramana Maharshi. Amazon. Com
14. Fic, Victor M: The Tantra. Abhinav Publications, Delhi. 2003.
15. Leaman, Oliver: *Key Concepts in Eastern Philosophy*. Routledge, 1999, page 269.
16. Śarmā, Candradhara: The Advaita Tradition in Indian Philosophy: A Study in Advaita Buddhism.

Motilal Banarsidas, First Edition: Delhi, 1996. Pg. 125.
17. Singh, N.K and Mishra, A.P., Eds: Global Encyclopaedia of Indian Philosophy, Volume 1, Global Vision Publishing House, 2010. pg. 303.
18. Sunday, Patricia Ann: Nostradamus, Branham and the Little Book: God's Masterpiece, AuthorHouse, Nov 1, 2012.Germans refer to themselves as "Deutschen, which is derived from the Sazon word for "Assyrian".
19. Chadha, Prem Nath: Hindu Law, Dedlhi, 1974. While the oldest dharm-shastra is Manu Smriti, the source and basis of all other smritis or dharmshastras, is, therefore, the entire Veda, which is the first source of dharma, and hence the sacred law, next the Smritis.
20. The Works of Sir William Temple: Part II University Microfilms, 1990, Miscellanea, p.157.
21. Ibid.
22. <u>The Earliest Surviving Manuscript Closest to Euclid's Original Text (Circa 850)</u>
23. Lawlor, Robert: Sacred Geometry: Philosophy and Practice, Thames and Hudson, London, 1982.
24. British Archaeology at the Ashmolean Museum, Highlights of the British collections: stone balls; the internet link is:

http://ashweb2.ashmus.ox.ac.uk/ash/britarch/highlights /stone-balls.html.

25. Pestritto, Ronald: Woodrow Wilson and the Roots of
Modern Liberalism, Rowman and Littlefield. Page 15.
26. Hennessey, Andrew: HX Assembler SoftwareManipulating Chaos. Outshore Multimedia, Lulu Press, 2011. Page 24.
27. For an acute insight into Brihaspati's life, see, Amish Tripathi's, *The Immortals of Meluha*, Westland Ltd, Chennai, 2009.
28. Ingerman, P.Z: A Syntax-Oriented Translator, Academic Press, New York, 1966.
29. Jacquette, Dale: The Philosophy of Schopenhaur, Routledge, 2005. Pg. 43.
30. Ibid, 225.

NOTES

Notes:

ancientindianwisdom.com, 1 Aug 2002

In 1978, Dr. Abraham Seidenberg, a professor of mathematics at the University of California in Berkeley, as noted in a paper called The Origin of Mathematics (p. 301, 1978) mentioned two different forms of mathematics, namely the algebraic and the geometric. Therein he explains, "If it could be shown that each of these has a single source B and there are many rather familiar facts that suggest this is so B and if, moreover, in both cases the sources turn out to be the same, it would be plausible to claim we have found the unique origin of mathematics."

He concluded, Old Babylonia (1700 BC) got the theorem of Pythagoras from India, or both Old Babylonia and India got it from a third source. Now the Sanskrit scholars do not give me a date so far back as 1700 BC. Therefore, I postulate a pre-Old Babylonian (i.e. pre-1700 BC) source of the kind of geometric rituals we see preserved in the Shulba Sutras, or at least for the mathematics involved in these rituals. In this paper, Seidenberg established that the Shulba Sutras were the basis for the mathematics in Egypt, Babylon, and Greece. In this way, Seidenberg also recognized the similarities of the Shulba Sutras with Pythagorean Greek mathematics. He went on to trace the unique origin of these forms of mathematics to the Shulba Sutras. His research led to the conclusion that the Sutra literature preceded the mathematics of both Old Babylonia (c. 1900B1750 BCE) and of the Egyptian Middle Kingdom (c. 2100B1800 BCE). However, even more than this, Seidenberg showed that the mathematics of both the Old Babylonia and Egypt must have derived from ancient India in the Shulba Sutras, as others have confirmed. As Seidenberg concludes: "The elements of ancient geometry found in Egypt and Babylonia stem from a ritual system of the kind observed in the Shulba Sutras. "

Bertrand Russell's famous quotation: *Mathematics is woven into the fabric of Existence.*

The Essence
of
Sat or Existence
As it relates to Consciousness

The Essence

of

Sat or Existence

As it relates to Consciousness

The Essence of Sat or Existence As It relates to Consciousness.

Sat is the root word of Satya, which in Sanskrit, means "to be", or Being, and has a number of connotative words. As such, Sat is a central concept in Hinduism and Hindu thought, which loosely translates into English from Monier-Williams Sanskrit-English Dictionary as "unchangeable", "that which pervades the universe in all its constancy". It is also interpreted as "absolute truth" or "reality". One such cognate is sattva, which means purity, and which forms one of the chief orders of "existence" in Hindu philosophy. Sat is not just a translation as being *Unchangeable* but is a manifestation of Being.

In its broader application the idea of Being, Existence and that which is Unchangeable, Sat fits out an entire new knowledge, in that there is an argument that moves on a plain of the highest reality. This idea is so very powerful that it gives birth to two earlier theories of "forms" and "archetypes" by Plato in The Republic, which will be investigated later in this paper. In the meantime, suffice to say that "unchangeable" is "that which has no distortion"; "that which is beyond distinctions of time, space, and person"; and "that which pervades the universe in all its constancy". As such, unchangeable is "absolute truth", which in Vedantic modality is the only "reality". Perhaps this is why Mahatma Gandhi said in his autobiography that he worshipped Truth as his God.

In this paper, although facets of truth will be considered, such as the Greek Aletheia, the greater emphasis will be put on the thought that moved Hindu sages to speak on the derivative, Satya, which connotes to truth in the same way that Kierkegaard tried to deconstruct Aletheia: "A human being is spirit. But what is spirit? Spirit is the self. But what is the self? The self is a relation that relates itself to itself or is the relation's relating itself to itself in the relation" (1)

This idea may sound as gobbledygook to most but it is Kierkegaard's attempt at "deconstruction" that later came into vogue with continental philosophers, and which injected "method" into reasoning when dealing with esoteric philosophies that required the need to move with the Cartesian scientific method, which came with the famous phrase, cogito ergo sum – "I think, therefore I am". Indeed, this was nothing new; it had started a long time ago with Euclidian geometry, which was demonstrative by amassing a series of valid deductions from self-evident truths, rather than something rooted in observation and experiment. However, this method of individualistic knowing founded on razor-sharp reasoning did not fit well with Kierkegaard's philosophy; his was more concerned with the individual human condition, compared with Spinoza, Hegel, and even Carl Marx, for whom the individual was more or less irrelevant, "a dissolute pantheistic contempt for individual man" (2)

So passionate was Kierkegaard, that he can be called a romantic in the same vein that we find William Wordsworth in his poem, "The World is Too Much with Us", complaining about "the decadent material cynicism of the time", and the need for humanity to get back in touch with nature in order to progress, spiritually. For this reason Kierkegaard believed that the whole history of thought has been preoccupied with the wrong concerns. He particularly criticized the Greeks and those Continental philosophers who concentrated on "architectonic metaphysical schemes, venerating reason in order to comprehend and make sense of the world", even though none of these philosophies take into account the fundamental human condition. In this regard, Kierkegaard is quite emphatic about his dilemma as he writes in his Journals: "What I really lack is to be clear in my mind what I am to do, not what I am to know."

It is a pity that Kierkegaard came so close to the Hindu approach to knowing, and hence to 'real knowledge', but which he eventually denied in his confusion over the difference between religion and philosophy: "the thing is to find a truth which is true for me, to find the idea for which I can live or die" (3). And, therein he found his answer in religion, which he holds as a matter of passion and not reason. Indeed, he justifies this by saying that reason undermines faith. Here he conveniently ignores those philosophers who offered rationalistic proofs for God's existence, such as Anselm and Thomas Aquinas, even though he argues that, "An authentic belief acquires its force from within, as a 'leap of faith' without the guidance of reason to reassure us that what we are doing is 'right' or 'true'" (4).

Kierkegaard's method of investigation, though close from where the bulk of Hindu philosophy starts its investigation, is a total contravention of the Hindu approach to "real" knowledge, which stems from being experiential in that, intuition is the a priori "first step", which is discovered in meditation, rather than Descartes' "a priori", captured from "innate ideas" that yields intellectual knowledge.

Intellectual knowledge appears at a lower level of understanding in Hindu philosophy: at a halfway point between Sat and Satya. After all, there are no shades of meaning in Sat, which carries the meaning of Existence,

Being, or the Supreme Reality. Satya on the other hand connotes Truth, as in the aphorism, "Satyam eva jayate": Truth alone wins, or "Satyam muktaye": Truth liberates. There is this statement, *"Satya 'Parahit'artham' va'unmanaso yatha'rthatvam' satyam"*: Satya is the benevolent use of words that come from outside the mind for the welfare of others; or, in other words, responsibilities is truth, too, as upheld by Patanjali, "When one is firmly established in speaking truth, the fruits of action become subservient to him (5). Or, as is given in one of the most important Upanishad, *"The face of truth is covered by a golden bowl. Unveil it, O Pusan (Sun), so that I who have tenets of truth as my duty (satyadharma) may see it!"* (Bṛhadaranyaka Upanishad V. 15, 1-4 and the brief Isa Upanishad 15-18). Truth is superior to silence (Manusmriti), is a comparative statement that carries "value" but it is still at a lower ebb of Sat (6).

Combined with other words, Satya acts as modifier, like "ultra" or "highest," or more literally "truest", connoting purity and excellence. For example, satyaloka is the highest realm or heaven, depending on one's understanding of Hindu cosmology, while Satya Yuga is the "golden age" or best of the four cyclical cosmic ages in Hinduism, and so on. Perhaps the greatest relevance to Sat or Being or Existence, is the contention by Hindu sages that Sat equates with Supreme Consciousness, or Brahman. Here the mahavakya Prajñānam Brahman, equates with the notion in Advaita Vedanta that Consciousness is Brahman. Indeed, this is followed by Satya, which refers to *Chitsvaru'pa* as the

Supreme Consciousness, or Param Purusha, the Supreme Being. In this regard "Sat" is one of the three characteristics of Brahman, as proclaimed in the aphorism, sat-chit-ananda: existence-consciousness-bliss.

There is certainly merit in also looking at how Buddhist thought may contribute to this investigation into the nature of Sat, especially as it pertains to Benevolence, particularly so of "Metta" and "Karuna". These two Buddhist terms equate to transcendence of love but embrace compassion. However, what is even more relevant here is that, "Truth equals love". Even so, it is important to note that this concept of truth is not merely a synonym of fact or correctness, but is more metaphysical, like the difference between brain and mind. This 'bigger picture' contains the notion that truth implies a higher order, a higher principle or a higher knowledge. Thus, the connotation of "Satya" is what one becomes aware of upon becoming a Bodhi, an enlightened or an awakened person. Thus, this is more akin to the sum of the rules of the universe or the universal reality, which is common in Indian philosophy. Even so, it is not the same as Existence and hence it lacks the deeper measure of the highest reality.

This idea of benevolence is also an important dimension in Greek philosophy, which is borrowed from both Hindu and Buddhist philosophies. Buddhist Metta relates to friendliness as is Hindu Mitrā (Vedic Mitrā as attested from the Rigveda onwards is one of the Adityas; as Mitrā, one of the twelve sons of Aditi), a solar deity and the god of honesty, friendship, contracts and meetings but later merged with Buddhism as Maitriya to become an important Bodhisattva. Both of which are at variances of Satya or truth, but which has the potential of merging into love. Indeed, some even go so far to claim that, in Roman Catholicism, Mithra is no other than the Pagan Christ. S.D. Murdock quotes Gerald Berry in Religions of the World:

> "Both Mithras and Christ were described variously as 'the Way,' 'the Truth,' 'the Light,' 'the Life,' 'the Word,' 'the Son of God,' 'the Good Shepherd.' The Christian litany to Jesus could easily be an allegorical litany to the sun-god. Mithras is often represented as carrying a lamb on his shoulders, just as Jesus is. Midnight services were found in both religions. The virgin mother...was easily merged with the virgin mother Mary. Petra, the sacred rock of Mithraism, became Peter, the foundation of the Christian Church" (7)

This is only the tip of the iceberg as far as comparisons are concerned: other than the fact that personalities such as Augustine, Firmicus, Justin, Tertullian, and many others vehemently denied that Mithra had any influence on Christian theology, history proved them wrong since Mithra was not only associated with early Christianity but with a host of other cultures and religions. As a major deity associated with the sun in Hinduism it was first transplanted from India into Persia, before it was imported into Greece;

then it was grafted onto Turkey, before being absorbed in the Roman Empire as one of their principal Gods. Finally, Mithra became a major cosmological figure in Christianity at a time when the struggling Church was sheepishly trying to consolidate its hold on the valuable infrastructure of the dying Roman Empire, both as a model for expansion, and as a method to save the new religion from extinction. No wonder, so much of early Hindu and Buddhist theology played a major role in shaping the tenets of early Christianity, which is only now being openly examined without the threat of violence that played so heavily on the early critics. Indeed, some of the finest precepts from Hinduism and Buddhism, such as Bhakti and Karuna, or devotional love and compassion, had gone into Christianity to make it what it is today. Still, some might say this idea of Bhakti and Karuna is nothing like Agape, which has more to do with Christ's love for humankind, rather than the devotee's binding love for the Lord.

There might be some truth in the Christian interpretation of the original Agape; nevertheless, the short of it is that while the idea of love was new to the emerging Judea-Cristo religion, that which is referred to as Bhakti in the practice of Hinduism, is a state of Being. It is the act of merging with the Divine in a permanently raptured state of love that goes by the name of sat-chit-ananda, or existence in a blissful state of Consciousness. However, mergence with the Divine, is not a philosophical construct as is the case with Metta (friendliness) in Buddhism; it comes after a long period of practice with meditation in a disciplined manner commonly referred to in Hinduism as Sadhana or spiritual practice. In this instance, the meaning of Satya as given in the earlier mentioned Sanskrit phrase, *"Parahit'artham' va'unmanaso yatha'rthatvam' satyam"*. Satya here is close to Buddhist's benevolent use of Metta, but in Hinduism the philosophical connotation has a greater application in word, thought, and deed, outside of the mind for the welfare of others. Therefore, a benevolent sage must be truthful, regardless of the meaning of Satya in the same way that Christ is truthful within the context of Agape.

Human life progresses through different stages—from childhood to adolescence, from adolescence to youth, youth onto maturity, and maturity to old age. It is through these changes that people progress in the manifest world. Human life or its receptacle, the body, is not Satya, not completely true, as they change with time. Sat here operates outside the mind and body; it is permanently related to the Divine, and as such, it acts as an extension of the Divine independent of mind and body but at the same time, it remains in sync with humanity. Indeed, in this sense it has the potential to move independently of thought and intellect at remarkable speed, even faster than the speed of light.

And yet, because of its "unchangeable" nature, it is not just durable; it is imperishable. Even more pertinently, like the Divine, it is ever omniscient, omnipotent, and omnipresent. In this sense Sat does not move; it just Exists in the same manner that Consciousness exists: as particles so infinitesimally small that the ancient seers likened it to being smaller than that of the expansionary particles of space. In this case, the human soul that has risen to that state of consciousness becomes one with the Divine, in the same manner, that the Divine is everywhere at any given time, and as such it is attuned to everything in creation. It becomes the knower and anticipates action before it even takes place, which makes it so very fast that it outruns even the speed of light.

In the Yoga Sutras of Patanjali, it is written, "When one is firmly established in speaking truth, the fruits of action become subservient to him." According to Paramahamsa Yogananda, during deep, dreamless sleep (*sushupti*), akin to Samadhi brought about by meditation, the yogi abides in his true nature and the soul cognizes Absolute Truth (*Paramarthika*). This idea, which was echoed by ancient Hindu sages, was picked up by Socrates and became central to the Socratic Method, in so far as his philosophy is concerned. Indeed, instead of an argument or a discussion he would use the Socratic Method, not to discover the truth but to find out what theories were not true; his purpose aimed at arriving at Truth by testing truthful definitions of questions. In "The Republic" the question was brought up, "Is it better (or more beneficial) to lead a just life or an unjust life; the answer then sought to be plumbed from, "what is a just man", and then eventually from the question, "What is Justice".

Even though Socrates has immensely influenced Western philosophy, especially in the pursuit of Truth, all that remains in the twenty-five hundred years of Continental philosophy is "method". Indeed, there is much to say about the man, Socrates, as a lover of Truth, as well as practitioner of Truth but to say that he was anything akin to the ancient Hindu Seer or the Buddhist Bodhisattva, is inconclusive, especially in the manner in which the idea of Sat or Truth is presented in this paper. Indeed, it is a mistake to think that ordinary persons are never in communion with God or the Ultimate Truth. If all men did not occasionally pass into the state of deep, dreamless sleep, even if only for a period of minutes, they could not live at all. The average person has no conscious recollection of his soul experiences; but, as a part of the Universal Whole, from time to time he must replenish his being from the Source of Life, Love, and Truth. The *Shanti Parva* of the *Mahabharata* declares, "The righteous hold that forgiveness, truth, sincerity and compassion are the foremost (of all virtues). Truth is the essence of the Vedas." Furthermore, Ethics in the Vedas are based on the concepts of Satya and Rita. In a broader sense, pertaining to religious practice of Hinduism, Satya is the principle of integration rooted in the Absolute, whereas Rita is the expression of Satya, which regulates and coordinates the operation of the universe and everything within it. Likewise, in Jainism Satya is considered to be one of its five core principles and all *sadhus* usually take a vow to adhere to it.

In Buddhism Sat manifests as Satya with its equivalence in Pali as Sacca, and translated in English as "reality or truth". In terms of the Four Noble Truths, in the Pali, or *Magadhi Prakrit*, it is found *as sacca, tatha, anannatatha and dhammasacca,* which all equals Truth. However, there are 'two truths' here: conventional and ultimate, or *sammuti sacca* and *paramattha sacca*. These two phenomena have their own characteristics; while some are conditioned, Nibbana, or Nirvana, is unconditioned, and are collectively called "ultimate reality". Uncharacteristic as they are in terms of Hindu philosophy they can be found collectively but not in the unsubstantial; in any context, they come under the conventional Four Noble Truths; within the modality of *ariya-sacca*, are the briefest synthesis of the entire teachings of Buddhism, since all those manifold doctrines of the threefold canon are, without any exception, included therein. They are the truth of suffering, reflected in mundane, mental and physical phenomena, and the origin of suffering, extracted from the Pali, *tanha* that equates with thirst or craving. By contrast there is the extinction of suffering that comes with Nibbana or Nirvana, or through rigorous training from lessons learn in the Eight Fold Path leading to the extinction of suffering, interpreted as the eight supra-mundane mind factors.

In Buddhism, 'mere suffering exists, but no sufferer is found. The deed is, but no doer of the deed is there. 'Nirvana' is, but not the man that enters it. The path is, but no traveler on it is seen' (8). The Buddhist practice is mainly relational and deals with ultimate reality while the Teaching prevails in both. However, Anatta or non-atman, contradicts the supremacy of Sat, or pure existence, found in Hindu philosophy and Consciousness theory.

Similar ideas can also be found in Neoplatonism, which originated in ancient Greece, and shares common grounds with Indian religions via the Proto-Indo-European religion: "Hè idea tou agathou", which means 'Reality in her most true appearance', equates *The One* and *The Good* are identical to *The Good*. But there is no Sat, even though Plato went to great lengths in The Republic and The Phaedo to arrive at his theory of forms and his drive to prove the immortality of the soul. Even so, with Socrates as his mouthpiece, the idea never went beyond theory and, consequently, Sat never had the chance to rise up with sufficient conviction to make the case of Unchangeable Reality, a reality.

In reality, except for a few Indophiles, because Continental philosophers were largely clouded by Christian dogma and an inherent prejudice against the wisdom of Hindu thought, as observed in the in-fighting among early Catholic writers' insistence that Mithra had no influence on Christianity and his appearance came long after the arrival of Jesus. In fact, they not only failed to recognize the impact of Mithra as an important Greco-Roman mystery cult, long before the advent of Jesus and Christianity, as well as the acute resemblance between Mithraism and the religion of Christ. Or, to inject fear into the hearts of the new Christian converts , this is what Mithraism meant to the later Church: "the devil, jealous and malignant, induced the Persians [who worshipped Mithra] to establish a religion the exact image of Christianity that was to be—for these worthy saints and sinners of the church could not deny that the worship of Mithra preceded that of Christ—so that, to get out of the ditch, they summoned the devil to their aid, and with the most astonishing assurance, thus accounted for the striking similarity between the Persian and the Christian religion." (9). What is interesting here is that these critics of Mithra did not care to know the extent to which Mithra or Mitrā had evolved in Hinduism, long before its tenets reached Persia, Greece, and the Roman Empire. Indeed, at least eleven hymns are offered to Mitrā in the Rig Veda, which is more than seven thousand years old, especially if we take into account that Rama's birth in the Valmiki Ramayana is given as 5114 BC, according to astronomical co-ordinates given in the text that correspond with Rama's birth. And since the Rig Veda existed in the Satya Yuga, a period of four thousand years in duration, and Rama was born in the Treta Yuga, a difference of three thousand years between the two yugas and Rama's birth, this makes the Rig Veda at least ten thousand years old. Even so, Mitrā predates the Vedas, for in the Tantras, a pre-Vedic text that predates the Vedas, Mitrā is depicted as representative of the Dawn; here he is even older than Agni, the deity who receives the sacrifices in the oblations and then takes them to the respective deities for whom the offerings are made. Likewise, Mitrā is the deity who not only ushers the dawn to supplicants, but who receives the Soma on behalf of Mahadeva who precedes Rudra mentioned in the Vedas. This Mahadeva is none other than Śiva, who is associated with the bull, Nandi. This is a key point in the Mithraism of the Greeks and Romans, which was picked up from Zoroastrianism associated with the eastern Persians from about the 6th century BC, at which time Zoroaster modified the Persian State religion to bring about two opposing forces, Spenta Mainyu and Angra Mainyu. Spenta is the Persian word for Hindu Spandana or Spanda, which suggests slow movement that mimics the creative or expansionary impulse of the universe. This idea of Śaivism, which was divined in its early stage from Mitrā as a solar deity to infuse luminosity in Mitrā's votaries. Indeed, it was this aspect of Mitrā that was incorporated into the early Vedic religion, and for whom hymns of praise were sung in the Rig Veda (10).

There is little doubt that the philosopher Zoroaster was greatly influenced by Mitrā's Spandana, while denigrating Vedic Aryaman to lesser importance, even he too is a solar deity associated with the sun. However, Aryaman is also considered to be chief of the manes, those venerated ancestors who are classified in Greek mythology alongside the inhabitants of Hades. In Zoroaster's scheme of things however, Aryaman is renamed Ahriman, who represents Angra Mainyu, translated as "destructive mind" or evil spirit, or the god of darkness; it also connotes "death and destruction" as an appellation of the enemy of Ahura Mazda. Epistemologically speaking however, "Mainyu originates from the Sanskrit, and carries several meanings: other than man, mind and sacrifice, it also means grief, sorrow, distress, or affliction. Both "mind" and "mainyu" connote to something higher, which is illumined wisdom that is the aim of Zoroastrianism. But while higher consciousness in Zoroastrianism remains dualistic in the belief that there is one universal transcendental supreme God in the person of Ahura Mazda, it undercuts the ultimate aim of Sat, Chit and Ananda, which is the aim of Advaita Vedanta. Zoroastrian votaries remain separate from their God, Ahura Mazda, and go in separate ways by virtue of the division created by Zoroaster that keeps the less intelligent and dark in the category Angra Mainyu while patronizing those in the category of Spenta Mainyu, who are bright and in the light in pursuit of illumined wisdom. However, unlike Advaita Vedanta where there is ultimate union with Brahman in Bliss consciousness, Ahura Mazda is aloof, and feared.

Six hundred years later when Mitrā is fully integrated in the Greco-Roman system of worship, as Mithras, Mitra is again drawn away from the possibilities of Sat and Existence to one associated with animistic tendencies. The Hindu Mitra that was associated as friend to all, including plants, animals, and humans; who was the receptacle of light and wisdom, even to the early Persians, and one who could fulfil the needs of all, is now the sacrifice. In this role, Mithra violates all that is dear to Śaivism and slays the bull in sacrifice. However, this is in keeping with Bull worship that was a common practice in most proto religions in Asia Minor. Long before Mithraism was imported into Asia Minor, Bull worship was already in vogue with certain Jewish sects, as seen most prominently in Aaron's attempt to re-install the golden calf as an intermediary between his votaries and God, which would lead the Israelites out of Egypt. Such is also the case with the Apis Bull of Memphis in Egypt, which was regarded as the all-powerful Ptah (Sanskrit, Pitah) that interceded between humans and God. The all-important significance of Mithra is the comparative treatment given in Hinduism and the religions that absorb him in their belief systems outside of India. Prior to his absorption in the early Vedas, he is associated with the generative Soma, not as liquor, but the Moon that influenced both agriculture and the mind of his votaries. Then his influence widens with the rising sun;

these early rays are as powerful as the moon rays, in that the early hours of the morning is associated with Brahma, known to Hindus as Brahma Mahurat. The significance here is that Mitrā's votaries believed that prayers offered during these early hours reached God through the benevolence of Mitrā's light rays.

Indeed, as one of the Aditya's twelve sons associated with the twelve months of the year, as well as having an influence on the planetary system, Mitrā was uniquely situated to affect "Chit" or Consciousness, which he transmitted to his votaries, especially if they obeyed the laws, and were just, equitable, and compassionate, as dutybound citizens. There is no doubt that it had to do with these concerns that caused Mitrā to be absorbed in the Hindu Pantheon among the major Gods, and for which he was offered praise in the Rig Veda. Perhaps, this was also the reason why he was considered the friend of the people, and as the society shifted with greater emphasis on governance of material values and the promulgation of laws to hold the individual responsible to the society, his worth increased in measure concerning oath, treaty, and covenant. Interesting, too, these qualities are found in Mithra of Zoroastrianism and the broader Iranian Mithraism. However by the time Mitrā is absorbed in the Greco Roman context he is downgraded to fit in with the host's shifting prejudices and sentiments. It was in this mode that those Romans that usurped the Catholic Church, which not only influenced dogma for almost a thousand years, in the same way that they used Jesus as a Roman to mould Mitrā as a soldier to bring quiet among the rebellious Christian converts that had swollen the ranks of the Church (11). Thus, within the parameter in which Mitra was boxed in, his usurpers had taken away all that was good and beautiful in terms of Consciousness and Existence, as was the case of Christ's early teachings, which was borrowed from Hindu Mitra, Vedanta, and Buddhism. In fact, everything that Mitra had taught about Love and Bhakti, loving from the bottom up to reach into the Divine, was turned around by the Church by way of Christian dogma of Agape: "God's love is displayed most clearly at the cross, where Christ died for the unworthy creatures who were "dead in trespasses and sins" (Ephesians 2:1).

Indeed, as long as one is obliged to follow Church creed or be bound by the norms of western philosophy, such an enquirer could never penetrate the essential elements of Hindu philosophy that could take them to the inner domain of Sat. For one thing, few western philosophers have ever got beyond Śūnyatā in Buddhist philosophy, which to this day have compromised their efforts in their attempts to broach such an important philosophical model as essentially "nothingness", rather than "absolute reality". Moreover, the unwillingness by western philosophers to grasp the essence of "wholeness" or "nearness" to the Hindu concept of the Absolute, known as Brahman, has been limiting to enable a full spectrum approach in coming close to an understanding of Hindu philosophy. However, even when western philosophers got seemingly close to the all-inclusiveness of Brahman, they became anchored on the idea of Maya, which they continued to interpret as illusion rather than getting anywhere close to how Sri Krishna explained this in the Bhagavad Gita:

Ajo 'pi sann avyaatma bhutanam isvaro 'pi san
Prakritim svam adhisthaya sambhavamy atma-maya

This quotation from Chapter IV, verse Six of the Bhagavad Gita, says that Krishna manifests Himself by His Self as pure sattva or goodness by His internal potency known as Yogamaya through prakriti or material nature, which is completely under His control. However, eager to employ deconstruction methodology at work, Continental philosophers arrived at an idea of this verse, as nothingness or illusion. Indeed, it is conceivable that, because of cultural differences, there could be inherent difficulties in understanding the gamut of "prakriti", which is commonly interpreted as "nature". Prakriti has to be understood within the context of consciousness, or as Sri Krishna puts it, as part of His Being; as such there is a higher element of His Being just as there is a lower element. The higher relates to Sat and Existence or the unchanging reality of the Divine, while the lower corresponds to Krishna's lower nature manifesting as Prakriti or the ever-changing mass of matter, which includes human beings that function on the lower ebb of consciousness.

The idea of Prakriti expressed as the lower nature of Krishna raises some imponderable questions for western philosophy. To begin with, how is it possible, even though being eternal, can Krishna manifest himself through a material father and mother that is part of prakriti, interpreted in the most simplistic way to mean "nature"? And yet, given the even more simplistic European understanding of esoteric "mystery" as to why is Krishna's birth so different from the "miracle birth" of Jesus! No doubt, there is resistance here complicated by prejudice, largely because it is inconceivable to the Christian world that such a birth could take place in India three thousand years before the birth of Jesus Christ. However, outside of this inherent prejudice, there is the unwillingness to accept, rather than try to understand that Lord Krishna is capable of establishing his "parents" in pure sattva, as well as by His Yogamaya potency and manifesting Himself through them while appearing to be "born" by normal human perception. Even so, as Lord of Creation, Krishna is not dependent on anything, for according to the understanding of the immortality of the soul, Krishna is never born, nor does he ever die; he appears whole without the use of prakriti to manifest himself. Indeed, he maintains that prakriti is part of his lower nature – *bhumir apo 'nalo vayuh mano budhir eva ca/ahankara itiyam prakritirastadh* "Earth, water, fire, air, ether, mind, spiritual intelligence, and false ego, are thus the eightfold divisions of my external energy or lower nature" BG: VII, 4 – in the same way that everything in creation is part of his lower nature. He enters every aspect of creation and simultaneously resides there, while at the same time He continues to perform his duty as Lord of the universe. In this way His true form, which is Sat, is transcendental and complete in itself, while prakriti, which is the substratum of all material existence, is subservient to Him. In this sense, "Atma maya" infers the consciousness of the soul, and maya is understood to be referring to yogamaya or the consciousness of Lord Krishna's internal potency. Thus, yogamaya arranges the situation and all the details with phenomenal alacrity and intricacy so that Lord Krishna appears to be born like a normal human being but factually this is not so. He appears to be born from a mother and a father but actually, it is not the case. Isha means great but Ishvara means greater than isha. Therefore it is stated that since Lord Krishna is superior to those who are isha such as Brahma, Śiva and Shesha, but according to the Isha Upanishad, only He (Krishna) is to be known as Ishvara or the greatest of the great and none other.

Which brings into play the idea of Brahman: earlier in this paper, Brahman is equated with Consciousness, which is sometimes marred by scientific enquiry, or by the methodology employed by latter-day philosophers eager to change the manner in which philosophy is arrived at, known as deconstructionism. In a manner of speaking, the western approach to philosophical understanding is one of analysis, which is an extension of academic training based on analyzing complex scholarly commentaries while comparing and contrasting viewpoints. Overall, this approach to the study of esoteric literature leads to highly intellectual exercises that dampen the inner flow of "real knowledge", which originates from the inner being of the individual researcher; over a long period of discipline, this methodology conditions the person to be wary of so-called extraneous observations, which do not follow the norms of the scientific method. This is the real dilemma with most western philosophers who tackle Consciousness from the viewpoint of pure science. Even physicists who have approached consciousness studies have warned about the pitfalls of the "pure science" approach, especially in dealing with particle physics as a tool to tackle the expansionary nature of the universe, as a means of finding answers about the nature of God.

By contrast, the ancient sages and seers of the Indian subcontinent who have approached consciousness theory, even though knowledgeable about the Vedas and the Upanishads comprising of hundreds of thousands of verses, prefer to forgo "academic" analysis in favour of reciting just a few aphorisms, such as the four Mahavakyas that deal with the nature of Brahman. In the monastic tradition, a Swami may contemplate exclusively on just one of these esoteric sayings over a period of time, but deep enough, to displace the mind so that real knowledge about the Self emerges to bear spiritual fruit in the form of Sat or acquisition of knowledge of the Ultimate Reality. Surely, the liberator needed is the inner self when tapped deep enough to render the mind still and serene rather than being a surging ocean ravaged by cross currents caused by monstrous typhoons. Moreover, within the serenity where the mind practically banishes unnecessary moorings, ghosts of past disciplines bearing false knowledge no longer can tempt the suppressed ego with their fatalistic offerings – as had been aptly demonstrated by The Buddha in his encounter with Mara at the time of attaining Nirvana.

To be sure, the Mahavakyas are the great sayings distilled from the Vedas and found their way into the literature of Advaita Vedanta and Jnana Yoga, after parsing the scrutiny of the Upanishads. Etymologically speaking,
Maha means great and Vakya means sayings. They are surprisingly so very short in length but, in the tradition of

the aphorism, they are loaded with meaning. Thus, while analysis is of little use, contemplation and meditation yoga is the key to the extraction of meaning, which has to be churned from Sat or existence of the Self. Even so, what is eventually gained is revealed knowledge about the nature of the world.

The four Mahavakyas with their approximate meanings are: Prajñānam Brahman: Brahman is Consciousness or Supreme Knowledge; Tat Tvam Asi: That is what you are; Ayam Atma Brahman: Atman, or the soul, and Brahman are the same; Aham Brahmasmi: I am Brahman. It is interesting to observe the order in which these saying are laid down, which does not necessarily mean that the yogi, sadhak or student, has to tackle all of them at once, or even in a piecemeal fashion. As hinted in the above one can work with any one of these aphorisms in one's meditation to yield meaningful results. However, at a quick glance at the order of their appearance, there seems to be the suggestion that, by approaching Brahman, the yogi or student's mind is readily open to Consciousness in which real knowledge is given birth. Similarly, *Tat*, or *That*, immediately refers to something of significance: it is either Brahman or Consciousness, or even Sat, a relative of Consciousness. Then, the most esoteric of knowledge: Atman, or the Soul, and Brahman are the same. There is no relativity: my soul and Brahman are the same! Imagine that: yours and my soul are not merely with the highest but are always together.

Finally, the end of mystery: "I am Brahman".

The ordering of the Mahavakyas may not have been intentional but they certainly convey a sense of cohesiveness that ties the text together in a holistic fashion. Indeed, even though one may choose any one of the Mahavakyas to meditate upon, they are intended to work together with astounding cohesiveness.

The most important thing for the yogi or student of yoga, who are the real philosophers, is this: until the mind is brought under the control of the Self, the attention span bounces from object to object, or from image to image in a seemingly endless sort of way. However, if the meditation is prolonged, the intellect will gradually come under the "guidance" of the Self and, consequently, those objects and images become *relatively* real until they disappear altogether. Thus, as the meditation further deepens with the wellspring of time, gradually, we come to see that no object exists independently from Brahman, the whole of Sat or Existence. Hence, it is said by the rishis of yore that Brahman satyam jagan mithya: Brahman is real and unchangeable, while the world is unreal, because it is ever in a state of flux (12). And so, as Consciousness rises, wherever the yogi looks, or whatever he thinks or feels, try as he might, he can find no second object or part thereof. Which is why the seers declare: *Ekam evadvitiyam Brahman*: there is only One, without a second. Everything is seen as a manifestation of something else, which the ancients call Brahman or Sat, or its English equivalent, Existence.

But how does the Western mind arrive at this knowledge of Existence? The Merriam-Webster Dictionary, as quoted in Wikipedia, says that existence "is the world one is aware or conscious of through one's senses, and that persists independently in one's absence. Other definitions describe it as everything that 'is', or more simply, everything." Some define it to be everything that most people believe in. In most cases, the common usage of "aware" and "conscious" have to do with feelings or emotions. One might be able to do away with these, temporarily, by administering external stimuli. Therefore, in this sense, common existence is largely a surface element related to the human body and can hardly be raised to that level of understanding in the manner in which Sat is presented in this inquiry.

Interestingly for this discussion, Buddhism speaks of "three marks of existence": anicca, dukkha, and anatta. These are all Pali words that are derived from Sanskrit: anicca stems from anitya, which means impermanence; dukkha, from dukha, which means suffering; and, anatta from anatman, which means "not-self" or no-soul. In each case, there is the perception of a slight variance in meaning, but philosophically the apparent twist given in Buddhism not only alters the intent but fabricates an entirely new religion and philosophy. Anicca, for instance, pushes forward the idea away from Sanskrit impermanence to "conditioned existence", in which Buddhism now claims that existence, "without exception, is transient, or in a constant state of flux." It is just the opposite of Hindu thought of impermanence in a philosophical vein: here it means "inconstant" largely because Buddhism nullifies atman which is permanent. Likewise dukkha, the second mark of existence, brings suffering to the forefront as one of the four major pillars of Buddhist cosmological beliefs (13). By contrast, in Hindu philosophy, dukha or suffering depicts a state of wrongful living but which can be reversed by the practice of artful living, as prescribed in Patañjali's eight-fold system of yoga. And, herein, we find the real difference between annata and anatman: annata speaks of "non-self" as that which has no soul, and by extension it implies that the atman or Self does not exist, whereas anatman upholds the permanence of atman or soul that exists (14). Here Buddhist thought totally radicalizes Hindu thought of "not-atman", which means something like 'this body is not atman', or that since the soul or atman is distinctly different from the body, 'I am not my body,' or that body which is confused with the atman, is not atman. After all, atman is not part of "conditional existence"; atman is Existence because it is permanent, and as such is different from Hindu impermanence. This has more to do with that body of knowledge that relates to prakriti or the lower nature of

Krishna or the Divine; it is permanent in the same way that the Self or Brahman is permanent.

There is little doubt that this notion of "non-existence" or "impermanence" in Buddhist thought has been responsible for Western thought that continues to grapple with the idea of Maya as illusion or non-existence in Hindu thought, and "nothingness" in Buddhist Śūnyatā. Maya is not merely "illusion" or "non-existence"; it is related to what can be called mistaken identity: a state of being when the soul mistakenly identifies with the body; 'I am this', or 'I am that.' Under such a state, of Being, the soul operates under the influences of the "gunas" rather existing in transcendence of prakriti or materiality.

However, the gunas (tamas, rajas, and sattva), which correspond to ignorance, passion, truthful existence, have a marked impact on every living entity but because the human brain is more evolved, it is incumbent on every individual to either hold the gunas in balance or transcend them, which would enhance the ability to merge with the Divine. The gunas are important for the behavioural characteristic of all beings and create bondage. In this way the mind mistakes the body for the soul and becomes bonded to material existence and becomes addicted by the five kleshas or afflictions commonly identified as anger, attachment to desires, lust or covetousness, pride resulting from false ego, and hate or jealousy resulting from low esteem.

The gunas are derived from the Divine or from Krishna's lower nature known as prakriti. They are not permanent in themselves but exist in a state of flux, which is conditioned by rising Consciousness in beings. Without this rise in Consciousness, beings remain in perpetual bondage trapped by the kleshas; however, in the Divine, they remain in perfect balance, which serves as a magnet to draw the beings into the Divine. But when there is disturbance due to the imbalance of the gunas, creation takes place. At such times beings absorb these gunas in different proportions, which restrict their abilities to recognise their true relationship with the divine. In a nutshell, this is the essence of Maya, which has nothing to do with non-existence; it is the reaison d'être for the need for understanding man's place in the universe and human relationship with the Divine. As such it is at the heart of another doctrine in Hindu thought known as Śankara: 'that which has been put together' and 'that which puts together'. It is essentially a mental process but also emphasizes the changes brought about in the universe because of contacts with the five elements, as well as by the forces of mind and intellect. In this sense, which agrees with Buddhist thinking, "…only the appearance of a thing ceases as it changes from one form to another. Imagine a leaf that falls to the ground and decomposes. While the appearance and relative existence of the leaf ceases, the components that formed the leaf become particulate material that goes on to form new plants"(16).

As far as Maya or "non-existence" goes, Buddhism has something to say that avoids extreme views as taught in the Middle Way: it avoids externalism (all points in time are equally "real", as opposed to the idea that only the present is real). Here the issue is perception: 'there are vast differences between the way things are perceived to exist and the way things really exist.' And, this is where Śūnyatā enters the domain of Reality: "by addressing the existing object's served purpose for the subject's identity in being. What exists is in non-existence, because the subject changes." (17). Yet, to put this in proper perspective, what is changed cannot measure up to Existence in terms of Advaita Vedanta, since Existence is unchangeable insofar as Existence is equated with the Self or Brahman, the Supreme Reality.

The ill-conceived idea of Maya and impermanence, within the purview of Western thought strikes at another fallacy in the West in determining "personhood"; for many, since Advaita Vedanta seems to nullify the smaller "self" when the aspirant rises in Consciousness to unite with the Divine, the deduction arrived at in this phenomenal change is loss of personhood. Indeed, there is hardly any rational thought here other than prejudiced thinking against one of the most profound thought in Hindu philosophy. After all, when the individual, after years, or several lifetimes of practice, arrives at the highest state of Existence the body does not die. The change that takes place is solely one of Consciousness, which at once enriches the body in a new state of earthly existence, while the soul languishes as that free agent with the ability to be re-united with the Divine. Philosophically speaking, there is more to be had from Ontology, which is a branch of philosophy that tries to make sense of Being, Existence and

Reality. Even so, the approach here is very general in nature in that it deals more readily with "categories of being" as they relate to questions of metaphysics. On the whole, questions are asked about what "entities" exist or can exist. However, before these entities are investigated, they are grouped in the same fashion that every aspect of matter, mind, and intellect, are characterized and grouped in that division of Hindu philosophy known as Sāṃkhya. But, before any meaningful answers can be attempted, early ontologists touched hard on the branch of Hindu philosophy known as Sāṃkhya.

In a strange sort of way, Sāṃkhya might be one of the oldest of Hindu philosophies since a lot of it predates even the Vedas, although there are strains of it in the Rig Veda. This means that Sāṃkhya is not a single cohesive work, for strands of it appear in many different works, including the Bhagavad Gita and some of the Upanishads. However, although there has been joiners to it, the first name to appear as the founder of this philosophy is Sage Kapila. Even so, the name of Kapila is not without controversy; there is ambiguity as to time and place, as well as whether there are two Kapilas or just one. On the one hand, the Srimad

Bhagavatam mentions Kapila as a renowned sage and the incarnation of Truth; as such he is regarded as an expansion of Vishnu. On the other hand, from the same narrative, which is one of the eighteen histories that account for the lives of the gods, the culture which they established, their teachings and the expansion of religion on the Indian subcontinent, one of these, the Srimad Bhagavatam accords the other Kapila as being a descendent of Agni, the god of five variations, who predates the Vedas as one of the sons of Aditi, the mother of the twelve cosmic gods that help to uphold and sustain the Universe as *Rita (18)*. This particular Kapila, who is a descendent of Agni, the fire god praised in the Rig Veda as responsible for receiving oblations on behalf of all the gods, is said to be a conditioned soul, in comparison to the other who is an incarnation of Vasudeva or Vishnu. What is significant for this enquiry is that these two Kapilas represent the two distinct statuses, which relate to creation: *Nimitta* or the efficient cause, and *upādāna*, the material cause. To make sense of this, recall that Krishna spoke about two aspects of his Existence: his higher nature that deals with spiritual matters, and his lower nature, known as yogamaya, which deals with prakriti. Within this context, there are two separate worlds; one that deals with the material cause that manifests as the material cosmos that we know from scientific enquiry, and the other world, a corresponding spiritual cosmos that can only be known from spiritual enquiry. Interestingly, while the one indivisible God creates both worlds, the first Kapila, the descendent of Agni, is identified with the material cosmos and is a considered atheist. He could never see the need for such a world, nor did he believe that in the spiritual world there existed innumerable planets and universes, including the highest spiritual realm of Krishna's personal abode known as Goloka. In this regard, Kapila the atheist, could never get the support of the Vedanta philosophers, and as such he went his own way. Eventually he would influence the Nyaya and Buddhist philosophies, even though he accepted the dualist cosmic notion of two realities, with subtle differences: Purusha, not as supreme Lord, but as consciousness, and Prakriti, not as the lower nature of Purusha, but as unalloyed matter. In this way his influence on Advaita Vedanta, though piecemeal, steadily grew until it became a philosophy to reckon with, especially with the Greeks, and later with European philosophers (19).

Sāṃkhya was able to get away from the idea of atman or soul by almost re-inventing the concept of Jiva. Unlike what we learnt in the Bhagavad Gita that the jiva is the embodied soul in that it identifies with the body rather than its rightful place with the Purusha or Supreme Reality, Sāṃkhya appropriates the Jiva in which Purusha is bonded to prakriti. This totally contradicts the Bhagavad Gita, which clearly indicates that Purusha and prakriti are essentially one, although the Purusha can separate itself from prakriti and just be the objective observer, thus allowing it to move on its own accord. It is this idea of separateness that prakriti seemingly acts on its own, which gave rise to the notion that the universe independently moves on its own accord without the need of Purusha or God. Indeed, in scientific parlance, the universe is seen as an expanding mass with an intelligence of its very own totally outside the realm of any divine influence, and thus denies the existence of God. This idea, more than anything else is responsible for the notion that Sāṃkhya is an atheist philosophy, although it recognises Purusha as Consciousness in the same way that quantum physics recognises the intelligence behind the expanding universe as Consciousness (20).

Earlier the claim was made that, within the context of this paper, there is more to Sāṃkhya from the perspective of ontology in that it contributes to Sat or Existence, although it brackets Being from the main framework of Hindu philosophy. Thus from an ontological point of view, by its very definition, according to the Monier-Williams Sanskrit/English Dictionary, (Cologne Digital Sanskrit Lexicon, Germany) Sāṃkhya means "to reckon, count, enumerate, calculate, deliberate, reason, reasoning by numeric enumeration, relating to number, rational." It is the only philosophical school within the parameters of Hinduism based on a unique "systematic enumeration and rational examination" (21).

The word Tattva indicates a true or real state, truth or reality, or a true principle or category. In Vedanta, tattva is said to be a combination of tad and tvam, and indicates "That thou art", and is the Mahavakya by which the identity of the world with Brahman is revealed. This relates to Sat or

Existence but in a more commonplace sort of manner, in that tattva is an element or elementary property, the essence or substance of anything. However, from the point of view of philosophy, tattva jnana indicates knowledge or truth or true principles of something. Even so, tattva is not restricted only to Sāṃkhya; it is used as maps in various schools of philosophy. For instance, in Śaivism there are thirty-six tattvas, in the Mahabharata there are twenty-five, while the Bhavishya Purana lists twenty-three. However, the Lokayats, originally known as Lokayata Brihaspatya and connected to the Cārvāka, considers only the five elements, largely because theirs is an atheistic philosophy that deals mostly with pleasure and materialism.

In Sāṃkhya philosophy there are twenty-five tattvas or true principles. These are Prakriti or *avyakta*, the unmanifest or imperceptible state; *mahat* or *buddhi* that relates to intelligence; *ahamkara* or egoism as it relates to an overriding attachment to one's self; the five *tanmatras* or the subtle sensory qualities like colour, taste, smell, sound, and touch; these give rise to the *Mahabhutas* or the five great elements, inclusive of akasha or space; the eleven organs are made up of five external sense organs, one internal sense organ known as *manas* or mind, and five motor organs: *vāk* that deals with speech, hands that deal with doing things, feet for movement, and the motor organ for excretion and the genitals – five organs of perception, and five of action; and Purusha.

The twenty-five tattvas enumerated in the above illustrate the reason for the label that Sāṃkhya is an enumerative and rational philosophy. However, two of the tattvas, Buddhi and Purusha, indicate the extent of a throwback to the origins of Sāṃkhya that relates to its preVedic connections. All twenty-five tattvas pervade Śaivism, which has its origins in Tantra that is also pre-Rig Veda, but Buddhi and Purusha are insinuated from what is called pure tattvas in Śaivism, which encapsulates the *Bindu* within Śiva, illustrated by the dot within the triangle that represents duality within the One that is commonly referred to as *ŚivaŚakti*. Indeed, from this comes, Śakti or cosmic energy; *SadaŚiva* the ever-auspicious materialization of the transcendent god, *Maheshwara*; *Ishvara*, and *Videshwara* or *Shuddha Vidya*, which is considered as pure knowledge. Taken together these have the nature of *Chit* or pure Consciousness within the context of Existence and Sat. These may all relate to Purusha, but the remaining five emanate from Buddhi or intuitive intelligence: *Kala* or time, *Niyati* or law of destiny, *Kaala* or creativity that has the power to draw the soul to pure knowledge, *Vidya* or limited knowledge, and *Raga* or emotions drawn from attachment.

While Purusha is considered pure in Vedanta, in Śaivism it is likened to be impure in Sāṃkhya because of associations with Prakriti. Indeed, in the Bhagavad Gita, Sri Krishna clearly states that Prakriti is his lower nature, which is governed by him, even though beings are endowed with sparks of His intelligence to break away from the foibles of nature and unite with Him in order to be liberated. However, this spark of intelligence can only be ignited by what Krishna calls Self-knowledge, by knowing, by which Krishna says, "All the sages have passed from this world to the highest perfection." Furthermore in Bhagavad Gita XIV: 2, Krishna says:

> *Those who, having devoted themselves to this knowledge, have attained unity with Me, are neither born at the time of creation, nor are they disturbed at the time of dissolution.*

Indeed, in Bhagavad Gita, Sāṃkhya is understood to mean Jnana or the science of Divine knowledge, which is identified with Brahman. Now, such a person who has reached this state of knowing is considered to be beyond the modifications of Prakriti. That, transmigrations involving births and deaths, do not trouble or tarnish these, even though everyone is born of Prakriti. However, the three Gunas of Sattva, Rajas and Tamas do condition other individuals. Yet, this is precisely where classical Sāṃkhya differs from Vedanta or the Bhagavad Gita's explanation of Sāṃkhya. The Gita's position is summed up in Krishna's statement to Arjuna in Chapter II: "Arjuna, you lack Sāṃkhya – right understanding." From the point of view of a philosophy of history or a metaphysical process of human history, this statement might sound puerile or even childish, but it makes the point about, not just classical Sāṃkhya, just where western philosophy resides in comparison with the origins of philosophy that started with the Hindus. In

Chapter II, where the word "sāṃkhya" was first used, the point aimed at had to do with meaning and understanding of the true relationship between one and all others, and not just what "appears" to be around just one person, even though that person might have been Arjuna, the chief protagonist in the Bhagavad Gita.

Indeed, there are more important things that condition our existence, such as like and dislike. The very existence of human beings as individuals or isolated personalities is due to an event that has perhaps taken place in the process of the creational or the evolutionary activity of the whole structure of the universe. Krishna seems to have suggested that the individual or so-called "me" has arisen as a result of the split of the cosmic ahamkara, the original cosmic "ego" that was born with the Gunas. It is not the same as the ego of man, but an impersonal metaphysical reality, which is the "I am what I am" of mysticism and religion that manifested itself, as it were, as the objective universe of perception and the subjective individuality, which are the jivas. That jiva is conditioned by the five elements, and the internal components of prana, the senses, the mind, the intellect, and the large reservoir of what is called the "unconscious." However, this unconscious is not the same that is know from psychology, but the potentiality of every future eventuality, and even rebirth that is there at the root of our individuality. Transcendent to all these layers of our individuality is the 'Light Supernal' which is the Absolute peeping through our reason, through our mind and even the senses, and animating every cell of our body, making us feel "We are", "I am", etc. (22).

Though much of what is said in the above could be linked to Consciousness theory that touches on our theme of Sat and Existence, which classical Sāṃkhya could easily accept, the statement, the Absolute peeping through our reason, would be anathema to core of Sāṃkhya for the simple reason that there is no concept of the Absolute in classical Sāṃkhya, as there is in the Bhagavad Gita's notion of sāṃkhya. Even so, in the Bhagavad Gita, as given all through Chapter II, right understanding is the central focus. In this sense, sāṃkhya as the knowledge of harmony is underlined in this verse given in BG II: 48:

yoga-sthaḥ kuru karmāṇi saṅgaṁ tyaktvā dhanañjaya
siddhyasiddhyoḥ samo bhūtvā samatvaṁ yoga ucyate

The plea in the verse is the duty of everyone who is cognizant of "right knowledge" to perform action while being fixed in yoga; the key of which is renouncing attachments by being even-minded in success and failure, which would ensure equilibrium. Indeed, *samatvaṁ yoga ucyate* indicates that equanimity is yoga, just as balance and harmony is yoga. In this way, too, cooperation and not competition is yoga, just as battle, war, exploitation, animosity, and hatred are not yoga. Similarly, two verses later, Sri Krishna connects this idea to *yogaḥ karmasu kauśalam,* yoga as expertness in action. Work done to perfection is verily yoga, and it is only from this expertness of action can we get a true meaning of sāṃkhya as given in the Bhagavad Gita of "right understanding". Along with right understanding comes poised mind, calm attitude, and expertness in action; only then can one perform one's duty with equanimity. This idea is enumerated in the third chapter of the Bhagavad Gita, which is perhaps the whole gospel of human action, in so far as it is called *Karma Yoga*, or the yoga of action. The key to understanding what Sri Krishna means by karma yoga is the story of the descent of man from the higher realms, which contradicts classical Sāṃkhya that holds man is a composite of the elements but infused with right knowledge as a result of Buddhi or intelligence, and Purusha or Consciousness. In Chapter III of the Bhagavad Gita, however, we learn that we are not constitutionally separate from the structure of the world or the universe. Ironically, despite the fact that we descend from the higher realms our individuality is not different from the substance out of which the world is made. To put this in a nutshell, there is the *mulaprakriti*, the original material out of which the whole cosmos was formed, something like the space particles of modern physics or something subtler than that, from which descended the tanmatras: śabda, sparsa, rupa, rasa, gandha, the principles of sound, touch, colour, taste and smell. These concretised themselves into a greater density of substance and became the solid substances of what we have as the five elements: earth, water, fire, air and ether. These things are the building bricks of the cosmos, physically speaking, everything material is nothing but a formation of the five elements:

earth, water, fire, air, ether, from which are derived the modern periodic table as mentioned earlier in this book.

Now here is the big leap from classical Sāṃkhya: the mulaprakriti is constituted of three forces mentioned earlier in this paper called, sattva, rajas, and tamas. There are corresponding scientific words to these three, known as statics, kinetics, inertia and action; statics is something like inertia, which can be equated with tamas or non-action; kinetics correspond to rajas: movement and distraction; sattva on the one hand could be the balancing act between rajas and tamas. However, in Indian philosophy there is an element of purity to it, since sattva stems from the Sanskrit root, sat, which means Existence, Being; and the condition of being is called sattva, and the characteristic of being is equanimity. Hence, the condition of true being is called sattva. So, the nature of reality or true being is neither inert existence, nor loss or absence of consciousness, nor is it activity in the sense of distraction. Pure being is sattvaguna; it is neither rajas nor tamas. This sattva is a power that connects the two extremes of inertia and activity – rajas and tamas; and the whole of the world is nothing but this threefold activity of nature – sattva, rajas and tamas – which is the structure, the constitution, the basic substance of the tanmatras, the five elements, this body, and all things in the world. This, in a nutshell, is the essence of Sat, Existence and Being.

How does the clarity of Sattva, derived from the balancing act between rajas and tamas, arrive to make one pure and above the foibles of the common folk? The ancients asked four questions: Is your vision clear? Do you see the indwelling divinity or atman within all beings? Is the world seen as it is or as it appears? Indeed, these four questions are condensed into Sri Krishna's admonishment of Arjuna noted earlier, "Arjuna, you lack Sāṃkhya – right understanding," the right vision or insights that transform our perception of who we are, what this world is, and what is our relationship to it. A person with such insights or understanding is a designated Rishi or Seer in the ancient Sanskriti world, but in today's world such a person would be considered a philosopher. However, the Upanishads would say otherwise: such a person would be a knower of Brahman; one who is imbued with Consciousness to the extent that there is no difference between personhood and Brahman, even though in today's world where there is a multiplicity of empirical understanding of philosophical construct, consciousness remains an elusive concept with different categories.

For the purpose of bringing this paper to a close, it would be helpful to consider the four categories of Consciousness that helped to mould Advaita Vedanta into a distinct philosophy. These are Brahma Caitanya or absolute consciousness, Ishvara Caitanya or cosmic consciousness, Jiva Caitanya or individual consciousness, and Sāksi Chaitanya or the indwelling consciousness. At a first glance, anyone familiar with Advaita Vedanta would surely object to such *upādhis* or adjunctive distinctions since, unlike western philosophy where there are major divisions and categories, Advaita Vedanta is itself non-dualistic and hence all Consciousness. This is the essence of Brahma-Caitanya, from which the Rishis claim that there is a substratum of the universe, which is finer than anything that modern science can define in that it holds all of creation in its grasp. The nature of this phenomenon is pure being, and what the Rishis call sat-cit-ānanda, which connotes existence, consciousness, and bliss (23).

Yet in our commonplace world, despite what we learn from Advaita Vedanta, there is an intrinsic division in the affairs of thinking man. Most western philosophers cannot comprehend Advaita's (non-duality) claim of absolute consciousness that is undivided, unmoved and unchanging, since all that the untrained eye or mind, "without sāmkhya", knows is multiplicity and change. Or, for those who are willing to put Advaita's claim to the "test", there is at least a paradox, which Shankaracharya, the greatest of Advaita's defenders, ably resolved by his theory of *Vivartavāda* or superimposition: "From the ultimate standpoint, absolute consciousness did not become this world; it only appears to have done so." What this means is that beings causally superimpose the world of appearances on the Real or Brahman, in the same way that one may casually mistake a rope in the dark for a snake; however once light is shone on the rope, reality dawns with "sāmkhya" right knowledge that "the universe has no existence apart from Brahman." This idea of "mistaken identity" that, it is possible for something to exist without being real, makes it possible in Advaita Vedanta that something can exist and not exist; or to put it in Advaita language, 'this world is and is not' (24). What "is not" is the built-in suggestion of an "illusion", which is not Maya in a philosophical sense. This "illusion" does not suggest an existence without being real, but a parallel world without a base or without substance; it is not Sat in that it does not have absolute Existence. However, for one who has sāmkhya, who has "clear vision" as does a Rishi, the world is absolutely real in so far as he sees the whole of it as Brahman, although a mistaken world of matter. What makes the Rishi see through what others call "maya" or "illusion" is cosmic "imposition of the unreal on the real...which measures the immeasurable" (25). Nevertheless, real Maya comes into play when it shows, to the untrained eye or without the right understanding, "its twin faculty of concealing the reality and projecting the apparent, just as a magician uses illusion to trick his audience into believing what he so wills. For most, the magician's clever skills are real but there is Reality beyond measure of skill based on realization. The Taittiriya Upanishad says:

> *Anandaddhevya khalvimani bhutani jayante*
> *Anandena jatani jivanti*
> *Anandam prayanty abhisamvishanti*

Which translates as, 'From pure consciousness, which is of the nature of absolute bliss, all beings arise, in bliss they are sustained, and at death they reenter and merge again.' This is a subtle point that makes the distinction between body and Self, which is equated with pure consciousness. Because the Self, as opposed to the body-mind with which we mistakenly identify, is itself nothing less than Existence; when we become aware of this truth, bliss erupts from the innerness of the heart and floods the entire being. However, this eruption of bliss does not happen by itself; the yogi or Rishi makes a career of meditation, and after persistent inquiry into their true nature, the mind ceases its control of the intellect, and the Self emerges from the chasm of sub-existence, in an ocean of peace and joy that connotes Sat-Cit-Ananda, or bliss- consciousness in ultimate Existence.

Having that essential clear vision and sāṃkhya, the yogi becomes cognizant of two fundamental truths about the world: the Absolute and Relative consciousness. The Absolute is permanent, changeless, and lasting; it exists in all and it is real, regardless whether it is known or not, but once it is experienced by the seeker, there is a spontaneous eruption of bliss. With Relative consciousness, however, everything is connected with the body and the mind, as well as the energy that runs it, which is called ahamkara or ego. The ego is the identity each person begins to fabricate from the moment of birth, an identity that is shaped by the predilections of past lifetimes. From the point of view of Maya, the Relative consciousness is considered unreal only in the sense that it is neither permanent nor lasting. Advaita Vedanta considers Relative consciousness through what it calls īśvara-caitanya; the prospect where Brahman unites with the Creator, Preserver, and Destroyer of the universe. In this role as the combined force of the three tattvas in one, Brahman is designated as the ultimate cause of the universe; nevertheless, through yogamaya, the veil of appearance is superimposed over the world. Even so, Brahman does not transform itself or the world to affect this superimposed state, largely because Brahman, like Existence, is changeless and permanent in its designated status of Absolute Reality. In this sense, Brahman is without beginning and without end. However, Īśvara, is a Deity with attributes, a personal God in this superimposed world recognized by those without sāṃkhya. Even so, this does not mean that there are two or more than one Gods. From the viewpoint of Advaita

Vedanta, 'Brahman appears as Iśvara when viewed through maya.' From abstract Consciousness Brahman is approachable by votaries in a personalized form, and Iśvara might even be given a name, according to the socio-cultural customs in that particular milieu that breathes its peculiar human consciousness.

Indeed, human consciousness, as opposed to Brahman Consciousness or Absolute Consciousness, further descends from Iśvara consciousness to Jiva Caitanya or human consciousness. Rather than the ego identifies with Brahman or Iśvara consciousness, the ego endowed Jiva (the shadow aspect of the soul) is human consciousness bound, and hence identifies with the body and the mind. Swami Śivananda says that the superimposition of the ego-idea upon pure consciousness "is the individual's first plunge into the whirlpool of maya." While Shankaracharya says that "the lie of separateness—the claim that 'I am I (the lower I)'—is the initial act that produces the chain reaction of further superimposition and entanglement. Considering ourselves as 'individuals' is the implication of considering everything as 'individual'." It robs humanity of being part of the unifying force that is Brahman, and thus inexorably superimposes a world of multiplicity upon the one, undivided Reality that is the essence of Sat, Existence and Consciousness (26)

Unlike western philosophy that claims knowledge comes from sensory perception, based on what the mind accumulates through life experiences, Hindu philosophy posits that real knowledge only comes after the mind is cleared and the Self merges with Brahman. Thus after clearing the mind and bringing it under control to that state of the tabula rasa, when all accumulated wrong or impure knowledge of the world is removed, the individual comes to the understanding of the luminous Self, which now has the mind as the onlooker, or witness and known in Vedanta as *sākṣi-caitanya*. In this state, the Jiva is now tempered in the knowledge that it is not the body but is now superimposed by the sākṣi-caitanya to become the witness that transcends the changing states of the mind. However, having arrived at this "self-realization", the individual, with a clean slate, returns to normal consciousness with a transformed mind. It is from here where the world is now seen in a refined state, akin to a sheet of glass, through which sunlight can pass unobstructed to further enlighten the mind in order to move closer to the Self.

Even as the mind moves closer to the Self, it will take time before a remarkable change is seen: the mind must go through the rigours of continuous contact with the Self, before it loses its grip on the intellect. It is only when the mind willingly allows the light of consciousness to reach the body and its organs, unimpeded, can the necessary change take place. Here, as the witness, the sākṣi-caitanya sees the Self distinctly from the body and mind, which are now recognized as subjects.

It is only when the sākṣi-caitanya is able to harmonize with the individual body that a true knowledge dawns: that, it is the self-luminous atman, which governs one's psychophysical being, and not the intellect or the mind. Called the *Antaryāmin* or inner controller, it is known as the witness-self, akin to the intelligence that rides the intellect as Buddhi, rather than the intellect riding the individual with incorrect or impure knowledge. Implicit to this understanding is the relation between the intellect and the luminous Self; the intellect is not the driver, nor should it take clues from the mind; it obeys the Buddhi, which is intelligence reflective of the intellect but processed by the luminous Self. The luminous Self here is thus none other than Brahman that is the sum of Sat, Existence and Consciousness.

REFERENCES

References

1. Kierkegaard, Sōren: The Sickness Unto Death (A Philosophical Masterpiece) Start Publishing LLC, 2012. p. 13).
2. Durkin, Kieran: The Radical Humanism of Erich From, Palgrave Macmillan, 2014. pg. 174.
3. Kierkegaard, Sōren: The Soul of Kierkegaad: Selections from His Journals. Edited with an introduction by Alexander Dru from the original, published by Oxford University Press in 1939. Dover Publication. pg. 44.
4. Ibid.
5. Patanjali, Yoga Sutra number 2.36. Published by The Yoga Academy, (Big Nest) London, 2013.
6. Manusmṛti or Laws of Manu, also known as *MānavaDharmaśāstra*, is a discourse given by Manu, believed by Hindus to be the progenitor of mankind to a group of seers, or Rishis, who beseech him to tell them the "law of all the social classes". The copy that I have consulted is translated by George Bühler and

7. published by Dover Publications, Inc., New York in 1969 in conjunction with the original Max Müller series, the Sacred Books of the East by Clarendon Press, Oxford in 1886.
8. Berry, Gerald: Religions of the World, Barnes and Noble, 1956.
9. *Visuddhimagga. XVI or The Path of Purification:* Translated by Bhikkhu Nānamoli, Buddhist Publication Society, Colombo. 1956.
10. Hilgendorf, James: A New Myth for The World, The Tribute Series. Pg. 148. Compare also, Frazer, James Geroge, *The Golden Bough*. Originally published in two volumes in 1890, but reissued by Touchstone Books, in one volume 1995. Unabridged 880 pages.
11. See article by Subhasha Kak, The Vedic Religion in Ancient Iran and Zarathushtra, August 5, 2003. Link: http://www.archaeologyonline.net/sites/default/files/imported/artifacts/Vedic Religion in Ancient Iran.pdf.
12. Cf. Hilgendorf and Frazer in 9 above.
13. Vanamail: The Sciencde of the Rishis: The Spiritual and Material Discoveries of the Ancient Sages of the Ancient Sages of India. Simon & Schuster Canada. According to Pujya Swami Bhoomananda Tirtha Maharaj in his Forward in this book, he is explicit about Sat or Existence: Brahman alone is said to be sat, or pure existence. Brahman is beyond time. Hinduism

does not declare the world to be asat, or nonexistent. The jagat, or world, is mithya and not asat. It is called mithya because it has a dependent and relative existence. It is not eternal and timeless, but it exists on the substratum of the Brahman - See more at: http://books.simonandschuster.ca/The-Science-of-the-Rishis/Vanamali/9781620553862#sthash.aFls4OEQ.dpuf

14. Kapur-Fic, Alexandra R: The Jatakas: Times and Lives of Bodhisattva. Abhinav Publications, Delhi, 2010.

15. Ibid.

16. David Kalupahana, *Mulamadhyamakakarika of Nagarjuna: The Philosophy of the Middle Way.* Motilal Banarsidass, 2005, page 48.

17. Kuipers, Theo A.F in *General Philosophy of Science*: Focal Issues. North Holland. (2007). p. 326

18. Ibid.

19. Holdrege, Barbara A. (2004). "Dharma" in: Mittal, S. & Thursby, G. (Eds.) *The Hindu World*. pp. 213–248. New York: Routledge Holdrege (2004:215). Remarks: "*Rta* is the ultimate foundation of everything; it is "the supreme", although this is not to be understood in a static sense. [...] It is the expression of the primordial dynamism that is inherent in everything ..." Also compare, Heckaman, C. (1979). *Toward a Comprehensive Understanding of Rta in the Rg Veda.*

Master's Thesis: McMaster University.

20. Rajadhyaksha, N. D: The Six Systems of Indian Philosophy Mumbai, OCLC 11323515.

21. Sen Gupta, Anima: *The Evolution of the Samkhya School of Thought*, New Delhi: South Asia Books. 1986

22. Ibid.

23. Sri Aurobindo: Life Divine, Birth Centenary Library, Pondicherry, India De Luxe Edition.

24. Please read the dialogue between Gargi and Yajnavalkya in Brihadaranyaka Upanishad.

25. Loy, David: *Nonduality: A Study in Comparative Philosophy*, New Haven, Conn: Yale University Press, 1988.

26. Shankaracharya: Self Knowledge (Ātmabodha), trans. Swami Nikhilananda (New York: Ramakrishna Vivekananda Center, 1946), p. 94.

27. Ibid.

The Advaitin's Way: Ganesha Chaturthi As The Gateway to Consciousness

The Advaitin's Way: Ganesha Chaturthi As The Gateway to Consciousness

Not until I had read the third volume of Amish Tripathi's *"The Oath of the Vayuputras"* that I took Ganesha, the mind born child of the Hindu goddess Parvati, seriously. Here he is not an elephant but a human being who is grotesque looking: he is fat and has an extraordinarily large nose, but like his brother Karthikeya, he is a great warrior. What is even more interesting is that Ganesha is neither the offspring of Parvati nor Śiva; he is the biological child of Śiva's previously married first wife, Sati: a fierce warrior that equals or even surpasses Śiva, who constantly dotes on her. This reading is so powerful that I found myself repeatedly going back to reassess my evaluation of Ganesha, as given in the Puranas, and even what we first learnt about him from the Rig Veda, the most definitive of all of the Vedas, which is sufficient to raise pertinent questions about the significance of Ganesha with regard to Indian philosophy.

For me, Ganesha is not just a person, even though he comes across real and assertive: he is intelligent, quick of mind in a deliberative way, strong willed, as well as physically capable that demands feats of strength, while remaining calm in all his deliberations; and despite his awesome size, he moves like lightening in situations where stealth is necessary. What all of these suggest is what we get at when probing the most essential aspect of Indian philosophy, which is how one holds the mind at bay in the pursuit of the consciousness in Vedanta, especially human consciousness or Jiva Chaitanya, despite the fact that Ganesha is considered one of the most important of Hindu deities.

When I first encountered Ganesha in volume one of the Śiva Trilogy, *The Immortals of Meluha*, the character whom we later meet as Ganesha, is merely referred to as The Naga. Indeed, from Puranic readings, we get the idea that the Nagas are an ancient martial people and very war-like; they were hated by mainstream Indians, and even Śiva had difficulties putting them down, until he had obtained assistance from Krishna as told in the Mahabharata. Certainly this image of the Nagas were so corrupted that history have them being eventually evicted from India whereupon they found themselves travelling through Asia until they reached the Americas. Obviously this account is pre-Mahabharata, for when the Pandavas were exiled from

India, it is hinted that they had also reached as far as South America whereupon Arjuna took a wife from among a particular tribe that bears resemblance to that of a Naga woman.

The manner in which Amish chips away at the Puranic account of Ganesha is interesting: it took more than a thousand pages before we get anything that is divine about this Hindu deity that is the darling of the Hindu world. At first, he is robustly satanic, but gradually, Amish reveals his idea of Ganesha that is even greater than any deity. His ugly looks and his amazing prowess, and the dark clothes and mask that he wears trip up the unsuspecting reader into unquestioningly accepting what is given on face value. Even so, it even took all the discriminating powers of Śiva to see through the outward garb before he could arrive at possibilities, and even this took another five hundred pages before we are able to see Ganesha for what he is. For me, this is the most appealing aspect of the Śiva Trilogy: the ability to transcend prejudices pertaining to forms before arriving at myth, and then the greatest of all transcendence to finally arrive at the possibilities of history. And, in so doing, to straighten out much of our muddled thinking that is conditioned by how we approach scriptures and remain anchored by what is given on surface value, rather than looking deeper and arrive at what is intended. For me, this is the best argument against bibliolatry as earlier discussed in the first part of this book.

Reading the Śiva Trilogy provided the impetus for me to reorient my view of Ganesha as something much more than a deity, and perhaps to even reassess the entire purpose for the festival of Ganesha Chaturthi, which is perhaps one of the most lavishly celebrated event in all of India. It also convinced me to take a closer look at the Puranas associated with Ganesha and reflect on their purpose; or, at least to enquire what celebrants gain from the fifteen-day period set aside to celebrate this all-important deity. Indeed, some may have opted for the minimal observances: they might have offered puja, offered sweets to friends and family and even meditated for the greater part of the thirty-six hours set aside for the first period. Others might have observed five days of celebrations, while still others might have put through the entire first seven days that culminate in the procession from the temple to the nearby flowing streams when the murthi is immersed in running water or in the sea to be reunited with the elements at the end of the fifteen-day period.

Traditionally, Ganesha Chaturthi is celebrated on the day "Ganesha frequencies" first reached earth. Symbolically, this is the day on which Lord Ganesha was supposed to have been "born", which is given as the fourth day of the bright fortnight of the Hindu lunar month of Bhadrapada, which corresponds to August 21 to September 21 in the Gregorian calendar. Spiritually speaking however, because of the alignment of the planets, this period is best suited for the maximum benefits of meditation by those who are particularly disposed to Jnana Yoga. And, since Ganesha is the pre-Vedic deity associated with divine knowledge, Ganesha Chaturthi was originally set aside for this purpose.

Chaturthi, however, carries quite a different meaning within the realm of spirituality, concerned with meditation and consciousness. Chaturthi stems from the root word *turiya*, the prefix, *char*, and the suffix, *thithi*. Turiya is a stage in meditation, char is four, and thithi is a lunar day that carries certain significance. Thus, Chaturthi suggests, especially from Hindu philosophy that, Turiya is the fourth stage in the experience of pure consciousness. As such Ganesha Chaturthi is the background that underlies and transcends the three common states of consciousness of waking, dreaming, and dreamless sleep.

Indeed, the period specifically aims at arriving, through meditation, at *turiyavastha*, a state in yoga that is beyond the states of waking (*jagruti*), dream (*svapna*), or deep sleep (*sushupti*). This turiyavastha is itself the target of a seeker who goes beyond ritual to find the Supreme Reality that goes by the name of Brahman. Later in this article, in the section dealing with the eight incarnations of Ganesha, there is the assertion that Ganesha is equated with Brahman. This is the high road for the aspirant of Advaita persuasion, compared to what is prescribed in the Agni Purana for the practice of religious observance (*vrat*) aimed at the acquisition of worldly pleasures rather than True Liberation (*Moksha*).

The Puranic birth of Ganesha:

One day Goddess Parvati was at home on Mount Kailash preparing for a bath. As she did not want to be disturbed, she told Nandi, her husband's loyal friend, characterized in the Puranas as Śiva's Bull, to guard the door and let no one pass (historically speaking Nandi is a human being and a very close friend of Śiva). Nandi faithfully took his post, intending to carry out Parvati's wishes, but when Śiva arrived at his abode and naturally needed to get into his home, being loyal first to Śiva, Nandi had to let him pass.

Parvati felt slighted and even angry, but even more than this, she felt mortified in the thought that she had no one as loyal to herself, as Nandi was to Śiva. Therefore, being a spiritual adept from her thousand-year experience in deep meditation, Parvati created a being out of her own state that would be as powerful as her very own self and at least as powerful as Śiva.

There are two versions that account for the creation of Ganesha: the first given symbolically shows he is a combined product of her mind and body. The other is that she made an image of a child from the mud where she customarily bathed, mixed with turmeric paste that came off her body in the bath, which she had kept sacred for many years. Eventually she approached Vishnu and requested that he breathe life into the baby clay image, thus creating Ganesha, whom she declared as her very own loyal son.

The next time Parvati wished to have time to herself in her private abode, without intrusion of any kind, she posted Ganesha on guard duty at the door. In due course, after a long period of time had lapsed, Śiva unexpectedly returned home, only to find this strange boy telling him he could not enter Parvati's private abode! Furious, Śiva ordered his guards to remove the boy, but they all failed! Such power did Ganesha possess that the Puranas declare him to be the son of Devi that originated from the very womb of Aditi, the mother of all the gods.

The ease with which the child Ganesha defeated Śiva's powerful guards astounded Śiva. Obviously, this was no ordinary boy! And the usually peaceful Śiva decided he would have to fight him; and in his divine fury severed Ganesha's head, killing him instantly. When Parvati learned of this, she was so enraged that, she decided to destroy the entire Creation! Lord Brahma, being the Creator, naturally felt threatened, and pleaded that she reconsider her drastic plan. She said she would, but only if two conditions were met. One: bring Ganesha back to life, and two, that he be forever worshipped as host of all the other gods.

Śiva, having cooled down by this time, and realizing his mistake, agreed to Parvati's conditions. He sent Brahma out with orders to bring back the head of the first living creature he crosses that has its head facing north. Brahma soon returned with the head of a strong and powerful baby elephant, which Śiva placed onto Ganesha's body. Breathing new life into him, Śiva declared Ganesha to be his own son while giving him the status of being foremost among the gods, and leader of all the Ganas, the reference to all living beings in the universe. Hence, Ganesha became Ganapati.

Of course, the word, "gana" refers to the host of all living beings coexisting in creation, but which became instructive in the story of Ganesha. However, at first glance, this story just seems like a nice tale that we might tell our children, or a myth without any real substance. But, its true mystical meaning is veiled. It is explained thus: Parvati is a form of Devi, the *ParaŚakti* or Supreme Energy that pervades the universe. But she has a special affinity to the human body: in the human body She resides in the *Muladhara Chakra* as the Kundalini Śakti located between the anus and genitals at the base of the spine. It is said that when we purify ourselves, ridding ourselves of the impurities that bind us, then the Lord automatically comes.(1) This is why Śiva, the Supreme Lord, who had been in deep meditation while Parvati had been purifying herself, came unannounced, after her purification had been completed.

Nandi, Śiva's loyal friend manifesting here as the sacred bull, whom Parvati first sent to guard the door, represents the divine temperament. Nandi is so devoted to Śiva that his innermost thought is directed to Him, which is why he was easily able to recognize the Lord upon his arrival. This shows that the attitude of the spiritual aspirant is what gains access to Devi's (the Kundalini Śakti's) abode. One must first develop this attitude of the devotee before hoping to become qualified for the highest treasure of spiritual attainment, which Devi alone grants. (2)

At the very first time after Nandi had permitted Śiva to enter, Parvati took the accumulated *maila* (the natural waste product that comes off the skin in the wash) from her body that had been preserved with turmeric paste, and created Ganesha. Yellow is the colour associated with the Muladhara chakra, where Kundalini resides and Ganesha is the deity who guards this chakra; however, in Ayurvedic medical practices, turmeric is a cleansing, as well as curative agent. This act of creating Ganesha to guard Parvati, who is symbolical of Devi, is the opening account of the very beginning of Tantra, a body of work that is pre-Vedic and comprises an ancient science, the first science that is the essence of metaphysics. It involves a system of asanas and breathing technique combined with meditation practice known by the name of Kundalini Yoga – all of which contribute to a comprehensive system of philosophy.

Devi needed to create Ganesha, who represents real knowledge as distinct from that of earthbound awareness, as a shield to protect the divine secret from unripe minds. A secret that she alone knew, and which was revealed during her thousand years of meditation from where she could be enabled to bring Śiva into her inner being. This revelation could have only taken place when awareness no longer exists and the mind completely turns away from mundane matter of the world, to the higher realm of Consciousness toward the Divine, as Nandi had; only then could the great secret be revealed, and then only through deep contemplation and meditation. Indeed, this is how the secret is communed to advanced practitioners of meditation during the fourteen-day celebration of Ganesha Chaturthi.

What was the great secret that Parvati had learned from her thousand years of meditation? The secret of Tantra until revealed to her was kept tight by its originator, Śiva. Amazingly, not even he, in his conscious mind associated with body awareness was even aware of its existence. But as

Parvati began to probe Existence or the higher echelons of Consciousness, she began to "see" things in her quest to conquer Mount Meru, the sacred transcendental abode of Śiva. Soon, she found out that the spinal column is a cosmic replication of Mount Meru, and just as there are notches in this mountain peak from where the devotee can take rests in the suffocating climb to the top, so there are subtle divisions associated around the spinal column known as Chakras. Indeed, before Parvati had any knowledge of her inner self, she sat as a coiled snake at the base of Śiva's spine pining away for his acceptance. During this time, she was not only ignored, but she remained almost asleep, which also accounted for Śiva's thousand years of wandering as the wild ascetic, smeared in ashes from his frequent visitations of cremation grounds. During this time, Śiva is also often depicted as feasting on burnt flesh from cremated corpses. However, as often occurs, when the body takes rest, and the mind no longer torments the Jiva or body-bound-soul, meditation happens naturally; at such times, the sleeping serpent at the base of the spine charges and Kundalini awakens on her own accord. Recognition of her own yellowness is proof that she is not alone, for her brightness throws light on her keeper, the primordial elephant known as Airavata that were brought up with all of the jewels of creation from the churning of the Ocean of Milk by the Devas and the Asuras. This elephant at the base of the spine is shaped like the Swastika and is surrounded by four lotus petals; however each petal is pierced in the middle by a spear; four more spears separate the petals, which seem to be guarding the transcendent elephant, on which Devi resides. This very first chakra is known as Muladhara, or the root chakra, which is ever vigilant, even when Devi seems to be asleep.

The word Muladhara is a compound Sanskrit word derived from *mula,* and *dhara*. Mula means root or base; it also denotes "beginning", "foundation", "origin or cause", "basis", "source". The meaning of Dhara is more extensive: on the substratum level it means to flow like a stream of flowing water; on a transcendental level it refers to Earth as Prithvi, who is a goddess, and who gives support to the globe as the source of spiritual growth.

The idea of source and flow is essential to an understanding of Kundalini Yoga, which has its origins in Tantra. In addition to the psychic centres that are associated with the spinal column, there are also three primary entities that are referred to as *nadis* or streams, or canals; nadi comes from the Sanskrit root word "nad" that means movement. Two of these, the Ida and Pingala, are strung like two chains invisibly encased in a finely fibrous "lotus stalk" alongside the spinal column, which is seen by yogis as "spider's thread". The ida and pingala, although associated with the Śusumna, encased in the spinal cord, in that they spiral around it from left to right and right to left, they work independently of each other and have specific functions that deal with the primary ascent of Kundalini, which is channelled mainly through sexual energy. The aim at this level of activity is to move slowly by coaxing Kundalini to traverse the benign path of ida; however sometimes the yogi goes against the teachings of the guru and channels Kundalini through the right hand path of pingala, which is rapid but very fiery to the yogi, where injury could be sustained. The two nadis, ida and pingala, are regarded as feminine and masculine respectively; they start at the base of the spine and terminate at the right and left nostrils, just below the Ajna Chakra, which is associated with clarity of vision, deep spirituality, and psychic phenomena; they also aid in processing the vital breath into Prana that is essential for the rise of Kundalini, and the primary activation of ida and pingala. Through these primary nadis, which traverse the spinal column, Pranic or vital force flows between the base of the spine at the anus and the genitals, and rises to the top of the head, where the "thousand-petal lotus" resides.

The ancient Rishis believed that within the Śusumna there are three other nadis, charged with cosmic substance, which is subtle and cannot be seen with the naked eye; neither do they ride on the common arteries or veins. However, the anatomy of the spinal cord suggests that it is largely a body of brain-matter, which is modulated nerves and nerve cells and fibres; it is not a tight fit in the spinal canal but is suspended into the spinal canal, where it "floats" in the cerebra-spinal fluid in a casing of fatty tissues that guard against injuries. Even more importantly here, is the fact that the spinal cord comprises of two symmetrical halves by an anterior and posterior fissure; this is of enormous significance in that in the centre there exists the *canalis centralis*, so minute but nevertheless sufficient to allow for the passage of the Śusumna along with its otherwise significantly encased three nadis.(3)

Indeed, western science deals mainly with the gross form of the spinal cord, while the ancient Rishis dealt with both gross and *subtle* nature that goes by the name of *Śukshma*, the subtle body that is unmanifest or dormant. Also, apart from the three primary nadis given in the above there are eleven other nadis of major importance when studying Kundalini Yoga, which are outside the domain of western science. And yet, there are thousands more that proceed to different parts of the body to perform special functions, some of which are physiological, others psychological, while many more relate to a knowledge of the universe that links the astral body with physical body functions in both philosophical and spiritual ways.

In-between the two chakras mentioned above, the Muladhara at the base of the spine, and the Sahasrara at the crown of the head, are five other chakras known as *svadhisthana, manipura, anahata, vishudha,* and the *ajna*. Their location in the human body corresponds to, below the navel, above the navel, at the center of the chest, at the base of the neck, and between the eyebrows. All of these subtle or psychic centres, other than having a profound spiritual influence on the individual, also contribute to the overall well-being of the individual. The muladhara for instance, aids in physical survival; the svadhisthana, to emotional balance and sexual proficiency; the manipura, to personal enhancement as well as charismatic control over others; the anahata, to love, friendship, compassion, and altruistic concerns; the vishudha, to confident communication, in the arts, letters, and general self-expression; the ajna, to reliance on the intuitive self and seeker of wisdom, clarity of vision; and, finally the sahasrara, to discharge of the spirit as the springboard to unite with the Universal Self or Brahman.

The above seven chakras are the main psychic centres that deal with Kundalini Yoga in the gross physical body but Tantra believes they are also in the astral body, and remain so even after the human body perishes after death. In other words, the chakras exist in a subtle state because gross matter results from metaphysical subtle matter, which argues that without the subtle body the physical body would not exist. Indeed, even though one cannot see the chakras with the naked eye, the yogi feels them during meditation. (4)

Physiologically speaking, just as there exists plexuses in the human body due to the cross-over of nerves, arteries and veins, similarly there are interlacing nadis or plexuses that branch out of the Śusumna to cross over to subtle centres around the chakras to form pools of consciousness or *chaitanya*. Prana charges these subtle centres of vital energy, which are constantly picked up from the Śusumna nadi. Interestingly, it makes sense to mention that there exists important lesser nadis and chakras here. There are, in addition to the seven already discussed, another seventeen chakras, and thousands of nadis located in different parts of the body, from toe to crown; the purpose of these is to serve all of the functions of the body in a similar fashion as do the major organs of the body. However, at each of the subtle centres of the major chakras there is a presiding deity, represented by a particular animal, which denotes the guna or manifest quality of that animal (5). Depending on preparedness and the degree of practice, before Kundalini awakens and passes through the different chakras, the yogi will pick up the raw masked quality of that animal, which could be frightening or experientially mortifying. However as the yogi progresses and the body is cleansed through maintaining a healthy diet of thought word and deeds, the essence of that particular animal, which should be the ultimate divine tattva or quality, would surface above the animal mask that would provide blissful experiences.

Animal Symbols Aligned with the Seven Chakra Centres:

Image	Chakra	Animal Symbol	Animal Attributes	Animal Message
	Root Muladhara	Elephant	Charges through blockages. Protects. Remembers. Loves closeness. Social. Effective.	I provide

	Chakra	Animal	Qualities	Affirmation
	Sacral Svadhisthana	Crocodile	Encourages creativity. Balances. Goes deep and resurfaces. Changeable.	I develop
	Solar Plexus - Manipura	Ram	Motivates. Determination. Will. Expansive power.	I recharge
	Heart Anahata	Antelope	Inspires. Tenderness. Leaps over pettiness. Grace.	I share
	Throat Vishuddha	Elephant	Purifies. Mastery. Harmonizes.	I express

	Third Eye - Ajna	Black antelope	Explore inner realms. Journeying. Trust. Vision. Truth.	I guide
	Crown Sahasrara	Egg	Divine connectedness, pure being Potential. Purity. Limitlessness. Ascension	I reveal

In addition to animals associated with the seven chakras there are also seven female divinities associated with each chakra; starting from the muladhara to the sahasrara, these are: Dākinī, Rakinī, Lākinī, Kākinī, Shākinī, Hākinī and Sri Lalita Devi. However, it should be mentioned that while this is the generally standard allocation of divinities to the different chakras, in most of the acceptable ancient texts there is neither an animal nor a feminine divinity allocated to the Sahasrara chakra. Moreover, the *Sat Chakra Nirūpana (6)* places Brahma, Vishnu, and Śiva (the principal deities of the Hindu pantheon) in the first, second and third chakras respectively, with different forms of Śiva thereafter. Also, in the *Śiva Samhita* and a few other lesser valued works, Ganesha is placed as the presiding deity in the first chakra, Brahma in the second, and Vishnu in the third. It would seem, especially to the western mind, that there is an irrevocable discrepancy here; on the surface that might seem so, but not if it is remembered that in Hinduism there are many different sects that arrange their deities according to the degree of importance they ascribe to male and female deities. In both Tantra and Vedanta, Ganesha and Brahma are metaphysically related to the Earth: Ganesh, as host of the Ganas or Beings, is symbolical of Prakriti or Nature, and Brahma, as the creator, is synonymous with the essence of Prithvi Tattva that holds everything in creation together.

In the Bhagavad Gita, Sri Krishna spoke about his higher and lower nature; and in the Ganesha Purana, which is narrated by Sri Krishna, Ganesha is assigned a very special place in the affairs of man. He is as powerful as any god because of his dispassion, and as such all created beings must pass through him before they can approach the higher deities, as is the case in Kundalini Yoga regarding any of the divinities assigned either to the nadis or the chakras. And, regarding the position of Vishnu as the presiding deity of the Manipura Chakra, this too, might seem inconsistent with Vedanta, since Vishnu, as preserver of everything created, is the second major deity of the Hindu Pantheon. However, purely from the point of view of Tantra the Manipura Chakra, located at the solar plexus, governs the life force. According to the Śiva Samhita, Manipura is related to the principle of sight, and since Vishnu sees all in creation and is the regulator of all life forms, he conquers disease and death. This idea is reinforced by the fact that the seed mantra for this chakra is Ram. Ram, who is considered a reincarnation of Vishnu, lived seventy-one hundred years ago, was the hero of the Ramayana, and his weapon was the bow, which did not only make him unconquerable but also indestructible. This idea of invincibility is particularly significant because the Manipura Chakra is likened to "the seat of Fire, both within the body and its cosmological connection with the god Agni, who is one of the sons of Aditi (the mother of all the gods) and who receives oblations from the fire sacrifice on behalf of all the gods. In addition to this, the energy generated by both Vishnu and *Braddha Rudra*, representative of the power of destruction although kind to his votaries in that all that exists return to him *(7)*; in this form he is visualized in meditation, in the form of Lākinī Śakti who wields the thunderbolt or Vajra. Vajra is one of the three nadis encased in Śusumna, which will be discussed later; suffice to say here that Vajra is associated with the sun and is one of the most difficult paths that any yogi can contemplate in meditation.

The seeming inconsistency addressed in the above goes further: as addressed earlier, the Śiva Samhita has the presiding deity of this chakra as Braddha Rudra, which is an earlier appellation of Śiva; although there are two distinct paths followed by Tantrics and Vedantists, there are instances in history where there is convergence. For instance, in the Ramayana, although Śiva originated from a different tradition, there is mutual respect and admiration for the two systems of yogic practice. Rama of the Bow is blessed by Śiva, especially in Rama's meditational practice where Śiva is seen as pure consciousness. This is the real significance of the strategic allocation of the three Gods to the first three chakras. Starting with Ganesha representative of Earth with all its mundane natural phenomena, the yogi slowly ascends the next chakra at a higher plane of consciousness where he is embraced by Brahma within all his creative elements. This is the world of man and mind, which further challenges the yogi to ascend even higher, where transcendence is the hallmark of existence. Vishnu offers some comfort, even though with him there is still that element of mind; what the yogi needs is transcendence, and by trailing the breath in pranayama, he encounters Śiva, who is pure consciousness.

By contrast however, among the Shakta sects, there are those who believe that the cosmos is created and managed by the generative and operative force of Śakti, rather than Brahma. Śakti in this context is not just a significant deity but a concept that means "power" or "force"; and since the core of Tantra is governed by meditation rather than by blind faith, the modus operandi is "thought power", which is described as "Śakti of the mind". Hence, in essential Śaktism, there is one of these feminine divinities noted above for each of the chakras – Dākinī, Rakinī, Lākinī, Kākinī, Shākinī, and Hākinī. However, it is important to take note that these divinities are not entirely independent; they only become responsive to body consciousness when they are struck by the rising Kundalini during her journey from the Muladhara to the Sahasrara. Indeed, the yogi becomes aware of the individual characteristic of each chakra by the colours emitted from each, which is signalled by the opening of the number of lotus petals ascribed: Muladhara 4, Svadhisthana 6, Manipura 10, Vishudha 16, Ajna 2 primary and ninety-six secondary, and Sahasrara 1000. It should also be noted that these lotus petals hang downwards but as Kundalini pierces through each chakra the individual lotus pushes the petals to face upwards, from which the peculiar hue of that chakra radiates, as a signal to the yogi that the chakra has been activated. However, as soon as Kundalini moves on to the next chakra, the lotus closes and the petals turn downwards. This procedure goes on until Kundalini reaches the Sahasrara chakra and merges with Śiva. At such time the yogi experiences Sat-Chit-Ananda, which marks the yogi's ascent into pure consciousness (8). Yet, this union between Kundalini and Śiva is not permanent, for Kundalini will return to the Muladhara where she would take rest, until such time that the yogi calls on her again to repeat the journey during meditation. In this downward path, according to the *Sat Chakra Nirupana*, it claims that Kundalini sprinkles her ambrosia in all the chakras that leaves the yogi smelling sweet and feeling totally satisfied. Indeed, as this repeated journey continues in meditation, especially where there is no more effort to rouse Kundalini, it is what sets the physical body apart from the cosmically etheric body. The experience of bliss in pure consciousness brings to the yogi essential proof of knowledge of layers of energy fields, which the ancient Rishis spoke so amiably with irrevocable conviction in their esoteric philosophies.

Outside the realm of Tantra, as practiced by tantrics, it is firmly believed that the seven chakras noted above are associated with the three nadis that run from the base of the spine to the crown of the head. The non-tantric aim is to reach Brahman by way of the thousand-petal Śusumna, which is the gateway to the Divine, regardless if one believes in a personal God, such as Ishvara, Vishnu, or Śiva. However for the Advaitin, those who believe in Advaita Vedanta, in which uniting with Brahman is the goal, this can only come with exiting the body through the Śusumna. For the tantric, however, the Śusumna is a place to experience bliss, which for them is testimony that yogic fire has been risen sufficiently, through the grace of Kundalini, in order to experience that all-important state of sat-chit-ananda or bliss consciousness-bound Existence. However, even among the most advanced tantrics, there are variations on the theme of Bliss: some speak about Param Ananda (bliss from above or the highest source) as supreme bliss, while others speak of Nityam, (infinite) Vijananam (dispassionate) Anandam (bliss) as bliss in eternal knowledge. However, in the background of all this is the objective of the practitioner that Śiva-Śakti will, once the serpent power or yogic fire has risen, manifest in them as Supreme Consciousness from where they will merge with Śiva-Śakti, completely.

In pursuit of the Supreme Consciousness, the tantrics liken the Ida and Pingala as the moon and the sun, which they call Śiras and Śasi respectively, while the Śusumna in the middle is seen as responsible for the cosmic substance that channels the transcendental threefold Gunas of Sattva, Rajas, and Tamas. It is not necessary to go any more into details about the gunas since these have already been explained. However what is important to note is how they are perceived from other non-tantric scriptures, especially of a later date, such as the Bhagavad Gita. In Chapter VII-12, Sri Krishna says:

Whatever beings are of sattva, of rajas, or of tamas, know them to proceed from Me; still, I am not in them, they are in me.

Thus, since the three nadis are subtle and cannot be identified directly either by human faculties or by instrumentation, they are known to exist, experientially, by both the tantric practitioner and the yogi. Both the tantric master and the yogi will detect the gunas (innate nature) as they exist in varying degrees of concentration in human behaviour. This is to say that while there might be a preponderance of a particular guna in a particular person, there is never a clear-cut case where one particular guna is exclusively established in any given person. Indeed, Sri Krishna is clear about this: "they are in me". However, since these are said to have been scattered by Sri Krishna throughout the universe at creation, the objective of both the tantric and yogi is to know that they exist, even in their relative strengths that depict essential behaviour, and adjust their own nature to bring all three into a perfect balance. But herein lies the real challenge in dealing with balancing the gunas, believed to be the lower nature Sri Krishna and known from Hindu scriptures as Prakriti. Sri Krishna hints at a formula in Chapter VII-13 of the Bhagavad Gita:

*Tribhir guna-mayair bhāvair ebhih sarvam idam jagat
mohitam nābhijānāti mām ebhyam param avyayam*

Which is translated thus: Deluded by the threefold disposition of Prakriti – the Gunas, this world does not know Me, of whom I am above and immutable.

Had it not been for the two Sanskrit words, "param" and "avyayam" which means "higher and "immutable", the strength of the clues given here might be lost on the student of Bhagavad Gita. What is higher or "above them"? Elsewhere Krishna says Aham Brahmasi: I am Brahman, and the only thing that is changeless or beyond modification and hence immutable is Brahman. So, while it is clear that those who do not know Krishna or Brahman, it is because of the "threefold disposition" of the gunas embedded in Prakriti. Thus, the most certain method of defeating the gunas is, by knowing Brahman, or knowing Krishna. And the most reliable way of getting out of the gunas and entering into the very heart of Krishna, or the Divine, is by becoming a yogi and engaging in the four yoga systems taught to Arjuna in the Bhagavad Gita. Embrace actionless action by engaging in Karma Yoga; be a Jnani by seeking to know Krishna by studying his scriptures, singing his praise, and engaging in devotional services. Also, perform austerities in yoga meditation in order to arrest the mind and know the Supreme Reality that is Brahman. Finally, be a Bhakta by following the path of Bhakti Yoga with unreserved love for the Lord, while serving him in all. Indeed, while Sri Krishna earlier suggested that all beings abide in Him, but He not in them, he qualifies this statement with the following, which appears B.G. X-9:

Out of pure compassion for them, dwelling in their hearts, I destroy the ignorance-born darkness, by the luminous lamp of wisdom.

Thus, the only way of not being touched by the gunas, is the unquestionable conviction of Krishna's affirmation that comes out of His compassion (*anukkampārtha*), which is guided by consciousness and not by attachment or desires on the part of beings. This is backed up by what He says in the preceding verse: "To them, ever devout, worshipping Me with love, I give the yoga of discrimination by which they come to me." However, this yoga is not the type of gift that automatically opens up the channels strung along the spinal cord that takes the yogi to the gateway of the Śusumna; on the contrary, the gift must be unconditionally accepted with the promise of devout and continuous work, simultaneously practiced on Krishna's all-encompassing four systems of yoga.

The four-fold practice of yoga, which is *Karma* or right action, *Dhyan* or meditation, *Jnana* or seeking the right knowledge, and *Bhakti* or devotional services to all created beings as a way of serving the Lord, are not only to ensure a greater cognition of Krishna's glory, but the withering away of the gunas by objectifying the ego or *ahamkara* as the prima-facie cause of identifying the body with the soul or atman. Even so, as the yogi practices his four-fold yoga, the *budhi* or intellect becomes acclimatize with the sublimity of the Divine, until such time, as when *budhi yoga* bears fruit in the clear knowledge that the Self and the Divine are One. From here onwards notions of the Divine as some sort of mystical being falls away and Brahman, as the indivisible and immutable, becomes the Supreme Reality in the form of the Self but known to the philosopher as the Intuitive Self. The most important thing we learn from the Bhagavad Gita about the Gunas, as compared with what we learn from the Tantras, is this: once the sadhak or student of divinity, turns in systematic search for meaning of his place in the universe with regard to his relationship with the Divine or the Supreme Reality, there is a corresponding movement from the Divine toward the sadhak in the form of the Intuitive Self. What is so significant about this movement is prompted from compassion. Indeed, the compassion is so strong that the Divine, thenceforth takes up residence in the sadhak's heart from where it destroys "the ignorance-born darkness by the luminous lamp of wisdom." In other words, everyone is born with the gunas intact, which permeates the entire body, and the only way to bring the gunas in balance, as it exists in Sri Krishna, is by engaging in the four systems of yoga prescribed by Him, until the intellect is suffused with divine intelligence or budhi yoga. However, the key to this is meditation, which sparks the intuitive flame, fuelled by experiential knowledge emanating from interaction with the divine seated in the heart centre. It is what had caused Arjuna to proclaim in BG: X-12, once he had realized that Krishna was not just an ordinary friend who had taken pity on his helplessness:

> *You are the reflection of the Supreme Brahman, the Supreme Abode, the Supreme Purifier, the Eternal, Divine Purusha, the Primeval Deity, the Unborn, the Omnipresent.*

This declaration marks the point in the sadhak's existence where the mind is no longer influenced by the gunas, and where pure intelligence holds existence in total balance between prakriti and the atman or soul. It also depicts a state of existence where the *pañca kleśa* or the five primeval afflictions get absorbed by the sadhak's karma, as part of the Divine's compassion. These afflictions are: ávidyā or ignorance, as a result of misapprehension of reality; asmitā or ahamkara, translated as egoism due to erroneous identification of the body with the Self, or the Self with the intellect; rāga or attachment; dveṣa or aversion; and, abhiniveśāḥ or fear of death, which stems from the propensity to cling to desires resulting from anger, lust, anxiety, hatred, and possessiveness. All of these afflictions are of course eradicated once the sadhak or practitioner of yoga is embraced by the divine intelligence; awareness is also moved to that higher plane of Existence where Consciousness is equated with Brahman. This is not wishful thinking; in some ways it can be said that it is the fundamental appeal of the Bhagavad Gita as expressed in Chapter 18-65:

> *man-mana bhava mad-bhakto mad-yaji mam namaskuru mam evaisyasi satyam te pratijane priyo 'si me*

Which translates as: Fix your mind in Me; be My devotee and propitiate unto Me by just being humble and making obeisance unto Me, and in this manner you will come to Me. This I pledge to you in truth, because you are very dear to Me.

It is significant to observe that Krishna tells Arjuna to fix his mind on Him. It may appear simple in its understanding, but it is very difficult to execute, for earlier in the Bhagavad Gita, Chapter VIII: 9-10, Krishna tells Arjuna how anyone can be assured of reaching him, especially at the moment of death:

> ... *having confined mind in the heart, having fixed the prana or life-force in the head, while uttering Om in yoga on Brahman, and simultaneously remembering Me, he who departs, leaving the body in this, attains the Supreme Soul.*

What is significant about this is the extent to which a person of such calibre must be adept in yoga in order to do all that as decreed by Krishna. Confining the mind to the heart, which alludes to the anahata chakra, at such a critical time, is in itself a herculean task. After all, while this chakra does not only regulate compassion and harmony in the day-to-day life of the sadhak, it also deals with controlling emotions, most of which are spurred by the mind that is independent of all the organs in the body. Then, comes the next to a near impossibility: "fix the prana or life-force in the head. In tantric practices, practitioners are urged to hold the prana in the ajna chakra, the chakra that lies between the eyebrows, in order to keep the mind at bay. This is a very difficult practice, even for experts who have learned to raise the yogic or serpent fire from the muladhara chakra and take it up to the Ajna. In tantra, this is the goal, and those who become proficient in mastering this practice become High Tantrikas and designated as those who have achieved oneness with Śiva-Śakti. However, in Advaita Vedanta, the sadhak is pushed even further: the practitioner must also be absorbed in uttering Om, the mystical symbol and sound that cognates Brahman, while remembering Krishna who is equated with the Supreme Soul.

Indeed, what both verses imply is the intensity of a lifestyle for those who have come to an understanding of what Advaita Vedanta means: it is more than a lifestyle, for it cuts across the norms of religion while questioning the very basis of all philosophical understanding. And, at the base of this is the immense importance of yoga, and the method of achieving the goals of yoga. Nor is it theism, for theism aims at imprisoning the mind and turning it around for its own sake. Here, there is just the opposite; it is liberation at all levels of existence. Liberation from the demands of the body, family, groups, society, church and state, and perhaps even God; for in Advaita Vedanta, God, as known in western societies, does not exist.

Krishna is Brahman and Brahman is Consciousness where the liberated soul plays its part just as particles in space play their part in holding the universe together as a single pulsating entity. It is a play of consciousness, with the basic notion that we are all actors on a universal stage; we are put here to play out the part given to us by our limited intelligence ordained in Prakriti at creation, until we wake up and realize our true potential in the realm of pure consciousness. That, our true self exists in relation with other selves apart from the confinement of body, from which we can get only a glimmer of understanding by probing deep into the very essence of the nature of our being that is designated in scriptures as the Self. And, this is why we have scriptures such as the Vedas, the Bhagavad Gita, and the Upanishads; but they are only guides to test our intelligence, and determine for ourselves, whether we are ready to take the challenge and make the leap, especially so ordained in the Bhagavad Gita.

Indeed, in Chapter XIII: 12-13, we learn how the sadhak or practitioner of yoga brings his embodied existence to an end, which is the aim of every enlightened soul. In several of the Upanishads the individual consciousness is compared to rivers emptying all their virtues into the surging ocean. Tantrics also use this metaphor to compare how the yogi merges with cosmic consciousness. For them, the Śusumna embodies all the substance of the particle-universe, but it is only at the will of Ganesha, on whom Devi is seated, who prods the serpent power, Kundalini to rise and burn away the contaminants embodied in the Śusumna in order to enable liberation (9).

Kundalini usually travels up the Ida nadi in a very slow pace, giving the yogi time to adjust to the changes that take place in the different regions of the body governed by the six chakras. However, if the serpent power courses through the Pingala, the nadi that is located to the right of the Śusumna, the action is swift, thereby causing the expansion of heat that often does damage to the health of the yogi that can even result in death. Unlike yogis who follow the path of Advaita Vedanta, where the yoga is slow and follows an incremental pattern of practice, where result is measured, in tantra the practice has an ingrained dimension of sexuality, where the merging with cosmic consciousness has a different connotation. Here the sexual act is used as a pump to push the yogic fire upwards coursing through the chakras until it empties into the ajna chakra where a myriad of experiences are observed. This is likened to a modified form of the yogi experiencing *blissful consciousness*, where kundalini is first experienced as a flame between the eyebrows before it is transformed into the full dimension of the dancing Devi, and finally manifesting as Śakti, and thence to pure consciousness. Once the substance from the Śusumna is further pushed up into the thousand petal sahasrara to manifest as Siva-Śakti, the goal is achieved (10).

In Advaita Vedanta, even where there is no duality, Ganesha as Lord of the Ganas (Lord over beings, both sentient and insentient) acts as the remover of all obstacles, and thus helps the sadhak or practitioner in meeting the goal. In most cases, the yogi propitiates Ganesha with this in mind: that the aim in yoga is the merging of consciousness that is Brahman; and, with Ganesha's help all activities of the body, including the senses will cease to exist, as we know it in everyday awareness of body functions. However, there is one override that in which Ganesha transforms into, which is the exception of the sound of Om, usually felt throughout the body in a subtle vibratory form during deep meditation. This sound or Śabda, which is the subject of Part Four of this book, can be so compelling in that the body experiences a breakdown of sorts, even though the atman or Self is fully awake and acts as the witness-observer to recall every minute detail, which is then reported to the intelligence that is an extension of *Buddhi* and known as Brahma jnana. In this loss of body consciousness, the mind settles in the heart, especially so at the time of death. But in everyday practice, which some pursue as to aid the eventuality of death, the yogi experiences something akin to death that is known as Samadhi, a deathlike state similar to dreamless sleep but where a different kind of consciousness is experienced; here the yogi experiences sat-chit-ananda, or blissful existence in Consciousness, in which is located the immutable Brahman.

In Dvaita and Advaita Vedanta much of Tantric principles are either played down or not recognized, largely because of the sexual connotations, which make up the bulk of the science of Tantrica. However, as observed in the above discussion, much of yoga is derived from Tantra in a very subtle form, with the first presiding deity of Ganesha acting as host at the root chakra known as the Muladhara. So far, there is good reason why the intricacies of the chakras, and especially the three nadis of ida, pingala, and Śusumna, have only been touched upon. The above discussion was necessary in so far as having a "legend" of sorts, for the purpose of knowing the differences between Vedanta and Tantric practices. Even so, what has been given thus far about the nadis have been very basic and cursory.

Indeed, in tantric circles, before mention is made of the nadis it is not unusual to hear remarks about "the sprouting shoot of the yoga plant" of complete realization of Śiva (in Vedanta, Brahman replaces Śiva), which is to be achieved by the six chakras. However, there is a warning in the Sat Chakra Nirūpana Tantra, that Kundalini Yoga can only be learnt from experiential knowledge with the assistance of a bona fide guru who is a representative of the Divine. This may sound pompous to those unfamiliar with Tantra or Kundalini Yoga, largely regarding the symbolic nature of the language which attempts to explain basic concepts (11). For instance, the human spinal column is likened to Mount Meru. In most Hindu scriptures it is not just one of those very high peaks in the Himalayas; it represents the home of Śiva and his consort, Parvati. However, in Tantra, Mount Meru is not just a peak but the Axis Mundi or the "central pole of the world" that connects Heaven and Earth, and from which we are to deduce a direct comparison to the vertebral column of the human body. Also, the ida and pingala are compared with the moon and the sun. Besides the two "rivers", the ida and pingala, which flow alongside the left and right of the Śusumna, the heart of Tantra is explained in what is inside Śusumna, which is fire-red in colour. Other than the fact that

Śusumna is composed largely of cosmic substance, there are three distinct channels that are further described for classification purposes as follows: the first channel closest to Śusumna has the appearance of the glowing sun and is personified as Vajrini. The second is pale in colour like the moon and personified as Citrini. The fourth channel, which is the tiniest, is blue in colour and is personified as Brahma Nadi. However in pure tantra all four nadis are addressed as Śusumna since Vajrini, Citrini and Brahma Nadi co-exist with Śusumna in perfect harmony.(12)

Indeed, the literal translation of Śusumna from MonierWilliams Sanskrit Dictionary means "very gracious" or "kind" and lists it as "one of seven principal rays of the sun" that provides heat to the moon. From a physiological basis, the translation also alludes to the notion that the Śusumna enriches the prana as breath passes through it during yogic practice of pranayama in order to awake spiritual fortitude. However, it is understood that these four personified forms lie within their respective channels and remain inseparable from each other, which nevertheless make them spiritually one; and while they are not anatomical entities they are, within the philosophical framework of Tantra, anthropomorphized and deified. Even so, they remain independent of each other with specified functions ascribed to them, which is hinted in their names (13).

Citrini (affectionately referred to as Chitra) is derived from the root word, Cit (pronounced Chit) which refers to consciousness. Vajrini stems from Vajra, alludes to Indra's invincible weapon the thunderbolt, and suggests adamant impenetrability; it refers to a cosmic force capable of repelling anything, like Vishnu's weapon that either emanates from mind or his atomically driven Sudarshan weapon also used by later gods. Moreover, it also refers to a particular diamond symbolical of indestructibility, as well as an irresistible force, as far as Tantra is concerned. Vajra is also a name for Goddess Durga depicting her unusual fierceness, and a particular form of military array, as well as a particular soma ceremony associated with a phase of the moon.

The description of how the three nadis are arranged in Śusumna within the spinal cord with their different appellations, tells something about the practitioners who dare broach Kundalini Yoga from the perspective of the full scope of tantra: it is not something for the fainthearted or the casual observer who have the inclination to follow ordinary yoga methods. The appellation of *Chandra-Surya-Agni-Rupa*, which equals Moon-Sun-Fire-Form, depicts the movement which the serious aspirant must go through if success can be had. The passage from the soft moon-lit night into the fierce sunlight, and thence into the furnace of blazing fire, is very real; and yet there are those who have literally braved it and come out of it like the most sublime of goddesses and compassionate gods.

Symbolical of the Urogenital Triangle at the base of the spine, mention was made of Ganesha occupying this area as the seat of Devi in a sleeping state but who is easily awakened once the conditions for her rise are met. For this reason, the fabled Ganesha is removed from storytelling and placed in his original form as Airavata, the four-tusk white elephant, who were among the treasures brought up during the great churning from the Ocean of Milk. It is therefore no wonder that four white lotus blossoms surround Ganesha at the Muladhara Chakra. The lotus or *padma* blossom represents wisdom, purity and detachment. In Bhagavad Gita, Chapter V: 10, Krishna says:

One who performs his duty without attachment, surrendering the results unto the Supreme Lord, is unaffected by sinful action, as the lotus is untouched by water.

This, in the context of Tantra, tells us something about the reason why Ganesha in his Airavata form is framed by four lotus blossoms. Even though he is within such close range of the two excretory organs (two finger-widths above the anus and two fingers below the root of the phallus and yoni), like the lotus, whose environment is mud and water, he remains totally detached. This quality of detachment narrated to the aspirant by the guru is the first clue given when approaching Kundalini Yoga, especially while sexual practice is observed in attempting to raise the yogic fire, which characterizes Kundalini as the serpent power.

There is a very good reason why the muladhara chakra has Ganesha in the position he occupies: he is the host of the ganas, as well as all of the gods in Hinduism. However, once the aspirant mindfully steps into asana, and pays respect to Ganesha, henceforth the entire muladhara chakra becomes objectified as the bulbous root known as Kanda from where seventy-two minor nadis or nerves emerge to flow upwards; of these the most important ones are ida, pingala and Śusumna. According to the *Sat Chakra Nirūpana*, "Śusumna goes to the neck, emerges from the spine, goes to the forehead, passes between the eyebrows united with Kundalini, goes near the Brahma Randhara (at the crown of the head) and ends near the thousand-petal lotus." The *Sat Chakra Nirūpana* also says that Śusumn "clings to the stalk of Shankhini as it goes up the spinal cord." Shankhini is the lotus stalk that takes root in Ganesha, and which transform into the bulbous root known as Kanda. This stalk connects all the chakras, which are identified by the number of lotus petals ascribed to each. However, once the Shankhini reaches the throat chakra known as Vishudha, it splits into two stems, with one going to the left and the other barely bypassing the Ajna Chakra at the middle of the eyebrows and going directly to the Brahma Randhara at the crown. In the second verse of Sat Chakra Nirūpana it is said:

"Inside Citrini [which passes through the left side of Śusumna] who is lustrous with the luster of the Pranava and attainable in yoga by yogis, she is subtle as a spider's thread, and pierces all the lotuses which are placed within the backbone, and is pure intelligence. She is beautiful by reason of the lotuses strung on her; and inside her is the Brahmanadi, which extends from the orifice of the mouth of Hara to the place beyond, where Adi-devi is"

There are a few references here that are, although symbolical, instructive: pranava is compressed energy obtained from distilled oxygen taken from the breath by the yogi during the practice of pranayama, a system of deep alternating breathing through the left and right nostrils that interact with the ida and pingala in a rhythmic fashion through retention and exhalation. This exercise, which can last from a few minutes to over an hour, depending on the state of expertise the yogi has reached, is tactical to the awakening of Adi-Devi, generally known as Kundalini. Here we also get a view of Citrini, which is like that of a "spider's thread". But what is not said here is that inside her is Brahma Nadi, through which Kundalini goes from "the orifice of the mouth of Hara in the Muladhara through all the chakras until she eventually arrives at Param Śiva in the Brahma Randhara in the crown of the head. Param means "above" and in Śaivism, Śiva refers to the creator, and Hara stems from "harakukha-kuhara", which is the orifice at the top of the Svyambhu Linga in Muladhara. This is where Advaita borrows from Tantra, for Svyambhu is the self-manifested form of Brahman as the first cause of creation, which might be distilled from the sexual connotation pertaining to Tantric knowledge. Indeed, in some Vedanta text where Kundalini is part of the lexicon, Kundalini is treated as *Śabda Brahman*, since one of the characteristics of Kundalini's rise, is the vibration that the yogi experiences, accompanied by a unique sound that is interpreted as Om (14).

To get a better understanding of the four nadis or canals, think of three tubes of varying sizes, one inside the other held together by a fourth, which is the larger outer tube known as Śusumna. Tantric yogis see four nadis rather than three, in addition to the Ida and Pingala strung alongside the right and left side of the spinal column, and refer to all four nadis as Śusumna, although the outer tube is the true Śusumna. Think of the next tube that is within the first, which is the next largest tube that Vajrini passes through and is considered by yogis to be as lustrous as the sun. Within Vajrini's tube is Citrini, associated with the moon because of its paleness, and identified with Sattva guna, the purest of the pure. Lastly there is the Central Canal that passes through Citrini's tube, known as the Brahma Nadi, the tiniest of the four tubes, and which is associated with pure intelligence. It is through this central canal, the Brahma Nadi, which Śabda Brahman not only passes through but it is from here where Consciousness vibrates through the entire body. It is also because of this location, paralleling the central nervous system that is mostly responsible for the yogi's claim that those at a very high state of consciousness can identify with Brahman as Consciousness.

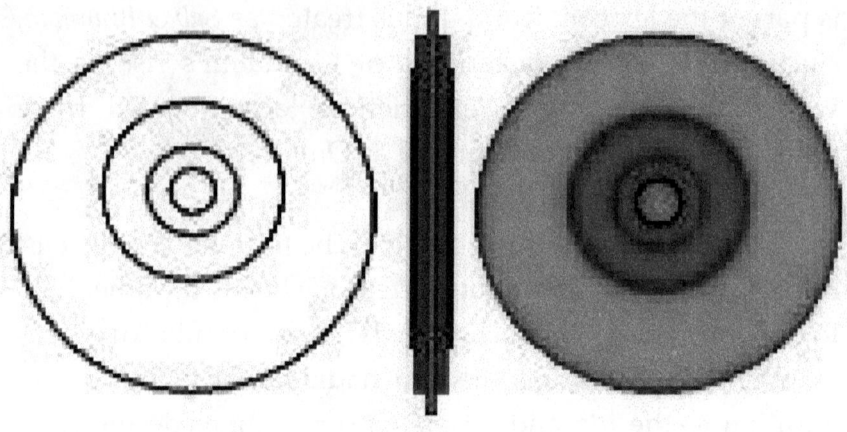

The explanation given in the above comes from verse two of the *Sat Chakra Nirūpana*, but the third verse has some stunning revelations that bring the entire nature of Consciousness into focus:

*Vidyamālā-vilāsā munimanasasilasat-tantu-rūpā susukṣmā
śuddhajñanaprobodhā sakala-sukha-mayi suddha-
bodhasvabhāvā
Brahma-dvāram tadāsya pravilasati sudhādharagamaya
pradeṣham
Granthi-sthānam tadetat vadanamiti suṣumnākhaya-nādya
lapanti*

Sanskrit similes are much deeper than what might be found in the English language and sometimes border on metaphor or metonymy. For instance, mention is made here of Śusumna as Goddess of Cosmic Substance and "beautiful like a lightening chain, thin like a lotus fibre and shines in the minds of the sages." What the passage subsumes is the composite relationship of all four "tubes" or channels coexisting as one, which connotes to the relationship between the atman or individual soul (in Dvaita or duality) and Brahman, which although different there is that very subtle difference of indivisible connectedness. This idea becomes clear when we look at the rest of the verse: "it is she who wakes up pure knowledge, by virtue of Śabda when Citrini flows through the Brahma Nadi, to incorporate bliss in the individual soul as proof of the existence of Brahman, and hence the true nature of pure consciousness. This is the secret of tantra that can only be known from specialized sexual practice whose object is not external ejaculation but the art of channelling the sexual energy upwards, which would awaken Kundalini who remains passively asleep on the "ambrosial" Knot or Mouth of the Spine, previously mentioned as *Hara*. Upon being awakened, her handmaid, Citrini, opens the doorway of the Secret passage given as Brahma Nadi, which causes Śabda to vibrate while Citrini glows in all her magnificent hues.

What is even more significant in the third verse is that Citrini, as an integral part of Śusumna, is endowed with the cosmic substance "scattered throughout the spinal cord", and with each emotion experienced by the yogi, different vibrations in tonality are created that is referred to as Śabda. Indeed, Śabda creates emotions by her vibrations but also monitors emotions from the yogi through yogic rhythmic breathing, as Citrini shines her angelic light (*lasat-tanu-ruba*) on the sub-particles that is the source of consciousness (*śuddha-bodha-svābhāvā*) during pranayama. This is where particles of cosmic substance embedded in Śusumna connect with cosmic intelligence in its raw form of consciousness and brings it to Brahma's opening gate (*Brahma-dvāram*), which then enables Kundalini to rise up and move with ease through the Brahma Nadi. This simple movement that comes about after concentrated yogic practice, sometimes takes a lifetime for some to accomplish, is the start of the journey of the purest of journeys, which will eventually end with the union of Param-Śiva and Śakti (*sudhā dharā gamayapradeśam*). And, to indicate how significant this doorway is for the ascent of Kundalini, whose mission thenceforth is to unite with Param-Śiva – the purest of the pure and highest of the highest – the doorway sanctified with ambrosia.

However, verse three does not only deal with the divinities mentioned in the above; it also deals with the yogi who has reached this high state of consciousness, which almost takes him to the rank of a god. This is indicated by the use of the term *sva-bhāvā* that also means "ones true nature"; after all, divinities do not have multiple natures; they are usually constant unless they assume a particular form to teach something of significance. But human beings true nature at most times remain shielded until it is necessary to show the individual's "true" nature. In this regard, Shankaracharya, the eight-century philosopher, links the idea of true nature with *jnana* or divine knowledge that is the essence of the Paramatma or the highest good that is sometimes brought down to humanity as evidence of the highest spirituality, which occupies the higher plane of consciousness and known from the scriptures as jnana (15). What is significant here is the status of the yogi who has crossed over from the "Knot" and is on his way to enlightenment; in an off-handed sort of way, it compares with the Bodhisattva who, after many lifetimes of spiritual travel, is finally on his way to enlightenment. But, enlightenment here comes from arduously conscious practice until the yogi enters with Kundalini, the Brahma Nadi stream that will take him, eventually with Param-Śiva, the highest of the highest that equates with Brahman.

In pre-Vedic time, Śiva, known by other names such as Mahadeva (Great God), Rudra, etc., is the Lord and Supreme Teacher. Ganesha here represents the ego-bound Jiva. When the Lord comes, the Jiva, surrounded as it is with the murky cloud of ego, usually doesn't recognize Him, and maybe even ends up arguing or fighting with Him! Therefore it is the duty of the Lord, in the form of the Guru, to slay the false ego, in the same way that Sri Krishna urges in Chapter XII of the Bhagavad Gita to pick up a sharp axe of real knowledge and cut down the Aishwatta Tree that represents false knowledge. So powerful is this ego however that, at first, the Guru's instructions may not work, as Śiva's guards failed to subdue Ganesha. It often requires a tougher approach, but eventually the compassionate Guru, in His wisdom finds a way.

Devi threatened to destroy the whole Creation after learning of Ganesha's demise. This indicates that when the ego thus dies, the liberated Jiva loses interest in its temporary physical vehicle, the body, and begins to merge into the Supreme. The physical world is here represented by Devi. This impermanent and changeable creation is a form of Devi, to which this body belongs; the unchanging Absolute is Śiva, to which belongs the Soul. When the ego dies, the external world, which depends on the ego for its existence, disappears along with it. It is said that if we want to know the secrets of this world, which is a manifestation of Devi, then we must first receive the blessings of Ganesha.

Śiva restoring life to Ganesha, and replacing his head with an elephant's, suggests that before we can leave the body, the Lord first replaces our small ego with a "big", or universal ego. This does not mean that we become more egoistic. On the contrary, we no longer identify with the limited individual self, but rather with the large universal Self that springs from real or spiritual knowledge known as Jnana. In this way, life is renewed and Jnana opens up the heart chakra where the divine resides; or, as in the case of Tantra in Śusumna, from where the Divine moves freely between chakras, until the atman either unites with the Divine, or it eventually exits the body to be incarnated again. From the vantage point of Advaita Vedanta, however, here we become one with the Self that can truly benefit Creation. Even so, until such time as real liberation dawns, we are restricted by a functional ego, like the one Krishna and Buddha kept. It is like a thin string (*lasat-tanu-rupa*: fine like a lotus fibre)) tying the liberated Consciousness to our world, solely for our benefit.

Ganesha is given dominion over the Ganas, which is a general term denoting all classes of beings, ranging from insects, animals and humans to the subtle and celestial beings. These various beings all contribute to the "government" of the Creation in the same way that Sri Krishna spoke about the Devas as his ministers; everything from natural forces like storms and earthquakes, to the elemental qualities like fire and water, to functioning of the body's organs and processes. If we don't honour the Ganas, according to Sri Krishna, all of our every action is a form of thievery, as it is not sanctioned. Therefore, instead of propitiating each Gana in order to receive their blessings, we bow to their Lord, Sri Ganesha. By receiving His grace, we receive the grace of all. He removes any potential obstacles and enables our endeavours to succeed. Or, in a nonreligious way, we care for the environment, as if it were a living deity – in the same way that the ancient Greeks spoke about

Mother Earth as Gaia, a pulsating entity that needs our protection just as it yields life for the protection of life.

Such is the greatness of Sri Ganesha! Jai Ganesha!

REFERENCES

References

1. This idea is repeated in many of the Puranas but it is brought to the point in Chapter Three in the Ganesh Purana. Obviously, cleanliness in both its internal and external forms is important to the rise of consciousness. Thus the story here is directly related to the wider perspective of Consciousness rather than the making of myth.
2. This idea, as it relates to Kundalini Yoga, has many facets to it, but none has shown ite relationship to Consciousness theory. Thus, this is the goal in this section of the book; it will also be further developed fully in the next section of the book entitled, Śabda.
3. Saraswati, Swami Satyananda: Kundalini Tantra, Yoga Pubns Trust, 2002. 453 pages.
4. Dahlby, Tenzin Wangyal Rinpoche; edited by Mark (2002). *Healing with Form, Energy, and Light: the five elements in Tibetan Shamanism, Tantra, and Dzogchen.* Ithaca, NY: Snow Lion Pub. pp. 84–85

5. Yoga-Age.com, an Online Resource of Yoga Practice. Go to: http://www.yoga-age.com/modern/kun4.html

6. Sat-Chakra Nirūpana or, Six-Chakra Investigation was written by Purnananda Brahmin 1n 1556. It was first translated in English by Woodroffe under the title, Serpent Power, in short condensed verses. These are terse and difficult to understand without a good knowledge of the Hindu culture. Since then , there have been many commentaries on this very important body of knowledge; perhaps the best is given by Veeraswamy Krishnaraj, following Kalicharran's commentary originally written in Sanskrit. Veraswamy Krishnaraj's commentary can be found in his book, Om Namasivaya, Nobel Press, 1901, or from Amazon. Com.

7. *Braddha Rudra*, another name representative of the Manipura chakra that utilizes the power of destruction in that "All that exists returns to him." Of course this is none other than Śiva, "who has camphor-blue skin smeared wit ashes and a silver beard, and sits in his wrathful form on a golden tiger skin " Tiger in Hindu mythology is symbolical of manas or mind. Thus his purpose here is to destroy the mind and bring the yogi to his true self.

8. Ledbetter, C.W: The Chakras, with a forward by Anodea Judith and Annotations by Kurt Leland. First

published in 1926 and considered a classic of insights into the working of the Chakras.
9. Sarasvati as in 3 above.
10. Carrellas, Barbara: Urban Tantra: Sacred Sex for the Twenty-First Century, Celestial Arts, 2007.
11. White, Davis Gordon: Yoga in Practice – Princeton Reading in Religions. Princeton University Press. 2011.
12. Sat-Chakra Nirūpana, as in (6)
13. Ibid.
14. This idea of Śabda Brahman is developed fully in the next section of this book.
15. Sastri, Kokileswar: An introduction to Advaita philosophy: a critical and systematic exposition of the Śankara school of Vedanta, Bharatiya Publishing House, Varanasi, 1979

NOTES

Notes:

The philosophical side of the Eight Incarnations of Ganesha is extracted from the *Mudgala Purana*:
'Like the *Ganesha Purana*, the Mudgala Purana considers Ganesha to represent the ultimate reality of being. As such, Ganesha's manifestations are endless but eight of his incarnations are of utmost importance. The eight incarnations are introduced in Mudgala Purana 1.17: 24-28. The text is organized into sections and each of these incarnations appears under sections 5 and 6. These are not the same as the four incarnations of Ganesha that are described in the *Kridakhanda* of the Ganesha Purana.' The first is *Mahotkaṭa Vināyaka,* who is reputedly born to *Kaśyapa* and *Aditi* in the *Krita Yuga*, the first of the Hindu era or epoch of the four life cycle of the universe that is characterized by Purity or Sat, or Existence; the second is *Mayūreśvara,* who is born to Śiva and Parvati in the *Treta Yuga* or second epoch where material and behavioral changes are observed; thirdly, is *Gajānana,* who is born to Śiva and Parvati in the *Dvapar Yuga* or third age or epoch where serious conflict arise from adharma or none righteous living; and fourthly

is, *Dhūmraketu*, who will come to end the *Kali Yuga* or the fourth epoch, which brings the four epochs, or *Pralaya*, to a close, and from where a new Pralaya starts afresh.

The incarnation described in the Mudgala Purana took place in different cosmic ages. The Mudgala Purana uses these incarnations to express complex philosophical concepts associated with the progressive creation of the world. Each incarnation represents a stage of the absolute as it unfolds in creation. The forgoing is a summary of each incarnation within the framework of the Mudgala Purana. However to keep the presentation short, only the philosophical interpolation are presented while leaving out much of the story line that accounts for gory details about puranic battles with demonic forces and even major gods. Thus, the incarnations that appear in the following order, represents Ganesha as the remover of the major kleshas or afflictions that befalls humanity.

1. Vakratunda, which is translated as "twisting trunk", represents Brahman as the sum total of all beings in creation. In the Puranic literature, this incarnation pits Ganesha against the demon *Matsaryāsura* that is the epitome of envy and jealousy. In this incarnation, his mount or vāhana is a lion.
2. *Ekadanta*, or the elephant with a "single tusk", represents the aggregate of all individual souls, which embodies one of the major characteristics of Brahman. In this incarnation, Ganesha overcomes the demon

Madāsura for the purpose of vanquishing arrogance and conceit. He has as his mount in this incarnation, his loyal mouse.

3. As *Mahodara*, Ganesha sports his euphemistic "big belly" as a composite of both *Vakratuṇḍa* and *Ekadanta*. He demonstrates right knowledge that is essential for creativity and the creative process. Here, as a manifestation of Brahman, he is an embodiment of wisdom. Indeed, it takes more than intelligence to overcome the demonic nature of *Mohāsura*, the archetypal demon that is proud of his delusional and ignorant behavior; in his vigilant combat against *Moha*, representative of pride and jealousy, Ganisha employs wisdom to conquer his opponent. Here his mount is again a mouse.

4. As *Gajavaktra* or *Gajānana*, Ganesha proudly displays his "elephant face" as a counterpart to *Mahodara*. The purpose of this incarnation is to overcome the demon *Lobhāsura*, who flaunts greed as a virtue. Here too, his mount is a mouse.

5. In this incarnation as *Lambodara*, Ganesha playfully displays his "pendulous belly", which represents contentment. However, this is the first of four incarnations that correspond to the stage where the Purāṇic gods are created. Here Ganesha corresponds to *Śakti*, the all-inclusive power of Brahman. Here the placid Lambodara dutifully takes on the demon *Krodhāsura* that is full of anger, hate, and vengeance.

Again, Ganesha's mount is a mouse.

6. As *Vikata*, Ganesha has an "unusual" or "misshapen" form, and corresponds to *Sūrya*, the Sun God. Yet, he is as bright and illuminating as the nature of the self-effulgent Brahman. Here Ganesha, as Vikata, overcomes the lustful *Kāmāsura* in order to bring balance and harmony on behalf of humanity. In this incarnation, Ganesha's mount is a peacock.

7. *Vighnarāja* as "king of the remover of obstacles", corresponds to Viṣṇu, and as such he symbolizes the preserving nature of Brahman. Here Ganesha takes on the demon, *Mamāsura*, as a warning to humanity of the evil nature of possessiveness. His mount is the celestial serpent *Shesha*.

8. Finally in his last incarnation as *Dhūmravarṇa*, whose colour is " smoky grey", Ganesha corresponds to Śiva. He lovingly but sternly demonstrates that, while Brahman is all-encompassing, there is that destructive side of Brahman that manifests as Śiva. The purpose of this incarnation is to overcome the demon, *Abhimanāsura*, who is symbolical of pride and attachment. His mount is a mouse.

ŚABDA

Śabda

Some time ago while attending a major musical festival in Trinidad I gave an introductory lecture on the subject of Indian music. Before this, I had given a public lecture on the origins of sound, known in Indian thought as Nada; this was in relationship to Nada Yoga, which I had experimented with for several years. The idea behind this discipline is to train the mind to look for that sound embedded in the original vibration from which creation ensued. It is a simple task, especially in the beginning, where most of the mind gives over to concentration on silence. However, as one gets deeper into the practice, problems emerge with the greater task of dismissing the mind and allowing the Self to be the guide. This arises when dead stillness begets total silence in an experientially subjective sort of way, which happens when the mind is dismissed and the outer state of existence merges with the self in Nada for the first Time. This is a major breakthrough for the novice, but the real task of Nada Yoga is evident when the novice pierces into the inner realm of Nada and journeys into its very centre, the inner core of

Existence and the seat of creation. Here, the novice will come face to face with the vibration responsible for creation known as Śabda.

Śabda is not just responsible for creation; it is responsible for the finer determinants of civilization, such as speech, the gradations of sounds that govern music, art, grammar, literature, and the finer determinants of natural law, all of which go a long way to make society what it is. Indeed, this was to be the purpose of my talk: to what extent it can be said that the concepts that gave rise to Indian music are found in the overall idea of Śabda? Knowledge of this type cannot be had from reason or logic. It has to be felt and experienced deep in the rhythm of the heart, as blood pumps throughout the body, coursing through arteries, veins, capillaries, where that primal sound is picked up and then transmitted through the intricate networking of nerves in tandem with synapses, neurons, electrons and protons, located in the brain but which has as its source as that when knowledge first emerged out of Śabda at the dawn of creation (1).

In direct response to Śabda, found primarily at the heart of cosmically transcendental sound, music is thought to orchestrate throughout the body apparatuses in a similar fashion accorded in the impetus of creation in the same manner in which Śabda erupted out of Nada at the dawn of creation (2). Indeed, that primal sound is the blueprint that manifests in all, characteristic of all living things, and which is why it is often said that musicians are not made but endowed. The notion that a person 'has an ear for music' is circumscribed in the Vedantic truism that all stems from

Śabda Brahman. Śabda is the sound responsible for creation, and Brahman is the Supreme Reality that is both the cause of creation, as well as the ongoing principle that affects creation. Taken together as Śabda Brahman, it becomes the most potent term that means transcendental sound (3). Transcendental sound goes back to the origins of time when Brahma, as the embodied Brahman appeared as the creator prior to the very first Pralaya, just when the very first wave of humans appeared in our universe. In this first appearance of the embodied Brahman the cosmic vibrations within his inner Self was heard: that vibratory sound welling up from Nada to manifest in his heart as Śabda, which he later interpreted as OM. This is more than a word: it is comprised of three syllables, A, U, M, which can be clearly heard during inhalation, a deliberation pause between exhalation, and at exhalation. The story that accounts for this is narrated in Brahma's account of Śabda. (4)

Having being Self-born, Brahma, who emerged from Brahman, found himself seated on a huge lotus afloat on a sea of Consciousness. A hint of "nothingness" pervaded as far as the eyes could see; there was nothing to touch; a total absence of scent; no concept of taste; and as for hearing, there was a stillness, so profound, since there was an absence of the elements as known to science. The only thought that came to him was, "Who am I?" After some time had elapsed, the answer came in a vision seated in the heart, "Meditate." Thus, with the eyes fixed on the tip of the nose, and the thought of "Who am I?" Brahma meditated on that question for one thousand days (5).

Eventually, Brahma was shaken out of his meditation in a vibration that slowly erupted in the heart centre, followed by the sounds, aa, oo, ma. Gradually, as he took cognizance of the vibration and carefully listened to the sound, he found himself uttering the word Om, which had a natural rhythm attached to his breathing. However, listening slowly crossed over to a spontaneous chant, which amazingly synchronized with air in his lungs lifting from the diaphragm, with a subtle push to other parts of his body. Briefly the breath took rest in the heart, before resonating upwards to lodge at the ajna chakra located between the eyebrows; from there it slowly dissipated outwards through the nostrils, while making that prominent m-sound one observes at the tail end of chanting Om.

The emergence of Śabda from the inner realms of Nada has very little to do with religion but much to do with the epistemology pertaining to the Sanskrit language and Hindu thought. This is clearly brought out in the Mandukya Upanishad, as well as in the Śiva Samhita, where Śabda is couched in the terminology of Spanda: 'whenever there is stress or Divine action there is vibration', which gives rise to sound. However, this is not ordinary sound; it is a movement, which has a will of its own that invariably connects to Consciousness. In light of the Śivastotrāvali, Śabda is equated with Spanda, which is claimed here as the heartbeat of the universe (6). As hinted in the above, Spanda is based on contraction and expansion that perhaps depicts the presence of the Divine in the form of the combined ŚivaŚakti, especially when Śiva wills creation and Śakti awakes to energise Śiva to act according to the combined intent. This is the state known in Śaivism as the rising of consciousness when the still point of the bindu (depicted as Śakti) in the triangle (depicted as Śiva) becomes a single pulsation and harmonizes with the breath, heart, and mind. Some of this was discussed in Part Three in this book; suffice to say here that the practitioner of Kundalini Yoga experiences the power of Spanda when the concept of individuality merges with that vast matrix of vibration known as Sat-Cit-Ananda or Consciousness. This is particularly noticeable when the yogi chants the three syllable mantra of AUM in the formula of inhaling with A, holding briefly with U, and then exhaling through the nostrils with the droning sound of M.

In a peculiar sort of way, the vibration created in the above willful exercise emulates the original Śabda sound that Brahma had discovered about the secret of his existence in that vast ocean of nothingness. Interestingly too, at that moment when Brahma had discovered the existence of Śabda born of the Self, something happened to him that immediately decries a very powerful trait: he felt lonely and the dire need for engendered company, which caused him to return to his meditation from where he was certain that answers would come. Indeed, just as the Self had given birth of the body in the form of Brahma, so, through the apparatuses of the mind, pulsating in that esoteric throb, Brahma brought forth the light of the Divine endowed in that subtler vibration known as *Parispanda* or the "blissful pulsation of joyful enlightenment, and created Sarasvati, whom he kept as his consort. This single act created a paradigm shift in the creation of the universe, from the task of populating the planet with all the varieties of life to that of creating language, art, literature, music, and all the martial and technical abilities to defend individual and collective interests with even the abilities of waging wars (7).

Indeed, Brahma's consort, Sarasvati is often depicted as the Goddess of Learning in general but also hailed as the initiator of speech, music, and the entire gamut of the sixtyfour arts, which includes the highly acclaimed martial arts that govern military formations, tactical strategies in time of war, and the training that goes to make definitive the art of warfare. However, it is important to keep in mind that, as a mind-born person from Brahma, Sarasvati was created from within the most interior region of Nada whereof Śabda later took the form of Śabda Brahman (8). And, outside the exclusive realm of relationship between Sarasvati and Brahma, or the spheres of communication among Brahma, Vishnu, and Śiva who were the first to have "spoken" to Brahma through the medium of suggestions, speech had been articulated through a codified form of gestures. But with the creation of Sarasvati, who became a manifestation of Śabda Brahman, this powerful Goddess was given the task to create speech or *Vac* to such a refined state that could be sufficiently understood by third persons. Thus, Sarasvati's major task on Earth had to do with giving the power of meaning to the spoken word, referred in the Vedas as Artha. Indeed, within the purview of Hindu philosophy, the greatest aim of any society is to be understood by all: to make sense of people's speech as well as others making sense of our own tongue. So important was this in ancient Vedic society that, in addition to giving meaning to life, Artha became one of the four goals of life. Its chief purpose was the ability to grasp the essence of the word regardless of the context in which it was used, which gave it a stable foundation in the world from which other related needs could be built upon. In this regard, as Sanskrit became known as the language of the gods and as it flourished and began to reach the lower worlds of man and woman, Śabda began to show a scientific side: the word manifested from sound could carry the quality of "verbal testimony", especially as later interpreted by philosophers from both Nyaya and Vaisheshika schools of philosophy. Consequently, Śabda was also accepted by both the earliest of Sanskrit Grammarians, Yaksha, and later by both Panini and Katyayana, as "a unit of language or speech or vac" (9).

While there may seem to be an element of divinity attached to this aspect of Śabda insofar as it has a definition linked to the sound of OM, there is that other dimension in its connection with Nada, especially in the discipline of yoga. In Nada Yoga there are four divisions or movements inherent in the discipline, which are *Vac* or *Vaikhari, Madhyama, Pashyanti,* and *Para* (10).

Vaikhari is what is known to all through articulated sound; etymologically speaking it is the grossest of sound energy, first heard among divine beings during creation.

Nevertheless it is considered to be the sound of the Divine or *Virat Purusha,* the one who sets Śabda in motion in the grossest form in order to be understood by all. At this state, Śabda is that quality of sound that pertains to the spoken word or listening, especially to music. *Madhyama* is heard at an intermediate range, which is a finer quality of sound that is barely audible but experienced in the heart. However, compared to the third stage of Nada known as *Pashyanti,* Śabda at this stage cannot be heard but can be "seen" by those yogis who are said to have that "inner vision". Indeed, sound at this stage has colour and form but which can only be seen internally in the heart. It operates in the realm of the Rishis or seers, one who sees internally by the grace of being one with Brahman. This is the realm from which a Rishi who has experienced Śabda can give reports about what is heard directly from the Divine and offer such statements as testimony that can be incorporated in such body of works as the Vedas, Samhitas or Upanishads. According to several works that have evaluated the place of Śabda in Hindu philosophy, as well as in the major bodies of Hindu scriptures, the fourth stage that goes by the name of *Para* is the highest state of Śabda, as derived from the wellhead of Nada (11). By definition, Para means "above" or the "highest" and suggests that Śabda equates with Ishvara or the highest divinity, especially for those who operate in the realm of a personal God. Moreover, Para, carries the unique quality of being transcendental and beyond the reach of the sense organs, even though, Para can be "heard" after engaging in a rigorous discipline of quieting the mind to the point where it no longer exists. From here, in the absence of the mind, the Self emerges to connect with the innerness of Para, where Śabda resides in the Universal Self known as Brahman, hence the expression *Śabda-Brahman*. In this sense, Para is that primal voice, which Brahma had first heard from within, in the pulsating vibration that erupted in his heart. This aspect of Para is also equated with the Divine voice that is not seen but which is heard through unspoken ideas or the germs of thoughts known to elevated souls as intuition by the Intuitive Self. It manifests and moves in the subtle body of divine intelligence, and remains in an undifferentiated form in the same way that Brahman pervades the entire universe.

Taken from both the Śaivite and Vedantic perspective, Pashyanti and Para constitute the two most significant basis of Consciousness in Hindu philosophy. Indeed, as a manifested word, Śabda having emerged from the deepest depths of Nada, first appeared in the Maitrayaniya or Maitri Upanishad (VI.22) to differentiate between two different forms of Brahman: the one with sound and the other without sound (Aśabda Brahman). Śabda without sound, like Brahman, is associated with the vibration of Divine Consciousness and, like Spanda, it pervades the entire universe.

Both Kundalini yoga and Nada yoga teach that the subtle body has a direct link with the physical body, which is responsible for the natural rhythm associated with speech, music, art, letters and all the creative elements found in civilization. It is the 'unifying continuity' between our bodies, our active mind, emotions and our internal awareness. In this way, we are intricately tied to the whole universe, and which determines our very thoughts, words and deeds. Indeed, from the perspective of Kashmiri Śaivism, Spanda – the Vedantic corollary of Śabda – 'the supreme vibration unifies and encompasses all that has emerged from it, and continually re-enfolds the manifest totality of all that exists back into the supreme light of consciousness'.

The light of consciousness undoubtedly alludes to the manifest energy of Kundalini discussed as Śakti in Part Three of this book. In a definitive way this condensed energy found in the body when Kundalini awakes and rises to touch all the chakras in the human body flows as consciousness in condensed waves of contraction, noted in the Śiva Samhita as *Nimesha*, which the yogis recognize as the constituent world around us that include feelings, thoughts, and the things we do. Nimesha is significant here because it has to do with absorption while at the same time corresponding to the speed of light in Sanskrit as far as it relates to what happens when a yogi engages in either Kundalini yoga or Nada yoga. During deep meditation in either of these yoga practices, the Self constantly monitors awareness at the speed of light, and there are times when instances of observations are picked in Nimesha, which has movement at the speed of 'the blink of an eye', or *Nimsharda*, half of Nimesha. These monitored "reports" are stored in the subtle body, and from time to time they are released to the physical body, which are then released as Intuitive Knowledge. The Self, will channel these through Kundalini or as pulses in the heart centre, or even in the Vishudha or Ajna chakras from where they are expressed according to the rhythm of the individual.

Along with Nimeśa, there is Vimarśa, which is the monitoring agent that is part of the Self, or from the point of view of Śaivism, the power endowed in Śakti. Even more precisely, verily the witness that feeds the individual intelligence in human beings in order to become aware of the world. In some respects, it is akin to "examination", for it examines and allows the person to become active and dynamically aware of the minutest details in the environment, in what is happening among others, or what is even heard or said in distant realms. In addition to this, Vimarśa is likened to the "I" behind the individual self: it makes the individual self not only conscious of all around us but continuously makes us conscious of our very own nature.

As the luminous and static "witness" Vimarśa moves the individual self to be closer to the Universal Self, which from the perspective of Śaivism, it aids us to be conscious of our own nature and our Existence, to the point where we develop the potential to become the Supreme in the image of Him. In this regard, Vimarśa is Śakti, the energies behind will, knowledge and the power of action, especially in empowering Śiva to create. Indeed, not even God can act outside of her realm of energies, which is why She is regarded as the eternal power behind Śiva known in the *Trika Darshana* as *Para-Śakti*, the Supreme Energy, existing in transcendence; the *Parāpara-Śakti*, the Supreme existing in both transcendence and imminence; and, *Apara-Śakti* existing in imminence. Such is the power of *Śakti* that, when touched by her in whatever form, human beings become something more than just limited atoms. Thus, according to the Trika, human beings are not just limbs of the Great God sharing some of His innate qualities but beings that have the potential to be one with Śiva, as if each being is part and parcel of Śiva. This is why, in the tradition of Śaivism, functional terminologies, from an etymological point of view, come in pairs of opposites. For instance, just as there is Vimarśa, there is Prakāśa, which connotes "light, brightness, splendour, clearness" and also "visibly manifested".

What is significant about the above, from the Trika literature (12), there are two aspects to the Supreme or Absolute: Śiva is static and Śakti is dynamic. Moreover, Śiva is considered auspicious largely because He is associated with "Prakāśa", which among other definitions it carries the meaning of light, luminosity, effulgence, illumination, Self-revelation, consciousness, the principle by which everything is known. However, none of this is possible without the power of Śakti, which is why Śiva and Śakti, or Prakāśa and Vimarśa, are inseparable. More than anything else, Śiva as the "Revealing Light" is manifested in beings in his static form but is potentially seen in all his splendour through illumination by the power of Śakti. Indeed, by her grace He appears within after Śakti courses through Śusumna from the Muladhara Chakra to the Ajna where she takes rest before making the final leap to the Sahasrara at the crown of the head. Here she energizes Śiva to the point where union is ignited in a flash of colours before transforming into a soft white glow; in this coupling, known as the Śiva-Śakti embrace, Śiva is enabled by Śakti to manifest in every pore and in every nook and cranny of the yogi, from head to toe. This is where the combined Śiva-Śakti principle, now acting as one, replicates in the yogi to make vision crystal-clear through the lamp of divine knowledge, now gleaned from the inner Self. At this moment where the yogi experiences sat-cit-ananda, thoughts, images, and even sounds that, until now, were hitherto blocked from the earnest seeker, are sharpened with a sense of infinitude, and illumination is rendered. Thus, rather than proclaiming to the world, "I think, therefore I am", the yogi sings out to himself, Aham Brahmasi, or Śivo ham: I am Brahman, or I am Śiva.

The moment of experiencing sat-cit-ananda, marks that auspicious stage in the life of the yogi known as *Pratyabhijñā* or "spontaneous recognition" as the essential nature in human life. This is different from the Vedantic notion, "to be known". Pratyabhijñā is derived from the Sanskrit stem, "prati", which means "something once known, now appearing as forgotten, while "abhi" relates to immediacy or immediate, and "jña" to know; hence the suggested meaning of sudden recognition of one's forgotten self. It is the essential breakthrough in divine knowledge that is the essence of Jnana, which yogis seek to know, but cannot know "It". In Śaivism, the knower can recognise his essential nature but cannot truly know it; that power of knowing belongs to the higher Self, while "nature" or Prakriti, according to Sri Krishna in the Bhagavad Gita, corresponds to His lower Self, and as such there is nothing to know but the need to recognise. Philosophically speaking, nature is not a knowable object but the "knowing" subject, and within the context of Pratyabhijñā, because there is the absence of *upāyas* or "means" there is nothing to observe, study, or do. There is neither will nor volition, and when recognition takes place, it happens spontaneously, outside of thought, mind, and motion, largely because all of these qualities have limitations, which block spontaneity that is the underlying basis of Pratyabhijñā.

The spontaneous recognition the yogi experiences in his encounter with his essential nature is another way of saying that is the first realization of his existence in the Self that is the same as Brahman or Śiva. However, all of this experience is given in the backdrop of Śabda or Spanda, which has been churning in the heart for quite some time. Even so, while it could be said that Spanda is the primary movement that allows the yogi to leap into consciousness, none of this is possible without Prakashā or light that exists in all bodies as Śiva or Brahman. Hence, there is nothing else to know once one experiences this. In a manner of speaking this experience is the principle that underlies absorption, which comes from illumination generated by Śabda Brahman or Śiva-Spanda. It also explains the claim that everyone has the potential to see sound, especially if one is on the path of consciousness moved by intense meditation, or engaged in Kundalini yoga, such as that discussed in Part Three of this book. The point about this is that sound that is seen, only happens with illumination: that aspect of activity when Kundalini pierces each of the chakras that causes an eruption of light. Indeed, each chakra emits a special quality of light, whose colour reflects a particular tonality that is different from the others. Gradually, the yogi tags these tones with the different colours that match both the different chakras as well as the different sounds remembered as having cosmic significance, as well as emanating from the greater depths of the universe. The light that the yogi experiences, which becomes more and more intense as Kundalini makes her rounds between the Muladhara and Ajna chakras, are subtle impulses that are simultaneously triggered by the movement of Kundalini Śakti and the dormant Śiva who remains inactive on the Sahasrara chakra located at the crown of the head. This movement is significant for the yogi, for the more frequent that Kundalini moves through the chakras the more elevated in the path to consciousness the yogi becomes. These movements also aid the yogi to build in the subtle body's consciousness a network of references to interpret the different colours emanating from the chakras as sound at the Para level.

Indeed, sound-vibrations at the Para level are so subtle that interpretation of the codes given in the several light colours, is needed. This is not any different from what happens when we "see" ordinary colours or hear different sounds from different locations: everything that we physically see or hear is dependent on the brain to interpret for us what is seen or heard. However, the light that the yogi experiences in each of the chakras remains dormant until the switch is thrown by the successive pulses sent out by Śiva. This switch is punctuated by the successive Śiva-Śakti embraces, which simultaneously triggers the light or Prakashā in the yogi's head; however the longer the embrace endures, the greater the intensity, experienced by the yogi as Śiva or Prakashā, along with the vibration that spreads throughout the yogi's body. Gradually, Intuitive Knowledge comes to the yogi that this light, which mimics the intensity of the vibration, is nothing but the presence of Śiva or Brahman. Eventually, however, the light subsides but the vibration is "seen" as any natural phenomenon, especially with the approach of the greatest of all experiences, known as sat-cit-ananda. This is the moment of the greatest of Bliss that connotes as the merging with Brahman or Śiva.

The experience of Brahman or Śiva marks the arrival of the yogi at the highest state of consciousness. Indeed, the Brahma Samhita declares that Brahman is Consciousness, commonly referred to as Prajñānam Brahman (13). However some interpret Prajñānam as intelligence. In Sanskrit the meaning of a word is based on the verbal root from which the word is derived. But this in itself is insufficient: to reach the meaning of the statement as Consciousness, one has to examine the etymology of the word "prajñānam". Taking a close look at the prefix "pra" it is not difficult to realise that there is something very significant that predicates "jñānam" or knowledge. Monier-Williams in his Sanskrit-English Dictionary, suggests that some of the meanings culled from different sources give "pra" as beginning, excellence, higher, greater, supreme, origin, source, perfection, purity. Jñāna, according to the Bhagavad Gita on the other hand, is defined as divine intelligence: that which comes from the highest source and which cannot be derived by reason alone. In this sense Prajñānam relates to the inner Self, which Vedanta and most of the Upanishad testify as Consciousness. It is *Śāstrayonitvāt* (14), the source of knowing from the highest authority, which requires no other references, or footnotes, not that which comes from inference or even perception. Brahman, on the other hand, is cause, as well as effect (15); and as the Supreme Reality, It manifests as well as reflected in the gunas known as Sattva, Rajas and Tamas. However, as intelligence, Brahman is seen through vibration, the very said vibration responsible for creation, in which colour and sound is the essence of knowing in that higher state of Consciousness. In this regard, intelligence is neither stratified nor appropriated in a given mode of cultivation. Hence, there is only one intelligence: that of Brahman and the same that manifests in beings, which is never differentiated; it is the one intelligence that pervades all.

However, what makes the difference is that, in which beings strive to know the Supreme Reality, although one may never know. This may seem contradictory but the idea is reinforced in the following statement:

> *One who says that I know Brahman does not know; one who knows the Truth says that I do not know. Brahman is the unknown to a person of true knowledge, it is known only to the ignorant* ---Keno Upanishad 2.01-03

However, what is certain is the recognition mentioned in the principle of Pratyabhijñā, even though that essential recognition may be limited by the extent of the gunas operating in the individual beings at differing states of existence.

From a practical angle of cognition, Prajñānam Brahma as Consciousness (Aitareya Upanishad, 3.1.1. attached to the Rig Veda) is endowed in all creatures that enable seeing, hearing, speaking and the distinguishing differences in tastes. However, as one moves away from instincts and dependence on reason and logic, Consciousness moves Being on a progressively higher state until one eventually merges with Brahman. At this eventuality, one experiences Brahman or Śiva in sat-cit-ananda and spontaneously declares, *Aham Brahmasi*: I am Brahman, or I am Siva (Brihadaranyaka Upanishad, 1.4.10 at the end of the Shukla Yajurveda).

The recognition in Consciousness marks a subtle move away from awareness to that state where the Self becomes the witness to all functions of the intellect, and in which Brahman equates with the indwelling Self in all. This is Sri Krishna's overall goal in the Bhagavad Gita. Such a person who has risen in Consciousness to the extent that the person is in full control of the senses, and mind, while being totally detached from expectations founded in pleasures and intense yearning for wealth and fame, is considered not only liberated but one who exists within the realm of Brahman. However, even from here where one has declared *Aham Brahmasi*, "I am Brahman", Consciousness continues to rise from where the yogi comes to the understanding that Brahman exists in all, in the same way that he experienced It in himself. At this level, the yogi declares *Tat Tvam Asi*: That thou Art (Chandogya Upanishad (6.8.15) attached to the Samaveda).

In the Chandogya Upanishad there is the delightful story of Śvetaketu whom, after returning home from his studies, his father, Sage Uddalaka, found him bloated with pride about his learning and therefore asked, "Śvetaketu, my child, you are so full of your learning and so censorious, have you asked for that knowledge by which we hear the unhearable, by which we perceive what cannot be perceived and know what cannot be known?"

The young man, conceding to the apparent shortfall, asks his father to instruct him. The father agrees and asks Śvetaketu to fetch him a fruit from the nyagrodha tree, upon which the father breaks it and asks Śvetaketu to identify what he sees. "Seeds", said Śvetaketu. The young man is then asked to break one and tell what he sees within the seed. Śvetaketu reported that there was nothing inside the seed, upon which the father said:

"My son, that subtle essence which you do not perceive there - in that very essence stands the being of the huge nyagrodha tree. In that which is the subtle essence of all that exists has its self. That is the True, that is the Self, and thou Śvetaketu art That."

The statement "Thou art That", is mentioned nine times in the Chandogya Upanishad and forms one of the fundamental principles in Hindu philosophy. The statement also takes us full circle to the very inception of creation, where there had been no such thing as duality or Dvaita, the idea that the Supreme Reality somehow exists somewhere up there while I am down here existing at his mercy. However, "Thou art That" suggests an Existence without name or form, which is depicted as "That". However, even more pertinently the statement brings into focus the idea that all is "That", and holds in balance the three previous declarations in which the only reality that exists, is Brahman, or in Śaivism, Śiva. It further implies that the indwelling Self transcends body awareness, mind, the senses, which is indicated by the expression "Thou". But the story of Brahman as It is linked to creation and consciousness, goes one notch further: there is not only equality among human beings but among all creatures, which is made clear in the statement from the Mandukya Upanishad attached to the Atharva Veda: *Ayam atma Brahma*, the Self is Brahman.

In many ways the last statement, *Ayam atma Brahma*, the Self is Brahma, ties together much of what has been said in general throughout this book, but particularly so in a more pointed manner in the way it was brought out in Part Three. However, from a philosophical point of view it challenges the western idea of the soul in that the soul is held as an agent totally apart from God. Etymologically "ayam" refers to "this" and atma is soul. But the statement will not carry the philosophical intended weight if attention is only given to the literal translation of "this"; in this regard, "thisness" is closer to the intentional use of "this", which refers to the self-luminous and non-mediate nature of the Self that is internal to everything, from the Ahamkara or ego down to the physical body. Even so, this is only part of the intentional meaning; what the statement suggests is that while soul is in every creature, the luminous Self, which is of a higher consciousness in human beings is that from which all things are made. In as much as it is everywhere, it is especially pronounced in human beings as Brahman; and, because of its omnipresent nature it pervades everything as it expands into Existence, which makes it beyond measure of perception or knowledge. Thus, by virtue of its self-luminosity, non-relativity and universality, the Atman or Self, and Brahman, are the same.

From the Brahma Sutras, a compendium of five hundred and fifty-five aphorisms, we learn that Brahman is Absolute Reality. The word Absolute has the quality of Existence, or the ultimate independence of existence of its own accord. There is nothing greater that can impinge on it as a whole or on its nature; hence the quality of its Reality, whose nature or substance cannot be subsumed or examined from reason, although all can meditate upon it. Indeed, Swami Sivananda boldly says in his commentary of the Brahma Sutras that while Brahman cannot be known, one can attain Self-realisation on Brahman but not through mere reasoning: "perverted intellect" (Viparīta Buddhi) is "a great hindrance"; it keeps one far away from the truth. However, from what were given in *Śrutis*, that which the ancient Rishis and Sages heard, it *can* be defined. In this regard, Swami Sivananda claims that a thing can be defined in three ways: by distinguishing it from others *Vyavartaka Lakshana*; by pointing out its apparent attributes *Tatastha Lakshana*; and, by describing its essential nature *Svarūpa Lakshana*. The statement, "That which is the cause of the world is Brahman", is *Tatastha Lakshana* by virtue of pointing out its "apparent attributes", which is essentially the origin, sustenance, and dissolution of the universe. This is the dynamic nature of Brahman in terms of what it does; however this is contrasted by the nature of Brahman in that, while the universe is in constant flux, Brahman does not change. This idea is supported by some of the highest "voices" affirmed as authority from Śrutis found in the Vedas and the Upanishads, which is definitive about Brahman: Satyam Jñānam Anantam Brahma – Truth, Knowledge, Infinity, is Brahman. This is an example of Svarūpa Lakshana. Thus from the Srutis (what is heard, as in Śabda) it would seem that Brahman is indestructible, and formless, without beginning or end; and because of its expansionary nature, like the very nature of the universe, it is limitless. Such is the nature of Brahman that, it is never seen, nor could it be described from observation with the naked eyes. However, it can be felt in meditation as the ever-present reality. This is why it is declared as Sat, which connotes Existence. And, since Consciousness is part of its essential nature as Cit in all living beings, it helps the individual to rise up from gross existence to that of Sat. Ananta is also the eternal nature of the soul, but when a person realises Brahman, recognition comes in a flush of enraptured experience of Sat-Cit-Ananda, or Existence in Consciousness and Bliss.

Śabda Brahman is an important concept in Hindu Creation theories in which vibration and light play an important role. Even so, Brahman itself has no will or movement in awareness without Maya or the lower nature of consciousness as Krishna explained in the Bhagavad Gita.

This is referred to as Mayavada, or as Krishna puts it in the Bhagavad Gita, "My lower nature." Thus, Maya in this context is the efficient cause of creation and is not separate from Brahman. Likewise, the material of creation or the material cause of creation is also in Brahman. Hence, Brahman is not only the entire creation, but also both the material and efficient cause of creation. It is the creator as well as the creation, all in one.

Until now, the idea of Maya has been deliberately sidestepped largely because it has been as badly misunderstood in western interpretation of it as "void" or "illusion" with regard to Hindu philosophy. However, in contradistinction to the Hindu theory of Existence and the role of Brahman, especially in the present need to usher in Siva, who have so far been kept at par with Brahman, the question might be raised: is Śiva the same as Brahman? There are differing views on this question, especially from commentaries given in the Brahma Samhita (same as Brahma Sutras commented in the above), an ancient body of work that, except for a few chapters, has been either lost or destroyed. However, the little that has survived has, since antiquity, caused a furrow of opposing views, which in many respects continues. For instance take the following verse, V: 45, of the Brahma Samhita:

> *kshiram yatha dadhi vikara-visesha-yogat*
> *sanjayate na hi tatah prithag asti hetoh*
> *yah sambhutam api tatha samupaiti* karyad
> *govindam adi-purusham tam aham bhajami*

The verse is translated thus: Milk changes into yogurt when mixed with a yogurt culture, but constitutionally it is nothing but milk. Similarly, Govinda, the Supreme Reality, otherwise known from Vaishnava literature as Sri Krishna, assumes the form of Lord Śiva (Śambhutam) for the special purpose of material transactions. This Govinda, also known as Krishna, is the self-same person as the formless Brahman. Thus it can be assumed that while Śiva comes from Krishna, Śiva nevertheless remains "tainted" by virtue of his material investiture, and thus he is essentially "yogurt". Krishna, on the other hand, who is declared as being the same as Brahman, remains pure milk.

Other than what is given in the above verse that is taken from the Brahma Samhita, the origins of Śiva are told in the Puranas, especially so in the Śiva Purana. Some accounts depict him as Supreme Reality, while others accord him equality with Brahma and Vishnu as part of the tripartite

Supreme Trinity in Hinduism. However, there are several mentions of Śiva in the Bhagavad Gita but what is most definitive is that, Chapter V: 23, which states:

rudrāṇām' śaṅkaraś cāsmi vitteśo yakṣa-rakṣasām
vasūnām' pāvakaś cāsmi meruh śikhariṇām aham

What is interesting about this verse is what Krishna says here about Siva: of all the eleven Rudras, He is Sankara. But along with this claim Krishna also lumps himself as also being part of lower order of creatures, which would assume that Krishna's intention in this verse is meant to suggest that He is talking about His lower nature that is the sum of Prakriti.

Etymologically speaking Rudra is derived from the root, "rud", which means to cry or howl, and has come down the ages to mean "howler" or "roarer"; it is from these defining words that gave Rudra the nickname, the Storm God, and which characterizes his "wildness" especially as depicted in the early days as he emerged out of Spanda. However, Rudra is also mentioned as the "Red one", or the "Shining one". In the Rig Veda the verse, *rukh draavayathi, iti rudraha,* suggests one who drives out sorrows or miseries. Hence, it would seem that what Krishna suggests in the above verse, is that his function as Rudra is to make men cry, as the first act of repentance; or to make them cry for seeking only enjoyment rather than seeking to gain the greatest good. In this regard, Śankara is the doer of "good", which emanates from *Śreyas* the principle of the greatest good, as opposed to *Preyas*, that good, which beings seek to enjoy, regardless of consequences.

Contrasted with the Yakshas and Rakshasas, who are celestial beings motivated to acquire wealth and hoarding it for the sake of power, as illustrated in the Ramayana with Ravana's grandfather, Kubera, who was such a person. Kubera who had a tremendous influence on his grandson, as not only a hoarder of wealth but the need to bolster his ever increasing stock of material possession to ingratiate his desire for power in order to conquer God. The Vasus on the other hand, who are eight in number, are compared with the Rudras, and Kubera as being able to manipulate the five elements together with the sun, moon and stars. Krishna's role as Pavaka, however, is to generate warmth for the welfare of all, especially in the expanding universe in this manifestation. Lastly in the verse the significant mention of Mount Meru, which had been explained in Part Three as representative of the Axis Mundi, is that around which all the heavenly bodies rotate. However, Krishna's manifestation here as Mount Meru is an allegorical account of what is given in Hindu philosophy as Brahma Danda (Brahma's Rod), which is representative of the spinal column in the human body. In Part Three, it is depicted as "the golden lustrous Śusumna from which all forms of sensation emanate" as well as the path by which Kundalini ascends from the Muladhara Chakra to unite with Śiva at the Sahasrara at the crown of the head, and which is accounted here for its vibratory nature that is Śabda Brahman. Indeed, it is the rising of Consciousness, which accounts for its brilliance.

Nevertheless, the comparisons and contrasts given so far do not adequately answer the question: is Śiva the same as Krishna? To examine this further it is necessary to return to V-45 of the Brahma Samhita, which purports to say that Siva is Krishna. Indeed, the analogy of milk turning into yogurt suggests a subtle "adulteration", which has the power to point to a significant phenomenon in Hindu philosophy known as Maya. For some, Maya is considered an illusory force that not only has the power to delude but also to stupefy. And, since Maya is associated with the generative aspect of Prakriti, which Krishna claims in the Bhagavad Gita to be his lower nature, this in itself would suggest that Siva's status vis-à-vis Krishna lies somewhere in the realm of beings in the same way that Krishna implies that he is the Self that lives in the hearts of all: *"I am the Supersoul, O* <u>Arjuna</u>, *seated in the hearts of all living entities. I am the beginning, the middle and the end of all beings* (BG: X-20). This signifies that, although Śiva is an important deity, like yogurt that is derived from milk, he is no longer Krishna. So, while Śiva is affected by Maya, Krishna is not.

In addition to the degree by which Śiva is affected by Maya, in that he is designated as the Lord of Jivas, this says something about the limitations of Śiva when compared to Krishna, who is regarded as the Self that resides in the hearts of all creatures, *aham ātmā sarva bhūtāśayasthitah*. At best, Śiva enjoys a marginal potency like a ghost that hobnobs with the shadow self of the conditioned soul attached to bodies. In the

Puranas, Śiva is identified with the lowly, the suffering, those in need of spiritual counselling, and even takes pity on those bereaving souls found in cemeteries and cremation grounds, where Śiva doused with ashes from the burning corpse. As such he is very much with all that needs to be uplifted, who he consoles wisely. Thus, Śiva shares the multitude of emotions experienced by beings, while Krishna as the Self in all remains detached, regardless of the situation. Indeed, the only time that Krishna responds to life situations is when an individual meets all the conditions of an avowed devotee; then Krishna meets that devotee as a friend and occupies a special place in the devotee's heart. However, nothing of substance changes: Krishna or Brahman remains the Supreme eternal and unlimited, *say nityo nityanam cetanas cetananam*, but the conditioned souls like humans or those deities like Śiva, although also eternal, carry a portion of the qualities of the human condition governed by Maya, and so, remain limited.

However, there are those who maintain that Śiva is not limited. This is justified in the Śaivite school of philosophy that, because Śiva enjoys a slight degree of "ananda" or bliss, there is also that ingredient of Cit or Consciousness that cognates with Śiva's plenary spiritual potency to raise him to that level of Brahman.

In a manner of speaking there is nothing strange about Śiva's plenum of spiritual potency, for indeed, humans who become sufficiently elevated in Consciousness, are often said to have risen to that state of Brahman or Siva-Consciousness, depending on the spiritual path they chose to follow. In any case, this is observed by Śaivites who often experience satcitananda, as much as it is observed by Krishna or Vishnu Bhaktas who encounter the same experience. Even so, it is the contention of scriptural injunction that while Śiva only has some portions of sat, cit and ananda, Krishna has it all. Even so, this might be irrelevant when the question is addressed from the point of view of the two constituent elements of Prakriti: material or inferior nature compared to superior nature that is living entity, the "life element by which this universe is upheld"(*jivabhūtām yaye 'idam dhāryare jagat*). In the Bhagavad Gita it is suggested in VII-5, that the five elements plus mind, intellect, and egoism, form the inferior Prakriti (apara prakritiṁ - "apara" here means lower) of the Supreme, while the cosmic life principle or that which constitutes the entirety of the Jivatman is the superior or higher prakriti (paraprakritiṁ) of the Supreme. However, both are under control of Krishna. In this regard, all living entities, although considered sparks of the Supreme, nevertheless remain part of Prakriti, which is subordinate and controlled by the Supreme. Moreover, the principal qualities of *apara prakritiṁ* constitute the three gunas of sattva, rajas and tamas, which, like the vibrating universe, are constantly in a state of flux, but contrasted with paraprakriti, although the gunas manifest from the Supreme, they have no effect on the Supreme or Krishna.

But how satisfactory is this? For the avowed Śaivite it is not very convincing, although there remains a glimmer of hope in this thought: the last line of the X: 45 suggests that while Śiva is the lord of the Jivas, yet he partakes of the nature of a separated portion of Govinda. Or put it another way: because of all the qualities Śiva takes on, he partakes the nature of the Jivas, which significantly reduces his potency as Supreme Reality. Even so, his role in Spanda is unaffected, which accounts for the essence of Śiva Consciousness that equates perfectly with Śabda Brahman. In this regard, just as Siva partakes the nature of the Jivas, so he also becomes charged from the vibratory power of the gunas that are part and parcel of the expanding universe. He is one with the nature of the Jivas in their emotions, aroused from pain and suffering, as well from the virtue of Love, like that which is aroused by Śakti in the need to create. Furthermore, Siva is humanized in a dynamic way by being one of the Jivas and yet sufficiently powerful enough to cause creation through the energy generated on its own accord by Spanda. This is the principal difference between Krishna as Brahman and Śiva: Krishna remains detached from the life of the Jivas; he leaves them to work out their own problems, even though he responds to the call of his Bhaktas or those who qualify as true Devotees. Śiva on the other hand lives among his devotees and shares all of their emotions, which amounts to a very large part of his personality. In this regard, while Krishna or Brahman is likened to the Akasa or space which contains in itself all of the elements and all of the universe, Śiva remains inert and ineffective until he is energized by Śakti; indeed, that very Śakti might be Krishna, whom Śiva never knows until he is summarily touched by Krishna's creative powers:

> etad-yonīni bhātani sarvāṇī 'ity upadhāraya
> ahaṁ kṛtsnasya jagataḥ prabhavaḥ pralayas tathā
> BG: VII: 6

Which translates thus: know that my higher and lower nature are the two wombs from which are the source of all beings; I am the origin and dissolution of the entire universe. In this regard, the higher and lower nature are considered as cit and acit, the sentient and insentient respectively; taken together they are the basis of Existence, which is characterized as divine power, as discussed in Part One of this book.

Indeed, once seen from the dynamic nature of Prakriti, the idea whether Śiva and Brahman are the same, loses its potency and the discussion comes to a close: the atma is an eternal spark of Krishna or Brahman, which enters into all sentient beings "as the witness and experience". Thus, as Krishna says in the above verse, He is the organizing cause from which everything comes into Existence, and as such he is the ultimate cause of creation. In this regard He comes to all creatures in different ways; and in Śaivism it is quite conceivable that Śakti, which unites with Śiva at the sahasrara at the crown of the head, is perhaps Krishna in that form. After all, it is no secret in any of the Śaiva literature that Śiva is nothing without Śakti; on his own, he is inert and devoid of energy; and it is only when he is pierced by Śakti that he comes alive. Comparatively speaking Krishna as Brahman is ever alive, albeit non-attached, in the hearts of all creatures: he is there as the Self, monitoring every movement of all, and when the individual creature qualifies as a true devotee, he draws that being into his eternal Existence.

The idea of Śakti and Brahman is akin to the two approaches to sound in Hinduism: "unstruck" sound connotes Śabda Brahman and struck sound equates to Spanda Siva. According to the Narad Purana, struck sound gives pleasures to the species, while unstruck sound, produced from ether, delights the gods and gives liberation to the yogi.

Indeed, sound, either as Śabda, or Spanda, plays a significant role in both creation and in the general affairs of all creatures that cannot be determined either through reason, inference, or perception. It is also beyond the reach of logic or any other scientific methodology that can either prove or disprove what has thus far been said of either Śabda or Spanda. In this regard, the human heart is considered the receptor of all rhythms emanating from Śabda Brahman, which is the heart of the Universe. It is not only fundamental to the theory of sound, but which also underlies the basic theory of art, language, music, and poetry, which is linked to the Religion of the Vedas. This idea germinates from the concept of Apara Brahman mentioned in the Mandukya Upanishad where theories of language and music are enshrined. And, as mentioned earlier in this part of the book, the Śiva Samhita states that "whenever there is causal stress or Divine action, there is vibration", noted as spandana; and wherever there is vibration or movement sound is inevitable. This movement or vibration is none other than Śabda, from which the vibration is caused by Pranava; it is the sum total of that quality of energy that binds the universe together, similar to ether or space, and which the yogis know as refined energy obtained from Prana. Hence the Vedas say that this Prana is the root and essence of everything: "it is Pranava and Pranava is Vedas, Vedas are Śabda Brahman. Consciousness in all beings is Śabda Brahman."

The idea that Pranava is Vedas, certainly takes a quantum leap of Śabda into the very realm of language; for here sound, as is known to the modern mind, now reaches into the sphere of metaphysics and even theories of physics, which the ancient Hindus were no stranger. Indeed, in the Gandharva Vedas (16), we get a clear insight and firm understanding of Hindu ideas on sound that, certainly opened the way to experimentation with both metaphysics and physics. Much of this is also reflected from the Hymns composed in the Rig Veda, which definitely illustrate the extent to which there was a move away from religion and the expansion of knowledge of the *science* of sound. Indeed, these compositions in the Rig Veda contain the earliest examples of words set to music, and by the time the Sama Veda had arrived to the general public, a complicated system of chanting had been developed. Here rules about poetics had reached such a state of advance renditions that only the schooled and able "chanters" could do justice to the compositions. However, the chanters were a special class of temple priests, considered to be descendants of Gandharvas believed to be divine beings, but with the expansion of Sanskrit education, and the arrival of the Yajur Veda, something out of the ordinary had seeped into the matrix of Vedic culture: 'a variety of professional musicians had appeared, such as lute players, drummers, flute players, and conch blowers.' But they had not just dropped from the sky; it took centuries of experimentation with the science of sound before musical instruments could even be considered to accompany the rigid grammar of music, which also had a lot to do with Hindu philosophy of language.

The cornerstone of this movement came with the concept of Sphota, which has a lot to do with the manifestation of Śabda in the processes of speech. It is such an old science, which some claim to have even predate the Vedas, but as it blossomed into the Vedic period and beyond, it had the power to push Hindu philosophy in the area of ontology and then to epistemology, which gave rise to theories of knowledge in India and even beyond its borders. However, this theory of knowledge is nothing like what Kant suggested in his Critique of Pure Reason. It implies a reappraisal of the relations between language that formulates our knowledge and the being of the objects that the human mind tries to know. In this regard, the scientific basis of Sphota lies in the hierarchical structure of the elements implicit in verbal communication, which constitute a model for the origins of the phenomenal world characteristic of Śabda, even though Sphota is not identical with Śabda; it is a permanent element of Śabda (17). While Sphota has a lot to do with rhythm that accounts for Hindu theories of music, the root of it derives from meaning. However this meaning is not calculated in a reasoned fashion but spontaneous. Indeed, the very nature of the word Sphota connotes "bursting forth" and has an element of light attached to it that inversely alludes to Śabda Brahman (18). Hence, the very expression of the meaning of a word, or the process of arriving at meaning is Sphota, which erupts from the wellhead of Śabda Brahman. In this regard, meaning is "manifested" or revealed in the same way in which Om was manifested in the two vowels or phonemes of AU, and then droned by "M" to bring the breath to a slow halt. In this droning space that naturally occurs to allow a slow and deliberate act of emptying the material aspect of the breath, the more useful and refined portion of the breath, accounted for by the vibration that has a cosmically primal quality about it, accompanies the chant in the divine aspect of the breath, which is now revealed as Pranava. This pranava is Brahman. In this process of understanding Sphota, we get a revolutionary account of the possibility of suggestion: every word carries the germ of an idea, which not only explains the working of the speech process but a Hindu theory of knowledge that is unlike anything ever considered in western philosophy. In this regard, Sphota is not applied to the elemental meaning of the word, but to the permanent aspect of phonemes, in the same way that OM carries the meaning of Brahman.

Related to Sphota, which is permanently linked to Śabda, are two relative principles that are integral to Hindu theory of language. These are "prakṛta dhvani" and "vaikṛta dhvani". Dhvani is a synonym of Nada or sound that is derived from a lower level of hearing referred earlier in this section as Vaikhari. It is a very old term that goes back to the Atharva Veda where it is associated with the rudiments of music, such as tone, echo, thunder, noise, voice, word; and as *dhvani prasthāpana*, it gives currency to an expression. At this level sound can be analysed from being picked up by the human ear but is restricted to their context, in the same manner in which a scientist might observe certain set of circumstances and draw conclusions just from what is observed. Thus, sounds emanating from prakṛta dhvani has much to do with related activities drawn from nature, while sounds related to sphota are not grasped by the ear but drawn from the elements associated with divine intelligence. Vaikṛta dhvani on the other hand suggests undergoing change, derivative of something but not natural; it is also subject to modification due to its secondary nature, or disfigured and perpetuated by adoption; there is also a semblance of hatred, hostility, and aversion brought about by agitation, enmity, abnormal conditions resulting in disfigurement. This list is not exhaustive but because of the nature of vaikṛta dhvani as an important characteristic of sound, it is suggestive of everyday language. It is best suited for the composition and choreography of dramas, which had greatly shaped the abundance of Vedic drama and music productions that dealt with themes of magic and mythological narratives concerning demonic behaviour anathema to a society that lived by the norms of Dharma. According to Patanjali, Sphota is not identical with Śabda; it is a permanent element of Śabda (19). Likewise, by its very nature as hinted in the above, dhvani suggests non-permanence in so far as it can be heard. Indeed, once the sound has travelled its course, nothing is further heard. However, quite the opposite of this like Śabda, Sphota is not audible but felt or intuited from vibrations that well up from within. In this way, Sphota is manifested by the articulated sounds, while the dhvani element of speech differs in phonetic value with reference to the variation in the utterance of different speakers. Like the sound of a drum, differences in speed of utterance and time distinctions are attributes of the two aspects of dhvani noted above, which cannot affect the nature of Sphota revealed by the sound. Depending on the tonality, rhythm, and the pace of the external sound, Sphota could manifest according to the extent of the vibration that spurts out from within. However, once sound is released from the speaker's lips, Sphota is instantly revealed, although the speaker might not be aware of the "silent" comprehension. In this way dhvani might be said to be the instrument that prompts the manifestation of Śabda. Thus the formula is, Sphota = Dhvani + Śabda. Sphota manifests Dhvani, and in turn, as dhvani continues to exist after the revelation of Sphota, Śabda by it dynamic vibrational "awakening", manifests to give meaning that only Sphota can decipher from the combined activities of Sphota and dhvani. In this regard Patanjali claims that the two dhvanis, as ephemeral elements are actualized attributes of Sphota. Even so, Patanjali claims that Sphota is revealed by the articulated sound; the only thing that is picked up is the phonemes or vowels in speech. In other words vowels are representative of Sphota, which again correlates with the experience of Brahma, the creator, when he heard AUM, which became responsible for his awakening and thus his elevation into Existence. Hence, according to Patanjali, "Sphota is a conceptual entity or generic feature of articulated sounds, either in the form of isolated phonemes or a series of phonemes. It is a permanent element of physical sounds, which are transitory in nature, and which vary in length, tempo and pitch of the speaker. It is an actualized replica of ephemeral sounds."

What has been presented thus far is a synopsis of the prevailing views on the nature of Sphota. In the Brahma kanda it appears at least nine times and is used in different approaches, sometimes relatively to the meaning of Sphota and at other times as synonyms, such as pada, vakya, dhvani, nada, prakṛtadhvani, and vaikradhvani. Obviously, this has caused confusion in works dealing with the study of Sphota, even among Indian scholars, but more so among those outside of India trying to get a handle on such an important field of ontology and even etymology.

Perhaps the most confident scholar who have contributed the most to the study of Sphota in relation to Śabda, is Bhartṛhari whose discussions on the nature of Sphota posits the need to be cautious in any approach to this "very high science", in which "words or sentences can be considered under two aspects as sound pattern, or its generic feature". He recognizes two entities, both of which may be called Śabda: one is the underlying cause of the articulated sounds, while the other is used to express the meaning. Thus it is said:

dvaavupaadaanashabdeSu shabdau shabdavido viduH
eko nimittam shabdaanaamaparo'rthe prayujyate. Bk. 44//

The translation is thus: The former, called Sphota, is the conceptual entity and permanent element of word, whereas the latter, called dhvani, is a sound pattern, which is the external aspect of the language symbol. Thus, Sphota as a mental impression of an audible sound pattern, is the cause of that sound pattern.

Bhartṛhari is not without critics, especially on his views of cause and corresponding effects of Sphota and Dhvani. Indian logicians in particular who are driven by pure reason resulting from mathematical models, believe that the two are distinctly different between cause and effect. The other predominating view observe differences as psychological, which however is not necessarily without realism. This view is supported by Vedantins.

The reason for introducing Sphota in relation to Śabda has to do with the overall philosophical approach to the study of language as it relates to knowing, in this book. Metaphysically speaking it has everything to do with "that in which the meaning bursts forth", which is the essence behind the entire philosophy of Sphota, and perhaps the single-most concern of Indian philosophers as to what precisely is the bearer of the meaning of the word. Indeed, this is one of the largest causes that gave the rise to the study deconstructionism, and which now stands firmly as an independent philosophy in the western world.

Deconstructionism was initiated by Jacques Derrida in the 1960s, even though he disclaimed any intention of introducing a brand new genre of philosophy to a somewhat cautionary world in the blackboard jungle of academia. And yet, even though deconstructionism took off like a rocket into space, none that has been engaged in deconstruction work is willing to acknowledge that there is a large body of work originating in India, which has given birth to this very important branch of Western philosophy. It is true that Derrida initially approached deconstruction as a literary tool relating to criticism about "traditional assumptions about certainty, identity, and truth," which is the general path that Sphota follows, once the "burst of meaning" dawns on the speaker or the listener. For this reason, Derrida also denied that his methodology ever intended to be anything more than a method, far more inventing a completely new doctrine of philosophy. He asserted, "Words can only refer to other words", although there is a progression that "demonstrate how statements about any text subvert their own meanings." Of course, Derrida has had his critics and some have even suggested that deconstruction is just another name for Nihilism, while others label his work as illustrative of the "limitations of Phenomenology" (20). Indeed, Phenomenology has its roots in the Mandukya Upanishad, rather than in the western claim of Edmund Husserl as its founder. Taken together with the importance of phonemes when dealing with elements of Sphota, such as Dhvani, it is not difficult to make the link between phenomenology and deconstructionism, especially noted on Derrida's "Speech and Phenomena". From here it is not difficult to spot the ongoing conspiracy among western philosophers that either ignore Indian contributions in the movement to arrive at established methodology of philosophical enquiry or deliberately undermine such methodologies that depict philosophical understanding, which has its foundation in that "spurt of meaning" that manifest in the Intuitive Self. Clearly, this idea is subverted, even when Derrida came so close to the Indian way of seeing the world in his 1967 ground-breaking work, *Of Grammatology*, in which he specifically asks such questions as, "What is meaning", or "from where does it come?" And, towards this end he mocked the western philosophical tradition by saying that it rests on arbitrarily dichotomous categories, recalls Pythagoras' pairs of opposites, such as the sacred over the profane, sign and signifier, or mind and body. For Derrida, it is from here where deconstruction begins, as these categories question any validity of certainty, identity and truth; for "words can only refer to other words", and attempts to demonstrate how statements about any text subvert their own meaning. There is little doubt that what Derrida alluded to here, is Ferdinand Saussure's linguistic structuralism in which sound and meaning is paramount to the two principal component of "sign" which Saussure termed the "signifier" and the "signified". To be fair to Derrida, his concern here, from which his entire philosophy is built, had to do with "language and writing are two distinct systems of signs; the second exists for the sole purpose of representing the first" (21). Indeed, whether

Derrida or Saussure even had an inkling of how close their combined theory of deconstructionism and structuralism has come from the inner regions of Sphota, is made clear in this statement: "...writing has been considered as merely a derivative form of speech, and thus as a "fall" from the "full presence" of speech"(22). There should be no quarrel with this but the most significant thing to remember is that while writing is a take-off from speech, the reader of the writing is ever cognizant of the internal structure of the linguistic sign, which is never differentiated from the sign as mere acoustic "things", nor from the mental process until that essential burst of meaning occurs.

Saussure's academic distinction made between "sign" and "signified" is no difference in *sphota*, which is whole and indivisible as compared to Nada, the sound which is sequenced and therefore divisible. The *sphota* is the causal root, the intention behind an utterance, in which sense is similar to the notion of lemma in most psycholinguistic theories of speech production. However, *sphota* arises also in the listener, which is different from the lemma position. Uttering the *nāda* induces the same mental state or *sphota* in the listener - it comes as a whole, in a flash of recognition or intuition (*pratibhā*, 'shining forth'). This is particularly true for *vakya-sphoṭa*, where the entire sentence is thought of (by the speaker), and grasped (by the listener) as a whole. This is the value of Sphota, which the true fathers of linguistics, such as Yashka, Panini, Kātyāyana and Bhartṛhari, bequeathed to humanity but which are applied in very dubious ways to the original purpose of linguistic studies for which India remains the original field.

However, there are those who would defend this assumption by saying that deconstructionism as a philosophical genre has not yet "arrived" since it is difficult to define. But so has been Sphota, which has a three thousand year-old history, and which has influenced a host of related disciplines, such as philosophy, linguistics, logic, philology, etymology, and even broad-based science. Not only that; it has also influenced the entire gamut of linguistics, as well as etymology, ontology, and how we arrive at a philosophy of language. Indeed, words like abhava (non-apprehension, anumana (inference), artha-patti (presumption), upamana (analogy), and of course, Śabda (as verbal or textual testimony), are customarily discussed among Indian scholars from time immemorial as the six means of knowledge. These were picked up by Greek philosophers, and later by western linguists and parsed as different units of language before being passed down to the panoply of the continental theatre. Unfortunately many of these major breakthroughs have not been formally recognised for the impact they have had in either the development of linguistics or philosophy of language. This is especially so with the tremendous contributions from such giants as Bhartṛhari who boldly articulated the theory that a sentence as a whole is understood in a sudden act of comprehension, and that the relation between a word and meaning is permanent and natural, and not based on convention.

Indeed, while there is a silent movement among Western thinkers that either play down Hindu contributions to the philosophy of language or out rightly disavow any contributions at all. There are some who recognise Pāṇini and the later Indian linguist Bhartṛhari, as having a significant influence on many of the foundational ideas proposed by Ferdinand de Saussure, professor of Sanskrit, who is widely considered the father of modern structural linguistics. Saussure himself cited Sanskrit grammar as an influence on some of his ideas. In his Memoire, *sur le systeme primitif des voyelles dans les langues indo-europennes* (Memoir on the Original System of Vowels in the Indo-European Languages) published in 1879, he mentions Sanskrit grammar as an influence on his idea that "reduplicated *aorist* (a class of verb form in Greek) that generally portrays a situation as simple or undefined, that is, as having perfect aspect, which represents the imperfect of a verbal class." In his De l'emploi du genitif absolu en sanscrit (On the Use of the Genitive Absolute in Sanskrit) published in 1881, he specifically mentions Pāṇini as having an enormous influence on the bulk of his work.

Indeed, Saussure was a talented linguist who spoke French, German, English, Latin, Greek and Sanskrit. His main theory was semiotics, borrowed from Greek but whose origins lay deeply in Sanskrit linguistics. From here he presented the idea that human language is a system of signs and signifiers whose origins were discussed in this section of this book. And because of this, he rejected the theory of language as being "a naming process only – a list of words with each corresponding to the thing it names", arguing that this "assumes that ready-made ideas exist before words, in the same way that Intuitive Knowledge erupts as demonstrated earlier in the formula: sphota + dhvani = Śabda.

REFERENCES

References

1. Alper, Harvey, P., Editor: Understanding Mantra, Motilal Banarsidas, Delhi, 1991: pp, 168, 228-229, 240, 380-382.
2. Ibid, page 80. Also compare with Bharata's Naryan Shastras, based on Vedic concepts, which is considered the bible of all branches of Indian art and poetics.
3. Singh, Lalan Prasad: Tantra, its Mystic and Scientific Basis, Concept Publishing, Delhi.p.98/
4. Ibid, page 99 as quoted here: "The Sanskrit alphabet is of Tantric origin. The letters are not called alphabet but Varnamālā. Its fifty letters from a to kṣa are the fifty basic vibrations of the Cosmos. Each letter is a bija mantra of fifty human instincts. Here bija mantra means the acoustic roots of different psychic expressions. It is said that the divine nectar that secretes from the pineal gland (located at the Sahasrāra) takes different forms of letters in the six different chakras or Padams.

Nair, Shantha, N: Echoes of Ancient Indian Wisdom, Hindoology Books (An Imprint of Pushtak Mahal) Delhi. Page 183.
5. Singh (3) page 99.
6. Cf. Compare Jose-Morales, Kundalini the Arousal of the Inner Energy, Suny Transpersonal Studies, with the innate self dwells there like the flame of a lamp. Contemplation of this radiant light as the luminous Brahman is the transcendental meditation. Gheranda Samhita, Vol V. 16. Ajit Mookerjee, *KUNDALINI!*, Dstiny Book, Vermont.
7. King, Richard: Indian Philosophy: An Introduction to Hindu Philosophy and Buddhist Thought, Edinburgh University Press, p. 49.
8. Bhattacharya, Umesh Chandra: Space, Time and Brahma, Jha Commemoration Volume, Oriental Book Agency, Poona, 1937, pp. 69-83.
9. Alper in (3) above, p. 229.
10. Taimni, I.K, The Science of Yoga, Quest Books, 1961. "The world is not only created by this Sabda which differentiates into innumerable forms of vibration which underlie the phenomenal world." Commentary on aphorism 27.
11. Kashmiri, Braj B: Kashmiri Literature (part of the series, A History of Indian Literature, OTTO HARRASSOWITZ, Publishers, Wiesbaden. Page 10.
12. Swami Sivananda: Brahma Sutras, Motilal Banarsidas, Delhi, 1949. Pages 417, 489-490.

13. Ibid, *Śāstrayonitvāt* is not just a word but an aphorism in the Brahma Sutras. The word Śāstra refers to scripture, and Yonitvat, the source of or the means of the right knowledge. Swami Sivananda explains thus, "The Omniscience Brahman follows from His being the source of Scripture." page 17
14. Ibid, pages, 171, 186, 213.

16. The Gandharvas, even from the time of the Mahabharata, were famous for their patronage for dance, music and art. A type of recital of Indian classical music is named after Gandhara. A form of sculpturing is described as Gandhara sculpturing. In Mahabharata, the art of music and dance is termed as Gandharva-Veda (meaning the knowledge of the Gandharvas). Arjuna is mentioned as learning this art from the Gandharvas.
17. Coward, Harold G and Raja, K. Kunjunni, An Introduction to the Philosophy of the Grammarians in The Encyclopaedia of Indian Philosophies, Vol 5. Pp 63-82.
18. In Swami Sivananda's commentary on the Brahma Sutras, he says that Brahman is the "Light of Light" p 116-117. This drawn from Sutras 3.22-23.
19. Patanjali discusses the idea of Sphota under P-1.1.170 of Taparastatkaalasya sphota is not identical to Śabda, but a permanent of Śabda.

20. Derrida, Jacques: "Genesis and Structure and Phenomenology," in *Writing and Difference* (London: Routledge, 1978), paper originally delivered in 1959 at Cerisy-la-Salle, and originally published in Gandillac, Goldmann & Piaget (eds.), *Genèse et structure* (The Hague: Morton, 1964), p. 167

21. Derrida, Jacques: Ethics, Institutions, and the Right to Philosophy (Culture and Politics Series) A collection of Derrida's writings, from 1975 to 1990, about teaching of philosophy, and the politics of philosophy in school, university, and the academic institution. Rowman & Littlefield Publishers (July 31, 2002) pp.6791.

22. Ferdinand de Saussure, Mémoire sur le Système Primitif des Voyelles dans les Langues Indo-Européennes - Scholar's Choice Edition Paperback– February 19, 2015

NOTES

Records show two totally contradictory views about these two different elements relating to the word that stems from Sphota and Dhvani. According to some, there is an absolute difference between these two elements, with cause and effect relationship between them. This agrees with the view held by logicians, who assumed total distinction between the cause and effect. According to the second view, the difference between these elements is mere psychological and not real. This is said to be supported by Vedantins, Samkhya, and grammarians, who believe that the effect is inherited in the cause. Bhartṛhari response is simply put: Sphota is always intimately related to dhvani, for "as soon as the sounds are produced the Sphota is cognized instantly. Thus, sounds are *manifesters* and sphota is manifested." Moreover, Bhartṛhari posits, "it is the articulate sound that reaches the listener's ear in the form of the sphota." Or, to put it differently," sphota is a replica of dhvani having phonetic features", which is why it is an "auditory image of the sound"

In an attempt to confute his logician critics, Bhartṛhari adamantly maintains that Sphota is one and without

sequence. Therefore, he concludes, "neither the question of parts nor the order can arise in the conception of sphota. It is sound or nada, which is produced at different moments of time, and the notions of sequence of plurality that really pertain to sounds are wrongly attributed to sphota".

> naadasya kramajaatatvaanna pUrvo na parashca saH|
> akramaH kramarUpeNa bhedavaaniva jaayatell
> Patanjali, Book 49:

Furthermore, pertaining to the relation between Sphota and Dhvani, Bhartṛhari firmly holds his critics at bay with his following three views: sound is closely bound up with sphota and is not perceived separately, like color, which is not separately perceived from the object; sound, without being perceived, causes perception of sphota, as the sense organ and its qualities, which being themselves unperceived, cause the perception of objects; and, sound is also perceived without giving rise to the perception of the form of sphota. In other words, the perception of sound is not regarded as identical with the perception of sphota.

The fundamental theory of Indian classical music, art and poetry is grounded in the theory of Nada Brahman or Śabda Brahman, and is linked with the Vedic religion. The Apara Brahman mentioned by Mandukya Upanishad is Nada Brahman or Śabda Brahman. Śiva Samhita states that whenever and wherever there is causal stress or Divine action, there is vibration (spandana or kampan), and wherever there is vibration or movement there sound (Śabda) is inevitable. "M" of Aum, the primordial vac represents Śabda which is the root and essence of everything; it is Pranava and Pranava is Vedas, Vedas are Śabda Brahman. Consciousness in all beings is Śabda Brahman. Śabda Brahman or Śabda-Brahman means transcendental sound (Shatapatha Brahmana III.12.48) or sound vibration (Shatpatha Brahmana Vi.16.51) or the transcendental sound of the Vedas (Shatpatha Brahmana Xi.21.36) or of Vedic scriptures (Shatpatha Brahmana X.20.43).[1]

Śabda or śabda stands for word manifested by 'verbal' sound and such a word has innate power to convey a particular sense or meaning (Artha). According to the Nyaya and the Vaisheshika schools, Śabda means verbal testimony; to the Sanskrit grammarians, Yaska, Panini and Katyayana it meant a unit of language or speech or vac. In the philosophical terms this word appears for the first time in the Maitri Upanishad (Śloka VI.22) that speaks of two kinds of Brahman - Śabda Brahman ('Brahman with sound') and Aśhabda Brahman ('soundless Brahman'). Bhartṛhari speaks about the creative power of Śabda, the manifold universe is a creation of Śabda Brahman (Brihadaranyaka Upanishad IV.i.2). Speech is equated with Brahman (Shatpatha Brahmana 2.1.4.10).The Rig Veda states that Brahman extends as far as Vāc (R.V.X.114.8), and has hymns in praise of Speech as the Creator (R.V.X.71.7) and as the final abode of Brahman (R.V.I.164.37). Time is the creative power of Śabda Brahman.[2][3]

The six means of knowledge (cognition) advocated by Upavarsha. These are, briefly: *Pratyaksha* (immediate); *Anumana* (inference); *Sabda* (verbal or textual testimony); *Upamana* (analogy); *Artha-patti* (presumption) ; and , *Abhava* (non-apprehension). He remarks that the *Vrittika-kara* (Upavarsha) believes that these six modes of acquiring knowledge are valid only until the Self is ascertained. But, once the subject-object differentiation is erased they no longer matter. He therefore makes a distinction between relative knowledge (*sesha-jnana*) and absolute knowledge (*asesha-jnana*). Upavarsha, he says, believes that absolute knowledge is attainable through *Adyaropa* or *Apavada* (*adyaropa-apavada-ubhayam nishprapancham prapanchate*). Sundarapandya explains: the attribute-less Brahman can be described by the method of superimposition followed by its withdrawal. The Absolute knowledge, however, is neither the process of superimposition nor is it the negation. Incidentally, Sundarapandya is also believed to have contemplated on the concept of Maya and on the pristine nature of Brahman without Maya.

(The *Adhyaropa-Apavada* method of logic pioneered by Upavarsha consists in initially assuming a position and later withdrawing that assumption, after a discussion.)

Apart from delineating the six means of knowledge that were adopted by the later Advaita Schools, Upavarsha is believed to have initiated a discussion on self-validation (*svathah pramanya*) that became a part of the Vedanta terminology.

Svatah pramana: true knowledge is valid by itself; not made valid or invalid by external conditions (*sva karya-karane svatah pramanyam jnanasya*). (As a general rule, knowledge (except memory) is taken to be valid on its own strength, unless invalidated by contrary knowledge.) Memory is not considered valid knowledge as it is dependent on previous cognition or impressions which might get faded or distorted; and, so is the dream.

Philosophy of Language Within a Hindu Context

Philosophy of Language
Within a Hindu Context

Philosophy of Language
Within a Hindu Context

Indian culture has its roots in the Tantras, the Vedas, the Puranas (such as the Ganesha Purana), the Upanishads, and the language of spirituality known as Sanskrit. Perhaps, of all the determinants listed here about the culture of the Indian subcontinent, it would be language; for from the very beginning of linguistic experimentation, there has been a tremendous preoccupation with language in the ability to be understood. The earliest of this, seen in the Rig Veda, has much to do with its august concern for economy, or as some have observed, its "power of limitations of language". For instance Pramana, claimed by Hindus to be the origins of Epistemology, arose out of one of the earliest works known as the Purva Mimāmsā related to the Vedas. The entire thrust of Pramana has to do with what is knowledge and by what means do humans gain accurate knowledge; what is the correct manner in which knowledge came to be acquired. However, insofar as spiritual or real knowledge is concerned, the overriding preoccupation is, how does one know, or does not know, or to what extent is this knowledge pertinent to one's being. Indeed, of the six theoretical branches of philosophy listed in the Vedas that deal with learning, four are closely related to language: etymology, grammar, lexicography, and poetry. Some of these are already touched on in different parts of this book from a different perspective, but the aim here is to bring together the essential idea of what intuition plays in the Hindu orientation of philosophy of language.

The development of an essentially Hindu philosophy of language goes back even further than the rise of Vedic epistemology. There is a vast body of teachings, which emerged with the Tantras; most of these are lost but managed, over millennia, to creep into the more popular works that are still with us today. As mentioned in the above, the Pramanas form the modus of Hindu epistemology, which essentially deal with the correct means of acquiring accurate knowledge and truths. These are *Anumana* or inference; *arthapatti* or derivation from circumstances, and postulation; *anupalabdi* or negatively derived cognitive proof or non-perception; *pratyaksa*, or inference; and *Śabda* or primordial sound that offers reliable testimony from past or present experts. These are thought to be the conditional categories that form the basis of Hindu epistemology; however, each of these are further split apart by the six Darshanas or āstika, which are the six major systems of

Hindu philosophy, in their attempt to offer "completeness, confidence and possibility of error." The older schools of philosophy such as the Mimāmsā and Advaita Vedanta, accept all categories listed in the Pramanas, while the Sāṃkhya, which in some respects even predates the Vedas, accept only three; however, the *Carvakas* (a materialist system of thought that arose during the 8th century BCE) only accepts perception as an epistemically useful means of acquiring reliable knowledge.

The chart provided below for quick reference shows the strategic space occupied by Panini and his level of achievement in his descriptive grammar, *Aṣṭādhyāyī*, as well

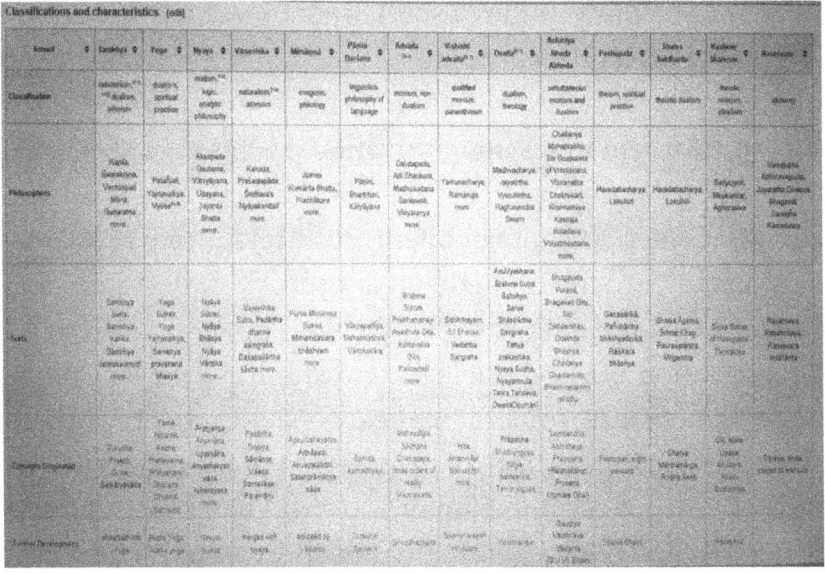

as the overall accomplishment attained by others in their quest to build consensus for a philosophy of language. Indeed, the level of scholarship demonstrated in Panini's descriptive grammar not only helped to pull together others who sought direction away from religious norms, hitherto guided by the lexicology of the Vedas and that portion of the Mimāmsā that dealt essentially with expert Hindu rituals – as opposed to the Purva Mimāmsā that dealt with epistemological questions about how true knowledge is gained and utilised.

It is important to note that the lexicology of the Vedas is quite different from other languages in that it is not just the study of word meaning or trying to make sense of symbols or their relationship to epistemology in general; it has its own rules of composition, especially in how morphemes are used. There is a greater emphasis on phonemes as they relate to sound units, and the relationship between words that evolve with semantics and derivation. In this regard there is tremendous emphasis in sociolinguistics, with special attention given to context, intent, cultural norms, especially the manner in which language is used by sub-groups that could have damaging effect on the laws governing rites and interpretation of religious texts. Indeed, in Vedic lexicology there is no place for pragmatics, as there are in western traditions. This goes back to the creation of the earliest Vedic texts: the Rigveda, the Samaveda, the Yajurveda, and the Atharvaveda. The basic texts that in effect govern Hinduism is layered over by perhaps the next most important text in Hinduism known as the Brahmanas, which consist of significant commentaries that usually relate to procedures, justifications, and explanations on the prose rituals of the

Vedas. There are two other major texts that are not only essential to a deeper understanding of the Hindu religion, but which form the core of both Hindu philosophy and foundation of Indian philosophy of language.

It is interesting to note that what we understand as Sanskrit or saṃskṛta was not known as the name of the language ascribed as Sanskrit during the Vedic period, which lasted for almost four thousand years. The term used for language was known as vāk, a term known today as either "voice" or speech. This voice was so sacred that it was protected from contamination from outsiders. Indeed, the sages reserved this voice for communicating with the gods or the unseen Divine entity known even then as Brahman. It would seem that, especially the sages who used language from two levels of communications, language had been perceived as something that had a divine element to it; it was something bequeathed to humanity for special use. As such there was an essential difference between everyday usage and the modus operandi fit for communicating with the gods. Indeed, according to Lalan Prasad Singh in his book, *Tantra, Its Mystic and Scientific Basis*, the Sanskrit alphabet is of

Tantric origin. They represent the different acoustic vibrations of the Cosmos, in which "the fifty letters are the fifty basic vibrations, which constitute the entire universe." They are termed the *bijaksara* of Tantric esotericism, largely because each letter, or even half letter, is a seed mantra, hence *bijaksara*. Thus a person who is aware of this phenomenon, also understands the power of incantation, for which the language was created. According to Singh, the use of Sanskrit, especially by those who follow the rules, "bring liberation from trifarious bondage – physical, mental, and spiritual"; for, it creates an "acoustic vibration in the psychic body of [the] sadhak, which awakens the Kundalini Śakti"(1).

This mystical idea behind the creation of Sanskrit is clearly seen in the word used for "God", which is Deva, and the language used to address the gods as Deva Vāk, or "divine language". In this sense the Rishis firmly believed that the language had not only been God-inspired, but were indeed created by the gods themselves. Thus only those who were qualified to speak to the Gods, through learning, intense meditation practices, and engagement in yoga asanas of the highest order, could speak this language, which in itself had its own rules of grammar, pronunciation, metrical context, etc. that differed so much from the animated world of man and beast. Indeed, Sanskrit as Deva Vāk was so mysterious that three-quarters of it were said to be hidden from ordinary humans, the non-Brahmins, who were barred from even trying to speak the language. Even so, this state of affairs was not ordained due to caste differences; the sages believed that due to their yogic discipline this divine language Deva Vāk entered their hearts as a gift from the Divine through mystical introspection. Hence Deva Vāk is the language of the Gods; and, by contrast, non-Vedic people, who did not necessarily occupy a different geographical area, were by definition Adevī or un-Godly, and the demonic, Asuryā (2). The Rishis approach to language as a means of reaching the Gods intentionally created a nexus of customs that enhanced religious practices while gradually reaching a state of esoteric consciousness where language could be seen, not just as a means for appeasing the Gods to gain favour, but the development of a deep mystical approach to language for language sake. In other words language was seen as a power unto itself; and the finer and more complicated it became, with rules that made speech precise, the wielder of this esoteric language – especially by the appointed priests – created a class of individuals that ranked with the status of gods. Indeed, so powerful they became that they did not only make language the currency by which one reached the higher realms, but whose actions such as those of linguists were respected to the point of even being feared. Thus, to give this language the birthright of divinity, it was necessary to find within the Hindu Pantheon the appropriate goddess to deify the language, which eventually led to the Goddess of Speech, or *Vac Devi*, which was later transposed to Sarasvati. But prior to this, we have in the Rigveda such notable personalities as *Brahmaṇaspati*, *Bṛhaspati*, and *Vācpati* as Lords of Speech. In Rigveda 1:40, this line makes the point, "As the patron deity of ritual speech, Brahmaṇaspati will make the poet's speech effective enough to bring the other gods, especially Indra, to our sacrifice" (*Rgveda*: 1.40: 12). And again in the Rigveda from Hymn XCVIII to the God: "Within my mouth, Bṛhaspati, deposit speech lucid, vigorous, and free from weakness. Thereby to win for Santanu the rainfall. The meath-rich drop from heaven hath passed within it" (3).

It is interesting to note, especially from the philosophical viewpoint of the developing Sanskrit language that, in contrast with the valorous deeds of the divine language, the language of the non-Vedic people "neither yields fruit nor blossom" (Rgveda, 10.71.5). "Yielding fruit and blossom" is a phrase indicative of the creative power of speech that produces the rewards for the worshipper. Indeed, from being a created but divine entity, the speech rises to the heights of being "a divinity in her own right and eventually becoming the substratum of the existence of the whole universe." The deification of speech is seen in hymn 10.125 of the Rgveda where the Goddess of Speech sings her own glory. In this hymn, one no longer hears of the creation of the speech, but one begins to see the speech as a primordial divinity that creates and controls other gods, sages, and the human beings. The idea that one can "see" the language, gives credence to the claim that Sanskrit is considered a perfect language, well made and polished, even though an "artificial language, par excellence," particularly due to its refinement. However, the refinement is not achieved by the exigencies of grammar but by close attention paid to soundby-sound bearing in all its details: "the imprint of conscious work, constructed on the very principle of thought, of creation, in a fashion similar to that of but more flexible and wide-ranging in its applications"(4).

And even though Sanskrit came into existence largely due to religious practices, the refinement was driven more so by a profound spiritual quests that desired to embrace all levels of being, including the emotional, intellectual and the dynamics of unexplained phenomena that pervaded the physical world. The need was so urgent that the very structure of words were formed from roots so small that they resemble what is known today as digitised particles that would eventually take on shapes, sizes and "particle perimeter" that is now identifiable with the help of computer technology. The attempts were made to find relationships and "resolution" and accuracy, especially mindful of convergence, confluence, and contiguity. In this regard, mathematics played a significant part, first as an intuitive tool and then, symbolically (5). This is especially seen later in the works of Baudhayana that went on to influence Pythagorean and even Euclidean geometry. This mathematical connotation is especially noteworthy, partly because of the multi significance of roots but intrinsically in the manner in which Sanskrit is engineered: it is crafted that way because 'virtually every word in the language can be derived from a root, a monosyllabic sound unit having a general significance in the sphere of action', such as sphota, dhvani, and of course Śabda. It is interesting to note Bertrand Russel's comment on the 'conscious work that went into making Sanskrit such a perfect language'; he is reported to have hinted that because of the nearly exclusive intellectual component of mathematics, "Sanskrit is ideally suited to describe and govern the nature of phenomena from the spiritual level to the physical".

Interesting enough, in the later Vedic traditions of the Brāhmaṇas, we are told that there is perfection of the ritual form known as rūpasamṛddhi (perfection of form) that, if certain recited incantations are done as intended, they will echo the ritual action that is being performed. This shows a notion that ideally, there should be a match between the contents of a ritual formula and the ritual action in which it is recited, further suggesting the notion that language mirrors the external world as well as the internal. In the Āraṇyakas and in the Upanishads, language acquires importance in different ways, too; the Upanishads while emphasizing the painful nature of cycles of rebirths, simultaneously point out that the ideal goal, which should put an end to these cycles of birth and rebirth and find one's permanent identity with the original ground of the universal existence in *Brahman*. The term Brahman had originally referred to creative ritual chants and the chanters, but after a millennia of use in this way, it gradually acquired the ultimate meaning that suggests the creative force behind the universe. As part of the meditative practice, one is asked to focus on the sacred syllable OM, which is the symbolic linguistic representation of Brahman. Here the language, in the form of OM, becomes an important tool for the attainment of one's mystical union with Brahman. Like the Sanskrit word akṣara, which originally referred to a syllable, but in the process of lexicon engineering it acquired the deeper meaning of "indestructible." Thus, the word akṣara allowed the meditational use of the holy syllable OM to lead ultimately to one's experiential identity with the indestructible reality of Brahman.

It is important to note that Sanskrit is not just a language that communicate ideas and images but also the expression of something about rhythm, and the music of poetry, and drama, as well as scientific, technical, philosophical and liturgical, which makes it the totality of life that carries through our day to day activities in the original. Thus, when considering the *Veda*, not just as a liturgical text but the full understanding of the word suggestive of "knowledge" of the totality of life, we are altogether confronted with a difficulty of another order of magnitude. This is partly because of the technicalities of the language, which for some it is considered archaic, and whose principles and usages are very different from those of our own language, but more pertinent is its symbolic nature. For instance words like Om and Swastika have such deep significance as representations of not just an idea but the bearers of separate bodies of knowledge, which encompass every aspect of life. The same can be said for words like Prithvi, Agni, Akash, Nag, and Trishul, all of which were codified scriptural bodies of work that taught values beyond religious norms, which is why the Indian government uses these words in military planning to capture major bodies of knowledge as they were used in ancient times.

The idea of Sanskrit being a symbolic language is clearly seen in this passage from the Ramayana, which is one of the longest and most memorable epic poems known to the world. The original author, Valmiki, invoked cosmological forces to narrate the unification of the Indian subcontinent at a time when Dharma was on the wane and adharma in its ascendancy. For this, Vishnu takes human birth to prove to humanity that every living soul can rise up from the material or gross body and become one with God in the idea of *Maryada Purushotama* or the perfect man who rises above materialism to discover his divinity. This is perhaps the most powerful demonstration of the possibility that the most powerful of human beings are mere children when confronted with the superior forces of the Divine, even though that divinity may seem helpless when contrasted with the supposedly superior demonic forces that control the affairs of man in a perfectly engineered manmade environment. In this regard the symbolic interaction between the forces of evil, represented by Ravana who is hell-bent in taking control of the subcontinent, and the forces of good, represented by Rama, is presented in a dialogue

between Rama and Vibhusana (Ravana's brother), just as Rama, the heroine of the epic, is about to engage in battle. Vibhusana cautions Rama, 'My lord, You have no chariot nor any armour to protect your body or shoes to protect your feet, how then can you conquer this mighty hero?'
Somewhat agitated, Sri Rama immediately said, "My dear friend, listen: the chariot which leads one to victory is totally different." Then, surmising his newfound friend who had decided to fight on his side, Rama continued in a more sombre voice while describing in detail the chariot: 'My chariot *Tehin Rattha* is that of *Dharmaratha*, the chariot of Dharma or righteousness, which gives everlasting victory in every situation of life. Sri Rama then points to imaginary wheels, 'The *Caka* of my chariot are valour and fortitude (*Sauraja* and *Dhiraja*). Then he went on to say, his invisible chariot is the epitome of Steadfastness (*Drdhata*), truth (*Satya*), while good character (*Sila*) are its flag and banner (*Dhvaja-pataka*)'. However, what Rama is equally concerned with is that which drives his chariot: 'what drives my chariot are not the horses (*ghore*) you see out there, Vibhusana, what is inside, my strength (*bala*), discrimination (*vivek*), self-control (*dama*) and care for others (*parahita*). Similarly, my reins are made of the ropes (*Raju Jore*) of forgiveness (*Ksama*), compassion (*Krpa*) and equanimity (*Samata*). But perhaps the most important ingredient that holds my chariot together is devotion to God (*Isa Bhajanu*) is the intelligent charioteer (*Sarathi Sujana*). Likewise, dispassion (within the context of mood, the word is *virati*, but the broader meaning of dispassion in Sanskrit is *vairagya*) is the shield (*Karma*) and

contentment (*santosa*) is the sword (*krpana*). Charity (*dana*) is the axe (*parasu*), understanding (*buddhi*) is the missile (*Sakti pracanda*) and knowledge of the self (*Vijnana*) is the relentless bow (*kathina kodanda*).' Furthermore, while describing the armour and other weapons of the person riding Dharmaratha (chariot of righteousness) Sri Rama explains the need for a pure and steady (*amala acala*) *mind* (mana), which He said is like a quiver (*trona samana*). However, the need for quietude (*sama*) is essential, and the various forms of abstinence (*Yama*) and religious observances (*Niyama*) are like sheafs of arrows (*silimukha nana*).

At this point Rama deliberates on what he considers pivotal religious rites established as Homage (*Puja*) to the Brahmins (*Vipra*) and one's own preceptor (*Guru*), as an impenetrable armour (*kavaca abheda*). Then he drives home the point of Dharma in one's life, 'There is no other equipment (*Upaya Na Duja*) for victory (*Vijaya*) as efficacious as this (*Ehi Sama*), my friend (*Sakha*): he who owns such (*asa*) a chariot (*ratha*) of piety (*Dharmamaya*) has no enemy (*ripu*) to conquer (*jitana*) anywhere (*Katahun*). Thus, concluding the "sermon", Lord Sri Rama urges us, "Listen, O friend of resolute mind, a person who possesses this strong chariot (of Dharma) is a great hero, and can conquer even the mighty and invincible foe, which is summed up as 'attachment to the world'" (6).

The significance of this dialogue between Vibhusana and Rama is not just the choice of words that are so symbolic in getting Rama's intent firmly understood by Vibhusana but what is actually heard by the listener in the unfolding drama. In fact, the drama itself presents an extended interpolation of cosmic forces that adjudicates with scriptural rites, which are further *underlined* by philosophical considerations. It is from this overlapping of ideas, which are ingrained in the actual construction of every word that make the drama not only instructional but highly symbolic. This symbolism is further brought out by what is seen in the spoken word while at the same time injecting in the listeners' mind valued considerations, which would have the power to raise consciousness at the level of simultaneous understanding. Thus Rama's words are not just soundbites arbitrarily connected with an object or event, but is, essentially, a voice, a force producing an effect directly on the substance of being. His speech becomes a creative living symbol, because it possesses the utmost power of any true and genuine poetry or music, to create a resonance in the subtler substance of being and to bring about in the listener a fine attunement to the experience of the seer, poet, or composer. Worked out in great detail by later tantric schools, this view of language is implicit in the utterances of the Vedic seers and forms the basis of their practice.

Tantra played an important role at a critical juncture in the main plot of the Ramayana, at which point Rama would either be crowned king of Ayodhya or thus remain in the capital city of Ayodhya to govern the Kosala Empire. Or, by virtue of Tantra, he be exiled to forest life for fourteen years from where Fate would arrange his meeting with his antagonist, Ravana, the archetype of adharma. To do this, Sarasvati, the goddess of speech, is invoked and thereby takes possession of a key character in the epic to instruct Rama's stepmother how to induce the emperor to banish Rama from the capital. It is interesting to note that Emperor Dasaratha, among other things, were a gallant military strategist and a profound Sanskrit scholar, as well as an important representative of Vishnu on Earth. This idea of a military strategist also being a Sanskrit scholar immediately conjures in the listeners' mind, in the drama, how effective Sarasvati's speech had to be in order to cause Rama's banishment, especially when the listener is reminded that Rama was not just a favourite son already anointed to be crowned king but considered by all as an avatar of Vishnu. Needless to say that, no sooner had Rama vacated the palace to embark on his exile, Dasaratha died of a broken heart. Indeed, Sarasvati is not just the Goddess of Speech; she is also the Goddess of language, the creative arts, music, and learning. She was created by Brahma to be his companion in a world devoid of human life, whom he not only depended on to finish the job of creation but in whom he deposited all of his creative intelligence, especially that of speech for which she is named, even before the Vedic period, Vac Devi. Even so, half of the physical make-up of Sarasvati belongs to Brahma, for which in this form she is known as Gayathri, and represented in art as having four heads that symbolises the four Vedas, and overseen by the highest of divinity, Brahman. Indeed, it is this aspect of Sarasvati that appeals to Tantrics. However, when they approach her in tantric rites, she loses her physical form and invoked through concentration on the Sarasvati Yantra, a geometrical rendition from which the deity's energy is linked, which enables deep meditation. Often, students invoke Sarasvati to gain mastery of their chosen subjects. However, her worship is also prescribed by siddhas (materially accomplished yogis who have mastered the art of manipulating the elements) to acquire supernatural powers, especially the free flow of wisdom. However, there are those who invoke her to gain control over enemies, or to attract people to oneself, while acquiring mastery over the arts and in their attempt to gain supreme knowledge.

Interestingly, while Sarasvati is considered a Vedic Goddess, largely because she is the consort of Brahma, and partially as the creatrix responsible for evolution of the intelligent universe, those who follow the teachings of the Vedas frown upon the tantric sciences. Nevertheless, the

Tantra does not see Sarasvati as being external of the human body: as the White Goddess, she is equated with the same powers as that of Sri Kundalini. Certainly, the practitioners of Kundalini Yoga approach her with the same discipline and cosmic reach without internecine factionalism, sometimes prompted by extremes that go by the appellations of "right hand" and "left hand" disciplines. Or, by those who visualize her in the mode of red-hued, which depicts her as the terrifying deity. The red colour of Devi, projected as Matangi, is a warning to those who approach her that they should be clear about why they go to her, as opposed to those who seek her grace in her normal hue of "white", like the snow-clad Himalayas, or "blue", as when she is invoked through the breath during concentration on her established yantra.

The point about addressing the presence of Sarasvati as the Goddess of Speech, has to do with the extent to which the connection could be made that the idea of a transpersonal force do exist in the human body, which equates with the living Goddess as part of the Intuitive Self. The idea that strength, wisdom, and intuition are natural to all, as they are to every sentient creature, is a strong point with the engineers of language. However, there seems to exist concurrently with a Hindu philosophy of language the idea of a gift of the Intuitive Self, which does not belong to us; our gifts and powers and talents are aspects of the divine energy that moves through everything in the world. And, although we can exercise them, while mastering these gifts, such as the expression of language, they are really never ours. Tantric masters recognize that fact in which they understood the power of archetypal energies. Their greatest insight, however, was to realize that all power could be traced back to a subtle sacred source, which they called Śakti, or cosmic power. However, this same Śakti, when it rises independently of our eighteen senses that provide body awareness, equates with the Intuitive Self, which is related to Brahman, and which provides for us divine knowledge expressed in language as the best of art, music, the sciences, wisdom, and the queen of all knowledge, philosophy. Having identified the Intuitive Self, does not necessarily mean the same as having a relationship with the goddess, as some practitioners of tantra may claim. The Intuitive Self, unlike the invoked deity, is archetypal, which is why many never know the Intuitive Self, far more to trust it when it subtly nudges the subconscious, even though it is the prime mover of knowledge and the purveyor of language, long before knowledge is recognized as knowledge. In this sense deities like Sarasvati, Durga, or Kali, are archetypes within each person, whether we know it or not. They are latent powers that personify energies within us that are always at play deep in the subconscious, as they are in nature. This is why Sri Krishna said in the Bhagavad Gita, "Prakriti (nature) is my lower nature. Indeed, the greatest of the ancient yogis and Rishis believed they are always present, they are always accessible, and they are, above all, helpful."

Indeed, in tantra, there's a recognition that all the energies in a human being and in the natural world are aspects of Śakti and as such, they are intrinsically divine. Thus, the Rishis believed that when the names of these specific Śaktis are recognize as goddesses, their latent powers can be activated to empower the tantric practitioner from within. Consequently, when the practitioner names the energy of abundance as Lakshmi, or repeat a mantra to Lakshmi, the sadhak or empowered practitioner is able to touch into the energy vortex that Lakshmi represents. In this way, by following the practice prescribed by the Guru that energy awakens in the body as the living Śakti and thus manifests according to the goals set by the practitioner, albeit a musical composition, a poem, solving a troubling scientific problem, or even striking gold on the stock exchange. Indeed, the goddess or Śakti element of the highest spiritual reserve intuitively gives the sadhak access to it. Hence, when Durga is called upon, the sadhak summons the deepest reserves of strength; similarly, when Sarasvati is invoked, inspiration intuitively creeps into the consciousness unannounced and from where the sadhak merely becomes the instrument to produce the most profound literary work.

*

Hindus believe that the core of their scriptures were created from the Intuitive Self and heard in the soul from the Causal Body. According to Sāṃkhya Yoga, given in Chapter II of the Bhagavad Gita, in the material realm, each individual soul is bound by three sheets or "bodies": gross body, subtle body, causal body. The Gross body consists of the five gross elements of nature, which are earth, water, fire, air, and ether or space. According to Bhagavad Gita 13: 6-7, the subtle body consists of eighteen elements—five lifeairs (Prana, Apana, Samana, Udana, Vyana), five working senses (voice, legs, hands, anus and genitals), five senses for acquiring knowledge (the eyes, ears, nose, tongue, and skin); then there is, mind, intellect, and ego. Concerning the third entity, known in Hindu philosophy as the Causal body, this is essentially the Atman or Soul. From the Bhagavad Gita it is believed to consist of the account of karmas from endless past lives, including the *vasanas* (latent subconscious tendencies that express as unconscious forward movement, ad infinitum from previous lives until liberation or Moksha is attained.

Indeed, the early scriptures were given to humanity as the Vedas and rendered in highly acclaimed Riks or verse collections: the Yajur or sacrificial formulas, the Sāman or metered hymn collections, and the Atharva. Because the Arthava (translated as wealth or what gives meaning to life) is different from the first three Vedas, it is considered to have been brought forward from a lost civilization whose practices are now identified as part of what is left, as Tantra, and whose followers are referred to as Bhaktas. These four collections, also known as Saṁhitas, the first three are basically mantras. The word mantra is translated by Monier Williams as "instrument of thought" or "sacred text of speech". This is particularly so of the Rik, Yajur and Sāman; however, the Arthava, and the later Upanishads and Brahmanas, are largely written in prose.

Each of the Veda upholds a vast body of knowledge that also comprises related commentaries or treatises attached to them; these comprise the Vedanta, or what appears at the end of the Vedas; and it is from these highly speculative works from which Hindu Philosophy is based. However, there is a mystical tradition that looks upon the Veda from another viewpoint and establishes only a triple distinction between them, based on the form of the mantras: metrical for the Rik, prose for the Yajur, and metrical chants for the Sāman. These three forms are said to correspond to the nature of the cosmos, conceived as creation governed by a triple force where the Yajur stands for the power of rest in the centre, the Rik for the principle of motion or expansion, and the Sāman for that of limitation or contraction. Under their mythological forms they are Brahma, Indra, and Vishnu or, in their psychological equivalents, the word of power and right action, the word of knowledge, and the word of peace.

The Vedas is more than what its scriptural attributes portend, nor is its symbolism of the language simply one of form, relying on images, parables, and myths as other poetic or religious compositions do. The substance of its language is based on its mantric character, which is so different from any other scriptural texts. Indeed, the language of the RigVeda is an extraordinary tool of unsurpassed flexibility and power of expression, richness, and versatility. Claimed as mantra, "an instrument of thought", whose rules are the rules of thought, it is said to have the ability to recreate in the prepared hearer the experience of the poet, of the Rishi. Thus, the word is not just a sound arbitrarily connected with an object or event, but is, essentially, a voice, a force producing an effect directly on the substance of being.

As seen in Part Four of this book, the concept of the word stems from nada, the original sound from which Śabda originated, and from which sphota erupts; from here the final process of forming the word, coalescence come from dhvani, which are the essential phonemes that give the word meaning. From this we can see the full spectrum of Bhartṛhari's theory that, despite the integral unity of the creation of the word, a sentence is an integral unit; and, analysing a sentence in terms of phonemes, morphemes or words, is useful for learning purposes, but the whole sentence alone is meaningful. When those who know a language hear an utterance in that language, they hear a sentence, not single words or phonemes; only those who do not know the language will hear individual bits of sound. As for the relation between word and meaning, Bhartṛhari holds that it is permanent and natural, and not based on convention.

From the viewpoint of the structure of the Sanskrit language, especially the manner in which it has evolved over several millennia of multiple use, Sanskrit is a creative, living symbol that possesses to the utmost, the power to create any true and genuine poetry, prose composition, drama, or music. It also has the built-in ability to create a resonance in the subtler substance of being and to bring about in the listener a fine attunement to the experience of the seer, poet, or composer. In a manner of speaking it is the embodiment of Sarasvati who lies dormant in every human being, which can easily be tapped from the Intuitive Self, if only we are willing to trust that part of being. Thus, worked out in great detail by later tantric schools, this view of language is implicit in the utterances of the Vedic seers and forms the basis of their practice.

Indeed, all of the six major schools of Indian philosophy were concerned with language; the earliest was the Mīmāmsā, which although chiefly concerned with the interpretation of the Vedas, the followers of this school of philosophy were particularly concerned with problems in the relation between words and sentences. The Mīmāṃsakas argued that, for a word to be intelligible, each utterance has to be identical with an earlier utterance that is later remembered. Thus, by extrapolation, words must be eternal, in the same way that the meaning of words is eternal, as is the relation between word and meaning.

Pāṇini had seen the need for a capacity for mutual connection between the meanings of words, and a set of conditions for meaningful and correct sentences. The idea ingrained in this was the capacity for mutual connection between the meanings of words and "mutual expectancy". Panini explained it thus, "he rides an elephant" fulfils the condition of mutual syntactic expectancy, but a string of words such as 'elephant, house, riding' does not. According to this condition, the sentence 'he rides a house' is also a sentence. So another condition, 'semantic compatibility', was added. In a sentence like 'he rides a house', the semantic compatibility is absent. Panini observed that the Mīmāṃsakas also required that the condition of 'contiguity' be fulfilled: words must not be spoken at long intervals or be separated by other words of semantic difference. Another condition was 'the intention of the speaker', about which there were varying opinions.

Each of the main branches of the Mīmāṃsā schools developed its very own theory regarding the semantic relationship between words and sentences; however, this was not only peculiar to the Mīmāṃsā school. Others believed that the meaning of a sentence arises directly from its collection of words, the idea being that each word in a sentence conveys both its isolated meaning and the syntactic meaning. However, others like Kumarila Bhāṭṭa and his followers believed that the meaning of a sentence arises indirectly. Each word gives its individual meaning, and this uses up its significative power (suggestive of Derrida's "sign and significance"); therefore the syntactic relation must be obtained by means of a secondary significative power (7). This view was also shared by the Advaita Vedantins, who, in order to be able to express truths about the Absolute, could not always use words with their primary meaning, but instead had to use the secondary meaning.

In his *Mahābhāṣya*, Patañjali had also distinguished primary and secondary meanings of words, while much later Bhartṛhari discussed the transfer of meaning (*upacāra*) through such tropes as simile, metonymy, synecdoche, and so on. However, by the 9th century CE, Ānandavardhana, in his exposition of literary criticism, had caused much debate among grammarians, philosophers and linguists, about the 'suggestive power' of words. Then, in hot pursuit, he had to contend with the extent that a text does not yield its full meaning to every reader, since the ideal reader must be trained in the symbolism and conventions of a text, and familiar with the realities to which the text refers. Perhaps the most important part of the debate was the suggestion that such a reader has an intuitive grasp of the text that untrained readers lack, which stems from the writers unconscious flow or from the Intuitive Self.

It is interesting to note that while the Nyāya school of philosophy, whose theories of knowledge is based on logic, moderately accepted the relation between the word and its meaning as plausible although not natural. At first, they saw the relation between word and its meaning as merely conventional in what they called "significative power" deduced from its connection with Śakti. However, theirs was a qualified acceptance in that Śakti applies only to primary meaning: that which erupts in sphota from within, as compared to secondary meaning, which is readily accepted by Nyaya even though they considered it only in terms of its relation to the primary meaning and can apply only to single words, not to whole sentences. It is further interesting to note that while Nyāya grammarians, known as *Naiyāyikas*, carried this seemingly illogical idea of word and meaning in their deliberations for many centuries, the concept remained strong even when the group changed from Nyāya to Navya Nyāya (New Logic), which signified the emphasis on logic as a persuasive tool in techniques of argument. Indeed, the Naiyāyikas and the grammarians stayed active for many centuries, in the course of which their teachings were transformed. The Naiyāyikas especially developed new terminologies and techniques of argument; this change was reflected in their adoption of a modified name, NavyaNyāya (New Logic).

It is interesting to note that the level of accomplishment attained in Panini's descriptive grammar, *Aṣṭādhyāyī*, invited a lot of attention by linguists, grammarians, lexicographers, and even philosophers concerned about language. From this point of view, it might also be interesting to speculate whether Patañjali's commentary on the Aṣṭādhyāyī in the *Mahābhāṣya*, can be considered a bridge in grammatical and philosophical concerns. After all, Patañjali lived in the third century B.C., before the appearance of the classical systems of Indian philosophy, and aspects of his thought that we would call philosophical, are concerned primarily with questions of meaning and meaning-bearers in language. In this regard, Bhartṛhari's Vākyapadīya, which stands four hundred years apart from Patañjali's *Aṣṭādhyāyī*, considers the faculty of speech to be an instinct or intuition. The point of departure is that Bhartṛhari compares human speech to animal instinct and does not believe that language is learned; he believes language accompanies cognition in that there is no cognition without language. His understanding of language is therefore rather metaphysical, as he equates language with Brahman. No wonder Bhartṛhari remained very close to the original idea put forward by the Mīmāṃsakas that Sanskrit was Devabhasa or God's language, and as such it is not only perfect in terms of structure, morphology, semantics, and so on, but also eternal (8). And even though there is an atheistic side to the Mīmāṃsakas, the divine nature of Sanskrit has never been ruled out as contradictory, largely because for the Brahmanical tradition, language itself is of divine origin: the spirit descending and embodying itself in phenomena, assuming various guises and disclosing its real nature to the soul.

The Mīmāṃsakas were often confronted by the nagging question: what makes a word meaningful? To which the answer finally came in the proposition, "the connection of the word with *akṛti*" that represents generic properties or class properties (9). This idea was originally put forward by Vājapyāyana but refuted by Patañjali, who finally concluded that both the individual instances and the class property must be included within the range of meaning; the supposition being that the uncreated idea is incomprehensible and never exhausted by the individual word. In this connection Śabda is invoked, because since the word is born in Śabda, it is ever present and eternal. Although its presence is eternally imbedded in the soul, it is not readily perceived, largely because its perception depends on its manifestation through the physical word sound. On this count, the Mīmāṃsakas agree that if the word were not eternal, it could not be understood every time it is uttered. In this respect, the connection between Śabda and Sphota is irrefutable, for sphota having been born from Śabda, and without parts, is the cause of the word, which also makes it eternal and verily Brahman. Indeed, Brahman is without beginning or end, and being indestructible as such, it is the essence of speech (10). According to Bhartṛhari, 'it shines forth in the meaning of all things and out it comes the whole world'.

Perhaps the most import reason for the sacredness of Sanskrit has to do with the language of the Vedas. Even before Sanskrit became a written language with its most scientific grammatical structure, it was the language used to transmit the Vedas from age to age through its oral tradition. This is the divine nature of both the Vedas and Sanskrit as a medium of instruction. Indeed, for both Kātyāyana and Patañjali, the Sanskrit language, at large, is not only sacred like the Vedas but its intelligent use, backed by the explicit understanding of its grammar, convinced them that Sanskrit leads to prosperity here and in the next world, as do the Vedas. Unfortunately, because of their propagation of this belief, it was partly responsible for the rift that occurred between the Brahmanas and followers of Jainism and Buddhism. After all, both Kātyāyana and Patañjali had strong associations with the Brahmanas, and since the reactionary Buddhists considered themselves as the natural heir to the new order, as opposed to the Brahmanas claim as the custodians of both the Vedas and the Sanskrit language, naturally, both the Jains and Buddhist viewed this supposedly theological "status" of Sanskrit as an implied criticism against them. Perhaps what made this viewpoint so acute is that both the Jains and the Buddhists, used vernacular languages for the propagation of their faiths.

Unfortunately, the grammarians did not accept the religious value of the vernaculars, since the vernacular languages, along with the incorrect uses of Sanskrit, were all lumped together by the Sanskrit grammarians under the derogatory terms *apaśabda* and *apabhraṃśa*. Both of these terms pointed to the two fundamental characteristic about Sanskrit: the fact that Śabda was the prime agent and its association with Brahman that provided its divine presence. But perhaps even more pernicious, the overriding viewpoint that also suggested that the vernaculars were degenerate or "fallen" forms of the divine language, such as Sanskrit.

While trying to soften the blow against the Jains and Buddhists, Kātyāyana said, "... the relationship between words and meanings is established on the basis of the usage of specific words to denote specific meanings in the community of speakers, the science of grammar only makes a regulation concerning the religious merit produced by the linguistic usage, as is commonly done in worldly matters and in Vedic rituals" (first *Vārttika* on the *Aṣṭādhyāyī*). At this point, Kātyāyana probably had his disgruntled critics on his side, but then he went on to say that, these "degenerate" vernacular usages most probably caused by the inability of the low-class speakers to speak proper Sanskrit. And, to make matters worse, other grammarians began to tell stories of demons that used improper degenerate usages during their rituals and hence were defeated. The most atrocious was Ravana of Valmiki's Ramayana fame, who although was a learned and Sanskrit scholar, also engaged in Shakta practices to increase his wealth and personal power, but who was eventually defeated, militarily, by Sri Rama.

In any case, while the concept of demons, such as Ravana in the Ramayana, arrived much later than the appearance of the Vedas, such as the Rik, Sāma, Yajur, the major preoccupation of the Vedas lie with creation and paying homage to gods in human form. Furthermore, while stories about demons were told by mere mortal beings, those divine figures to whom sacrifices were offered literally arose out of the sacrificial body of the cosmic person. Not only that, the incantations were considered to be done by the very Lord of Speech through creator divinities such as Brahma, Bṛhaspati, and Brahmaṇaspati. Interestingly, these creator divinities projected in the creative incantation through the priest, eventually came to assume in the Upanishads the meaning of the creative force behind the entire universe.

Nevertheless, it is true that, for a while in the early period, the Vedic hymns were looked upon as being crafted by particular poet-sages; gradually however a rising perception of their mysterious power and their preservation by the successive generations led to the emergence of a new conception of the scriptural texts as totally divine in origin and composition. Indeed, in the late parts of the Rgveda (10.90.9), we hear that the verses, known then as Riks, the songs or metric hymns known as sūktas characteristic of the Sāmaveda, and the ritual formulas pronounced as yajus in the Yajurveda, all arose from the primordial sacrifice offered by the gods. They arose from the sacrificed body of the cosmic person, the ultimate ground of existence. Thus began the tendency of increasingly looking at the scriptural texts as not being produced by any human authors, thereby taking many forms in subsequent religious and philosophical materials. Finally, there came the widespread notion that the Vedas are *apauruṣeya*, the claim by the highest authority of the Purva Mimāmsā that they are not authored by any human beings. Not only that, the Mimāmsā went further to pronounce that they are in fact uncreated and eternal, beyond the cycles of creation and destruction of the world such as the soul. Indeed, in late Vedic texts, we hear the claim that the real Vedas have the divine characteristic as *Ananta*, which makes them infinite, and that the Vedas known to human poet-sages are a mere fraction of the real infinite Vedas.

Concerning the Brahmanas criticism of the Buddhists and vice-versa, the root of which is said in this book, belongs to the approach of the Brahmanas' philosophy of language. The crux of this can be seen in Brahmanic value of the word Saṁnyāsin, for which the Buddhist reduced to "Bhikshu". From the Buddhist's viewpoint, a Bhikshu is one who is "above good and evil, who is chaste, who with care passes through the world"(11). As such, anyone can be a Bhikshu, so long as one subscribes to the rules of the Sangha. But contrasts with the saṁnyāsin however, there are qualifications embedded in the very language of the word: a saṁnyāsin is one who has reached the state of renunciation within the Hindu philosophy of four age-based stages known in Hindu cosmology as *ashramas*, whereupon the aspirant is heretofore a bona fide saṁnyāsa. The first three stages of the ashrama system begins with *brahmachari* or studentship, followed by *grihasta* or householder, then for the qualifying period of inner cleansing marked by retreat of forest life known as *vanaprastha*. Henceforth, once the aspirant emerges from his rigorous penance as a forest dweller, the community accords him or her the status of a saṁnyāsin, which occurs towards the latter part of one's life. However, Brahmacharis who demonstrate strong spiritual values from a very young age are allowed to renounce worldly pursuits and dedicate their lives to attaining *moksha* or spiritual liberation. Nevertheless, these aspirants sometimes distinguish themselves as great scholars, teachers, or spiritual leaders, who often leave behind great insights into the Shastras, linguistic problem solving, philosophy, and major contributors to the arts and sciences. Even so, the Buddhists never saw the need for an aspirant taking up the discipline of a saṁnyāsin towards the end of the aspirant's long life. The Buddhist take on this vital achievement of such an aspirant is that he is just a bhikshu, an ordinary mendicant with a begging bowl, emancipated from the tedium of Brahmanic studentship, or the duties of a Brahmin householder accompanied with the yoke of what the Buddhist considered "useless penances imposed on the Brahmanic dweller in the forest"(12).

That the Buddhists were a challenge to the Brahmanas system of theology is without precedent, especially in the Buddhist's wilful projection of the Bhikshu as a necessary challenge to the enormous esteem that the samnyāsin occupied in the Brahmana's social and spiritual field of activities. In this regard, for anyone to become a Bhikshu without the discipline laid out in the Brahman's ashrama system, was nothing less than heresy. More appalling than anything else was the challenge that it threw out to the social, intellectual, and spiritual order; for in the day-to-day teachings given by Buddhist masters in the Sangha, previous rules observed in the ashrama system were not only relaxed, but worst of all was the laxity observed in language of instruction. At the height of the Buddhist revolution, there were complaints of people like the Buddhists who wore red robes without having a right to them. Furthermore they read books different from the Vedas, against which the true Brahmans were warned never to interfere, even though they were extolling the virtues of the Upanishads with such a different flavour that the very essence of Brahman was passed over in preference for their idea or *anatma*, or no soul. Indeed, there were Brahmins familiar with Buddhist teachings who truly believed that although Buddhism leaned on some of the teachings of Hinduism, the Upanishads remained the germs of Buddhism (13). Indeed, while the Brahmanas believed that Buddhism were in many respects the doctrine of the Upanishads carried out to its last consequences, what became even more important were the belief that the Upanishads were employed as the foundation of the new social system. This view, which was current at the height of the Buddhist period, and which had garnered military protection under the Mauryan Emperor Asoka, was also held in high regard by the nineteenth century Indologist, Max Mueller who said:

> *In doctrine the highest goal of the Vedanta, the knowledge of the true Self, is no more than the Buddhist Samyaksambodhi; in practice the Sannyasin is the Bhikshu, the friar, only emancipated alike from the tedious discipline of the Brahmanic student, the duties of the Brahmanic householder, and the yoke of useless penances imposed on the Brahmanic dweller in the forest* (14).

Max Muller further suggests that a Bhikshu, any Buddhist monk, once so qualified, he or she enjoys the "spiritual freedom" of the saṁnyāsin while at the same time becoming the common property of the Sangha, which nevertheless paraded as the most respectable Fraternity. However, unlike the rigours of the Vedic ashram system, which the Hindu saṁnyāsin had to pass through before being recognised as such, the Buddhist monk became the common property of the Sangha and the Fraternity, which was "open alike to the young and the old, to the Brahman and the Sudra, to the rich and the poor, to the wise and the foolish". And perhaps, because of this "commonality" of approach, while conducting all their business in either the vernacular of the common folk, or what the Buddhist called the easier access to the Pali, linguists of the day saw an unfortunate demise of many of the rules governing Sanskrit, which had made it the queen of languages. Philosophically, Sanskrit did not fit in well with Buddhist cosmology, especially so that it catered to a wider range of social classes that cut across class, caste, and even tribal communities. In a manner of speaking, as the new religion, the entire length and breadth of India had not seen such an appeal to the common man since the time of Rama, as were seen in the Ramayana, where even animals heeded God's call. In this regard, Sanskrit for Buddhism was too heavy a load to carry on the backs of the lower classes, especially the demands it made on its adherents of semantics in its ongoing need to decode the essence of common words in order to arrive at intended meanings. This idea is particularly brought out in Maitrāyana-Brāhmana Upanishad in a small dialogue between Bhagavata and Gautama:

'It is said by Bhagavata: "O Gautama, on what does the earth rests?"
"The earth, O Brāhmana, rests on the sphere of water."
"O Gautama, on what does the sphere of water rest?"
"It rests on the air."
"O Gautama, on what does the air rests?"
"It rests on the ether (akasha)"
"O Gautama, on what does the ether rest?"

"Thou goest too far, Great Brāhmana; though goest too far, great Brāhmana. The ether, O Brāhmana, does not rest. It has no support."

Apart from the constraints on style, which clearly illustrate the extent to which Buddhists were beholden to Sanskrit logic, it is evident that they were also very much influenced by the style and methodology of the language of the Upanishads. In the dialogue between the sage and the Brahmana, the all-important semantic meaning of "on what does the ether rest? is totally lost on Gautama. He is so earthbound by Buddhist logic of "suffering" that the possibility of relationship between ether or Akash and anything else of a higher nature does not exist; that knowledge is so very far removed from his realm of consciousness that he castigates the Brāhmana with "going too far!" For him, ether is so light and its particles so very fine that functionally it cannot possibly rest on anything. Not only that; for Gautama, there is not an iota of semantic consideration as far as "rests" go. Is there any possibility of something beyond rest? Philosophically speaking such a consideration would involve a total re-evaluation of Buddhist theology concerning the idea of atman and Brahman or, at least, either a negation or re-evaluation of the Buddhist concept of anatma or no soul. This idea is clearly brought out in Bhagavad Gita 8:7:

raso 'ham apsu kaunteya prabhasmi sasi-suryayoh
pranavah sarva-vedesu sabdah khe paurusam nrsu

Which is thus translated as, O son of Kuntī [Arjuna], I am the taste of water, the light of the sun and the moon, the syllable Om in the Vedic mantras; I am the sound in ether and ability in man.

Semantically, Krishna explains something that the Buddhist is either incapable of understanding, or because of his aversion to the cosmogonic philosophy of the Vedas, the Bhagavad Gita, or the Upanishads, anything that is removed from his view of the universe is neither seen nor approved. Indeed, Gautama immediately stops himself by the statement, "Thou goest too far, Great Brāhmana; thou goest too far, great Brahmana. The ether, O Brāhmana, does not rest. It has no support." He cannot allow himself to see the possibility that Sri Krishna can be preliminarily perceived by his different energies: semantically, fire is one of the elements represented by the sun and the moon, the light of which is perceived by the eyes, which brings the colour, form, and beauty in them. The function of ether is likewise the glue that holds the universe together, the gases that is embedded in solid matter, as well as the vehicle of sound, the modification of which are the various languages and the synthesis of which is the syllable Om.

There is no doubt that Gautama is limited in his understanding of the truths and the facts in Nature conveyed in languages such as the Vedas, the Upanishads and the

Bhagavad Gita, especially when it is observed how Sri Krishna reveals himself as the five elements in Chapter Seven, verse 8 of the Bhagavad Gita. Embodying the five elements, each has a distinctive feature in the revelation of jnana, which is one of the four yoga systems Krishna recommends in the Bhagavad Gita for those who have a need to know. Interestingly, this important link is not limited to Vedic conceptions, but it is also reflected by Plato in Timaeus' exposition.

In a very peculiar way, Timaeus invariably points to the opening of Chapter 15 of the Bhagavad Gita. Here Timaeus boldly states, '...as regards the most lordly kind of our soul, we must conceive of it in this wise: we declare that God has given to each of us, as his daemon (i.e., "genius" or "guardian-angel") that kind of soul which is housed in the top of our body and which raises us—seeing that we are not an earthly but a heavenly plant up from earth towards our kindred in the heaven. And herein we speak most truly; for it is by suspending our head and root from that region whence the substance of our soul first came that the Divine Power keeps upright our whole body (90b).'

Compare Plato's words in Timaeus with that of Krishna's in Bhagavad Gita 15: 1-2:

śhrī-bhagavān uvācha:

ūrdhva-mūlam adhaḥ-śhākham aśhvatthaṁ prāhur avyayam
chhandānsi yasya parṇāni yas taṁ veda sa veda-vit
15:1 adhaśh chordhvaṁ prasṛitās tasya śhākhā

guṇa-pravṛiddhā viṣhaya-pravālāḥ adhaśh cha
mūlāny anusantatāni karmānubandhīni
manuṣhya-loke 15:2

The Supreme Divine Personality said:
They speak of an eternal *aśhvattha* tree with its roots above and branches below. Its leaves are the Vedic hymns, and one who knows the secret of this tree is the knower of the Vedas. To get to the real meaning spoken by Sri Krishna in these verses, ordinary translation will not suffice. The *aśhvattha*, although real and belonging to the botanical family of the fig tree (Ficus religiosa) is, because of its long association by yogis with Ayurvedic medicinal preparation, regarded as metaphorical. It is known by Buddhist as the Bodhi tree and by Hindus as the pippala or *aśhvattha* tree. Even for people who have seen it as described in the Bhagavad Gita, remain often mystified by its unusual presence. Incidentally, the largest *aśhvattha* in the world occupies three acres of land and is found in Kolkata in the state of West Bengal; locally it is known as the Great Banyan and takes on religious significance, as well as the bestowal of grace by those that meditate under its ever-expanding shade. As described in verses one and two, 'the branches of the tree extend upward and downward, nourished by the three *gunas*, with the objects of the senses as tender buds. The roots of the tree hang downward, causing the flow of karma in the human form. Below, its roots branch out causing (karmic) actions in the world of humans.' However, embedded in the sublimity

of the very word *ashvattha* is the clue that determines what is to come!

The mere mention of the words, "they speak of the imperishable Aśhvattha tree", alludes to something different about this particular tree, which is indicative of the uncharacteristic nature of its roots: "its roots are above and branches below", on the surface level quite contrary to what a tree is. Even so, an important clue is given to intent of the verse: "the leaves are the Vedas; he who knows it is the knower of the Vedas."

As have been discussed in this book, the Vedas are not mere scriptures, for it, and the language chosen to communicate its essence, is equated with Brahman and hence eternal. So, this Aśhvattha tree is no ordinary tree, for since its leaves are the Vedas, it is imperishable, even though by the very nature of its name is not constant and steady. From an ontological understanding of the name, *Aśhvatth*, it refers to a key concept in Hindu theory of existence known as Saṃsāra or phenomenal Existence (15). Saṃsāra here touches on the endless cycle of birth and death, while at the same time taking heed of the souls' search to find a way of taking permanent refuge in Brahman, but before that need of permanency can be established, the soul always returns to earth where attachment to desires and passions are anchored. Thus, the comparison with the specialty of the *Aśhvatth's* roots: it collects sap from the above while sending branches down to earth, which further advances the play of consciousness between the unmanifest state of Brahman and Śakti, or Purusha and Prakriti. Indeed, while Prakriti is constantly changing to meet the needs of Brahman's lower nature, it is, as Śakti, inexhaustible, which is designed to serve as the source of the secondary nature of Saṃsāra, and hence the seemingly endless play of consciousness. This play that is implicit in Saṃsāra is the central motif of the tree, which is in turn an ongoing extended symbol of the revelation of life itself. And, just as the Vedas aid in the study of life, especially as life playing out in Prakriti, such lessons of life are learnt from the leaves of the tree, even literally so, since the Vedas were originally written on Aśhvattha leaves.

But, is there a way to arrest Saṃsāra and hence bring an end to the souls' quest to merge with Brahman? Obviously, Plato missed the essential point from which he was inspired to write *Timaeus'* from his allusion to the first few verses of Chapter XV in the Bhagavad Gita; his dependency on reason as the vehicle of the intellect, kept him trapped in what he projected in Timaeus as the "effects of necessity". Unfortunately Plato saw the need for Intellect and Necessity to cooperate in the production of the psychophysical constitution of human beings, which suggests with little doubt that *Timaeus* was spawned from the atheistic side of Sāṃkhya philosophy. This idea is deduced from the main section of *Timaeus'* discourse, which explains the existence of the universe and some of its most general features. The universe exists and manifests goodness because it is the handiwork of a supremely good, ungrudging Craftsman or "Demiurge" (*dêmiourgos*, 28a6), who brought order to an initially disorderly state of affairs. However, while this thought could be modelled on the Vaishnava explanation for the purpose of the Avatar as spoken by Krishna in B.G IV: 7: *Whenever there is decay of righteousness, O Bharata / And there is exaltation of unrighteousness, then I embody Myself and come forth*. Plato's Craftsman is nothing like Vedanta's Brahman. In essence, Plato's Craftsman is an animal, largely because it possesses intelligence, rather than being anything near the Vedantic idea of Brahman as "the intelligence of the Universe".

Plato's dependency on reason as his raison d'être for his philosophy of language is clear: the acquisition of intelligence by anything requires the acquisition of soul. It is complete, and thus it includes within itself all the species of living things as its parts. It is unique, because its model is unique; the uniqueness of the model follows from its completeness. Here, Plato relies on "numbers" in the same way that the entirety of Sāṃkhya philosophy relies on numbers. However, while some aspects of Sāṃkhya use numbers to allocate the rational existence of the Universe as one composite whole, for Plato the uniqueness of the model follows from its completeness because as he sees it, the world's body is composed of the elements (another importation from Sāṃkhya). But Plato's, elements do not have equal value: fire is needed for sight and earth for tangibility, but they are dependent on wind and water to bind them together.

It is unfortunately that Plato misreads the Bhagavad Gita in which he seems to have missed the essence of what Krishna says about the element of ether: it is part of Krishna's invisible form, which holds the universe together. However if we consider Plato's Vedantic interpretation of the elements to be faulty, consider this exposition given by *Timaeus* in the transition to the second main part of his discourse (69a6–92c9):

> *The composition of the world's soul out of a harmonically proportionate series of portions of a mixture of both divisible and indivisible Sameness, Difference and Being, and the division of these portions into two intersecting circles (of the Same and of the Different) explain the cognitive powers of the soul in relation to the different types of objects of cognition: those that are and those that become. When joined with the world's body, they also explain the cosmological organization of the universe.*

Of course there has been serious objection to Plato's creation story as given in *Timaeus*. Aristotle for instance had dismissed it on grounds that it nonsensically required not just a beginning of the universe in time, such as what is given in the Pentateuch, but a beginning of time itself (Physics 251b14–26). However, there were those who albeit accepted the Aristotelian approach but had claimed that the creation story could not be read literally, but metaphorically. Nevertheless, this is not just erroneous reasoning on the part of Plato; by creating *Timaeus* on the foundational conscription of Chapter XV of the Bhagavad Gita, he had also resuscitated an earlier warning that Krishna urged Arjuna to keep in mind as a guide in Arjuna's quest to know. In B.G. Chapter II: 25, we hear: "This atman is said to be unmanifested, unthinkable and immutable." As such it cannot be perceived by any of the senses. This is a big statement on the philosophy of language, for as we have seen from some of the concerns of earlier linguists in this book, it is very hard to conceive of a thing that cannot be perceived. Contrary to what Plato suggests in *Timaeus*, the four elements – air, fire, water and earth – can be sensed because they undergo modification in that they yield new elements; even so, the element ether or Akaṣa does not undergo modification. It is ever in its original state, and as such, like Brahman, is immutable.

It is now time to return to the Aśhvattha tree, and this time take a look at verse two:

"Below and above spread its branches, nourished by the Gunas; sense objects are its buds; and below in the world of men stretch forth the roots, engendering action."

It is easy to see that, semantically, what is "heard of "as an Aśhvattha tree, is the metaphorical presence of something greater than this holy fig tree. After all, it is nourished by the Gunas, the three tattvas of satvika, rajas, and tamas, associated with principles of creation and the ongoing expansion of prakriti. The fact that they are brought in here, testify to the enormity of semantic meaning in this verse. The Aśhvattha is no ordinary tree; it is rooted in the highest region in Hindu cosmology, in an area of existence known as Brahmaloka, with its branches touching the highest of all the Gunas before it returns to earth in the company of men where the two lower Gunas reside and touch inferior beings with their desires unchecked. Contrasted with the sap that come from the higher regions through its areal roots, it nourishes enlightenment in men of superior intellect who are the product of superior birth; these men of lower intelligence are governed by the lower nature of prakriti, merely touched by the leaves, which although bears transcendental knowledge are always in a state of flux. This is especially so of men whose lives are governed by the ritualistic adjuncts of the religious side of religion written on Aśhvattha leaves. In this sense, the Aśhvattha offers no stability to a world governed by ritualistic behaviour, for this in itself becomes the master, and the ever-changing status that results in fickleness. Even so, it is incumbent on intelligent human beings to know this tree, and learn from it the highest secret of the universe, which is contained in the essence of Brahman.

But what is the secret gained from access to this knowledge, especially for those who look upon the tree as a spiritual portal, or a conduit of sorts to reach into the very essence of Brahman. The clue is immediately given in the next problematical śloka, verse 3, which states:

> Its form is not here perceived as such, neither its end, nor its origins, nor its existence. Having cut asunder this firm-rooted Aśhvattha with the strong axe of non-attachment.

Krishna seems to have deliberately paused here before he goes on to recite the next verse in the same chapter, which gives the listener time to absorb the shock of the need to cut down the great tree with "the strong axe of nonattachment". Obviously, we have something here that is more than a tree, and an instrument that is more than an axe, which suggests that the concept of Saṃsāra has moved from mundane existence, without stability – as the definition of the Sanskrit word, Aśhvattha, suggests: "that which is not today as it was yesterday" – to one of transcendence. The tree is not to be physically cut down but removed from the mind of the yogi as an object of dependence. One does not need the shade of the Aśhvattha to meditate and hence reach Brahman; nor does one need be prompted by what is given on its leaves to the extent that one becomes totally attached to its ritualistic side of life. Indeed, such actions are part of the ongoing attachment to this world, but through the real phenomenon of true knowledge anchored in the discipline of *Jnāna*, so-called spiritual portals are totally unnecessary. In fact, because these portals are regarded in Krishna's semantics as hindrances to the attainment of *Brahma Jnana*, the yogi is urged to "cut asunder the firm-rooted Aśhvattha with the strong axe of non-attachment".

The Sanskrit word for non-attachment is *asanga*, but for the yogi to reach the goal, he is urged to cultivate *vairagya* or dispassion, which is the benign outcome of non-attachment. To prepare the yogi for this, Krishna proclaimed in chapter six of the Bhagavad Gita dealing with Dhyan Yoga or Meditation that "the mind is restless and hard to control" (verse 35) but by the practice of *vairagya* or dispassion, nonattachment can be attained. Vairagya is a compound word comprising of two words, the adverb *vi* meaning "without", and *rāga*, which means "passion" or feelings that connote emotion or interest. In this verse Krishna appeals to the yogi to subdue all passions and desires in order to change his nature from the way of the world to that of the nurturer or abhyasa of dispassionate stance in life. Such a person who gains control of the senses is called a vairāgika. However, although Chapter VI in its entirety deals with Dhyan Yoga, here Krishna merely splices vairagya to prepare the listener for what is to come later; but by the time he gets to Chapter XIII, the language is more direct and instructive. Hence, on the subject of vairagya or dispassion, Krishna says in the first line of verse eight: *Indriyārthesụ vairāgyam Anahaṅkāra eva ca*

– strive for "dispassion towards the senses and absence of egoism. This suggests that there are two aspects of vairagya: the first has to do with deliberate action on the part of the individual, albeit controlled by ego or *anahaṅkāra* that might have been pushed on him because of some calamity. The other definitely has to do with the individual's resolve to train the mind to discriminate between real and unreal. The first is considered temporary, for the mind here remains fickle, and will always return to its former state whenever it is opportune to do so. The other is permanent, for here the yogi is motivated by spiritual discrimination or *vivek*, where the yogi experiences the illusory nature of objects. Thus, in his meditation, the yogi rises in consciousness and realization soon emerges with the understanding that it is the ideal life, to emerge from earthly existence into the realm of the divine, which can only happen with detachment. However, it is important to keep in the forefront of the mind that the purpose of engagement in the discipline of vairagya, is not just to modify the mind. This is done in conjunction with the practice of *abhyāsa* with the objective of bringing the mind eventually under the control of the Self, to the point where the mind is effectively no longer in control of the body senses (16). This is a very ancient discipline that goes back to pre-Vedic times – at least two thousand years prior to the Mahabharata which is conservatively estimated to have been at least 3000 BCE. Indeed, it was prevalent even during the time of Rama, which is illustrated in the Valmiki Ramayana under the section known as Yoga Vashista. It is such a tough discipline that Krishna reminds us of its rigour in BG: XIII, 9:

Unattachment, non-identification of self with son, wife, home, and the like, and constant equanimity in the occurrence of the desirable and the undesirable.

The above statement might appear very harsh, if not near impossible for some to incorporate into their overall lifestyles – especially so, if one is aware of the four goals of life set down by the ancient lawmakers for each individual to fulfill in order to meet the requirements for a happy life. However, there is neither sanction nor compulsion to prevent the habitual seeker of pleasure from chasing the illusory, or to prevent anyone from offsetting the objects of the senses that could bring the conditioned soul to a sudden and complete halt. Indeed, attachment to pleasures is an offshoot of the two fundamental goals of life in Hinduism known by the names of Kama and Artha. Simply put Kama means pleasure that springs from desires to sublimate libidinal needs. There is no end to what goes by the name of pleasure under the Dome of Kama, for this is not only driven by the complexities of the mind but also by the imagination. The other principle goal by which every Hindu is urged to participate is Artha; basically it means that which gives meaning to life in the broadest plexus imaginable. Of course, as one moves up the social ladder, regardless of caste or station in the web of societal renderings, two words play important roles in determining extensions of meaning, which is wealth and power. However, the two other goals,

Dharma and Moksha, might have been cosmogonically arranged with Kama and Artha as strategical norms to modify influences for no other purpose but to keep man tempered within the codified parameters of society. After all, Dharma means duty. But this idea of duty is very broad; it is not just living up to the standards that society lays down for all, for duty transcends law, and economics, politics and even religion. Just as an example, Krishna spent his entire sermon in the Bhagavad Gita in trying to convince Arjuna, not just why he must do his duty as a divine warrior, but what the term, *duty*, entails. In this sermon, every aspect of knowledge and the philosophy of language is brought to the fore, and at the end, the one word stands supreme among all others, which is Moksha, the last of the four goals of human life, but truly the goal of Yoga.

All of the four goals of human life, Dharma, Artha, Kama, and Moksha, are expressed under the philosophical category of Puruṣārthā, which literally means, "that entity that descends in the human heart by way of the Intuitive Self for the purpose of showing the way to human beings" or the intuitive "object of human pursuit" (17). It is differentiated from Tattva, which bears fruit from the truth of things, or Hita, which advocates the pathway to the Divine or ultimate reality, especially within the context of "that one who has descended for the benefit of all human beings". However to get to the depth of meaning in Purusārthā, it is necessary to look at the etymology of the word. It is a compound word that combines *purusa* with *artha*. Purusa is the embodiment of "human being" that gives the soul its unique personality. In Advaita Vedanta this soul is referred to as the Self, or Universal Soul or Ultimate Reality found in everything; Artha on the other hand, as we already know, is the tattva or principle that gives meaning to life, such as the object of desire or the ultimate purpose for the existence of human beings. Purusārthā then can be expressed as the essential nature of the inbound Self that knows its purpose from integrating the four tattvas known as Dharma, Artha, Kama, and Moksha. Thus, these four integrated principles can be said to be the methodology of knowing the truth, which could lead (hita) to the realizable goal of Purusārthā. In this sense, Moksha is equated with what might be called Param Purusārthā, the highest of the four goals. In this sense Moksha is not just liberation; it is the abandonment of all possible material gains, constituting the quintessence of *nitya kainkarya prapti*, attainment in the eternal service to the Divine.

It is claimed in the Yajnavalkya Smriti, a work that dates back to the time of Rama while Yajnavalkya was a guest of Emperor Janak of Videha that, the greatest quality depicted in those yogis that have achieved Moksha, is the absence of I-ness. And, in the Shrimad Bhagavatam IV. 4.20, it is observed "The quality of the liberated soul with Brahman simply means equality in the enjoyment of bliss. It is not equality of cosmic functions. The Jiva (the liberated embodied soul) can assume any form at will and wander all over the world in unison with the will of the Lord". Thus, Moksha or liberation can mean so much more, other than equality, enjoyment or bliss. In effect it can, semantically, "dispense" with the body in the same manner in which a snake dispenses with its skin, and still be its very true self. The secret behind this is that the liberated or disembodied soul that has gone through the rigours or discipline to arrive at transcendence over matter, eventually comes to the realization that the true being, the Self, is not the body. In fact this is what Krishna means in B.G: VIII, 15-16: 'Having obtained me, the Jiva-mukti, or liberated embodied souls, do not come into rebirth, the fleeting abode of misery: for they have reached the highest perfection: all the worlds, including that of Brahma are subject to return. O Arjuna, O son of Kunti, having attained Me, there is no rebirth, there is no suffering.'

For most readers of the Bhagavad Gita, and especially the above quoted passage, emphasis is put on, "having attained Me", for which interpretations are often linked to the afterlife. But in the entire Bhagavad Gita, Krishna has directed his entire sermon on the living: what can be achieved here and now, rather than what becomes of the soul after the human body ceases to exist. After all, the big question is what happens when individuals do not uphold the Dharma, or ignore the sanctity of the four principles that form the goals of life; or perhaps what is the outcome of both society and the individual person when choice is given to just one of the four tattvas on which to model their lives. But, rather dwelling on the negative aspects of unrighteous behaviour, Krishna prefers to urge the sadhak or yogi to look at the soul that has freed itself from the bondage of Karma as inspiration for acquiring powers of real knowledge or atma-jnana, which will fully developed all its being in the supremely blissful intuition of the highest Brahman. According to Shankaracharya, the mark of the Jivamukti or truly liberated person is one who have developed all his knowing faculties to trust the Intuitive Self; such a person is:

Beyond caste, creed, family or lineage,
That which is without name and form, beyond merit and demerit,
That which is beyond space, time and sense-objects,
You are that, God himself; Meditate on this within yourself.
Shankaracrarya — Vivekachudamani, Verse 254.

Balkrishna Naipaul, August 7, 2015.

REFERENCES

References

1. Singh, Lalan Prasad: Tantra, its Mystic and Scientific Basis, Concept Publishing Company Pvt. Ltd. Delhi. 1976. Page 101-102.
2. Ibid, Section 6, pp 96-101.
3. All references to the Rig Veda Saṁhita are from H.H. Wilson's translations from the original under the title Rig-Veda, A collection of Ancient Hindu Hymns of the Rig Veda. Cosmo Publications (reprint) Delhi, 1977.
4. Burger, Bruce: Esoteric Anatomy: The Body as Consciousness, North Atlantic Books, 1998. P333.
5. Ibid,
6. Goswami Tulsidas, Rāmcharitmānasa or Ramayana (With Hindi text and English translation) Gita Press edition, Gorakpur, India. 1968. Section entitled Lanka Kand; lines appearing just between Dohas 79 and Doha 80 on page 705 of this edition.

7. Matilal, B.K: Indian Theorists on the Nature of the Sentence (vakya) Foundations of Language, 2, 1966. Pp377-393
8. Devasthali, G. V: *Mīmāṃsā: The Vākya-Śāstra of Ancient India*. Booksellers' Publishing Company, Mumbai (1959). Scharf, P. M: The denotation of generic terms in ancient Indian philosophy: Grammar, Nyāya, and
Mīmāṃsā. *Transactions of the American Philosophical Society*, (1996), *86*(3), i-x,1–336.
9. Beck, Guy. L: Sonic Theology: Hinduism and Sacred Sound, Motilal Banarsidas, Delhi, 1995. P. 42. Also compare Chandogya UPANISHAD, (2.23.2-3)
10. The Dhammapada: An Anonymous Collection of Verses Being One of the Canonical Books of the Buddhist. Lulu Press, Inc. 2013. Chapter XIX, Verse 267. The Dhammapada is a versified Buddhist scripture traditionally ascribed to the Buddha himself. It is one of the best-known texts from the Theravada canon. The title, Dhammapada, is a compound term composed of dhamma and pada, each word having a number of denotations and connotations. Generally, dhamma can refer to the Buddha's "doctrine" or an "eternal truth" or "righteousness" or all "phenomena"; and, at its root, pada means "foot" and thus by extension, especially in this context, means either "path" or "verse".

11. Muller, Max F: Introduction To The Upanishads, Volume. 2: The Maitrayaniya-Brahmana Upanishad, Hindu Books Universe, Baroda, 2003. p 57 a.
12. Carus, Paul: The Open Court, Volume 4. Open Court Publishing Company, 1890. p. 2132.
13. Muller, Max F: The Upanishads, Volume 2. Courier Corporation, 1962. P. 1ii.
14. Barua, Arati, Schopenhauer and Indian Philosophy: A Dialogue Between India and Germany. Northern Book Centre, New Delhi. 2008. Page, 208.
15. Challa, Bhimeshwara: Men's Fate and God's Choice: An Agenda for Human Transformation, Trafford Publishing, Vancouver, 2011. Compare Krishna's advocacy of Abhyasa and what Challa has to say in pp 363-364 in this book.
16. Prasad Rajendra: A Conceptual-analytic Study of Classical Indian Philosophy of Morals, Concept Publishing, 2008, page 125.

Other Works Consulted:

Alper, Harvey, P, Editor: Understanding Mantra, Motilal Banarsidass, Varanasi, 1991.

Benedict de Spinoza A Theologico-Political Treatise / A Political Treatise (v. 1), Translated from Latin by R.H.M. Elwes, George Bell and Sons, Covent Garden, 1887.

Bennett, Jonathan (1984). *A Study of Spinoza's Ethics*. Hackett., pg. 276.

Bistrich, Andrea :"Discovering the common grounds of World Religions. pp. 19-22; For a critique of Karen Armstrong's work, see "Karen Armstrong," in Andrew Holt, ed. *Crusades-Encyclopaedia*, Apr. 2005, accessed Apr. 6, 2009.

British Archaeology at the Ashmolean Museum, Highlights of the British collections: stone balls; the internet link is:

http://ashweb2.ashmus.ox.ac.uk/ash/britarch/highlights/sto
ne-balls.html

Buhler, George: The Laws of Manu, Dover Publications, Inc.
New York, 1969. Republished from the original by Clarendon Press, Oxford, in 1886.

Chadha, Prem Nath, Hindu Law, Delhi, 1974. While The oldest dharm-shastra is Manu **Smriti**, the source and basis of all other smritis or dharm-shastras, is, therefore, the entire Veda, which is the **first source of dharma**, and hence the sacred law, next the Smritis.

The correspondence of Spinoza, G. Allen & Unwin ltd., 1928, p. 289. See also John Laird, Journal of Philosophical Studies, Vol. 3, No. 12 (Oct., 1928), pp. 544–545.

Curley, Edwin M. (1985). *The Collected Works of Spinoza*. Princeton University Press.

Eddington, Arthur, S: Space, Time and Gravitation. An Outline of the General Relativity Theory. Cambridge University Press, 1987.

Euclid's, The Earliest Surviving Manuscript Closest to the Original Text (Circa 850), British Museum, London.

Fic, Victor M: The Tantra. Its Origin, Theories, Art, and Diffusion from India to Nepal, Tibet, Mongolia, China, Japan, and Indonesia. Abhinav Publications, Delhi. 2003.

Kapur-Fic, Alexandra R: The Jatakas. Times and Lives of Bodhisattva, Abhinav Publications, Delhi, 2010.

Goodman, David, Ed. Be as You Are: The Teachings of Sri Ramana Maharshi. Amazon. Com

Hennessey, Andrew: HX Assembler Software-Manipulating Chaos. Outshore Multimedia, Lulu Press, 2011. Page 24.

Ingerman, P.Z: A Syntax-Oriented Translator, Academic Press, New York, 1966.

Jacquette, Dale: The Philosophy of Schopenhauer, Routledge, 2005.

Joseph, G. G: *The Crest of the Peacock*, Penguin UK, 1990

Lawlor, Robert: Sacred Geometry: Philosophy and Practice, Thames and Hudson, London, 1982.

Leaman, Oliver, *Key Concepts in Eastern Philosophy*. Routledge, 1999, page 269.

Nagarjuna, Mūlamadhyamakakārika 24:8-10. Garfield, Jay L. (1995), *The Fundamental Wisdom of the Middle Way: Nagarjuna's Mulamadhyamakakarika*, Oxford University Press.

Panikkar, Raimunbdo: The Vedic Experience or Mantramañjarī. An anthology of the Vedas for Modern Man and Contemporary Celebration. Edited and translated with an introduction and notes, with the collaboration of N. Shanta, M. Rogers, B. Bāumer, and M. Bidoli. Motilal Banarsidas, Delhi, 1977.

Patanjali, Astanga (Yoga. yogaś-citta-vṛtti-nirodhaḥ | |2| |)

Pbilostratus, *The Life of Apollonius of Tyana*, 220 AD (in Mountain Man Graphics, Australia, Southern Spring 1995),

Pestritto, Ronald: Woodrow Wilson and the Roots of Modern Liberalism, Rowman and Littlefield.

Rhodes, Ron. Reasoning from the Scriptures with Catholics, Harvest House Publishers, 2000. Paperback.

Roy, Sumita (2003), *Aldous Huxley And Indian Thought*, Sterling Publishers Pvt. Ltd.

Śarmā, Candradhara, The Advaita Tradition in Indian Philosophy: A Study in Advaita Buddhism. Motilal Banarsidas, First Edition: Delhi, 1996.

Seidenberg, Abraham: Elements of the Theory of Algebraic Curves, Addison-Wesley; First Edition (1968).

A Seidenberg, *The Origin of Mathematics* in Archive for History of Exact Sciences, 1978.

A Seidenberg, *The Geometry of Vedic Rituals in Agni, The Vedic Ritual of the Fire Altar,* Vol II, ed F Staal, Asian Humanities Press, Berkeley, 1983, reprinted Motilal Banarasidass, Delhi.

Singh, Lalab Prashad. Tantra, Its Mystic and Scientific Basis. Concept Publishing Company, Delhi, 2010

Singh, N.K and Mishra, A.P., Eds. Global Encyclopaedia of Indian Philosophy, Volume 1, Global Vision Publishing House, 2010, pg. 303.

Spinoza, Benedict: (as 1, above) The chief works of Benedict de Spinoza, Volume 2, Part Three, p.134.

Stiles, Mukunda, The Yoga Sutras of Patanjali. Red Wheel/Weiser, LLC, Boston, 2002. This is a remarkable clean and concise translation of Patañjali's Yoga Sutras.

Sunday, Patricia Ann, Nostradamus, Branham and the Little Book: God's Masterpiece, AuthorHouse,

2012.Germans refer to themselves as "Deutschen, which is derived from the Saxon word for "Assyrian".

Swami Sivananda, Brahma Sutras, Motilal Banarsidas, Delhi, 1977,

Temple, The Works of Sir William, Part II University Microfilms, Miscellanea, 1990.

Tripathi, Amish: The Immortals of Meluha, Westland Ltd, Chennai, 2009. For an acute insight into Brihaspati's life, see this book.

Younkins, Edward, E: Spinoza on Freedom, Ethics, and Politics. *Questions Libre*, Montreal, May 7, 2006. No 178.

Glossary

Glossary

Abhava: Non-apprehension, compared with anumana (inference), artha-patti (presumption), upamana (analogy).

Abhyāsa: The objective of bringing the mind eventually under the control of the Self, to the point where the mind is effectively no longer in control of the body senses. This is a very ancient discipline that goes back to pre-Vedic times – at least two thousand years prior to the Mahabharata which is conservatively estimated to have been at least 3000 BCE.

Aditi: Mother of the Gods, and as controller of the sun, the provider of light to all.

Advaita Vedanta: None dualism; the Self and the world have no independent existence but merely arise in that one Divine Reality.

Advaitin: Those who believe in Advaita Vedanta, in which uniting with Brahman, the Supreme Reality, is the goal.

Agape: From the Greek meaning love; however, Christianity makes this idea of love unconditional in that it makes no demands of anyone; yet, there is the notion that the price of sin demands of everyone, a particular code of conduct.

Agni: God of fire responsible for accepting the oblations on behalf of all Gods.

Aham Brahmasmi: Literally, "I am Brahman". However, philosophically, it is derived from a Sanskrit sutra whose English translation is "the core of my being is the ultimate reality, the root and ground of the universe, the source of all that exists." It is given in testimony by ancient Rishis that when repeated this sutra will resonate deep within, and expand awareness of one's eternal, unbounded nature.

Ahaṃkara: egoism relating to an overriding attachment to the lower self. As such the term that is related to egoism. It is a compound word: aham refers to the concept of the Self, or "I", while "kara" refers to a created being or "to do". Philosophically, Ahaṃkara refers to one of four parts of *Antahkarana*, as an inner organ, in Hindu philosophy; the other three are *Buddhi* or divine intelligence, Cit or Consciousness, and *Manas* or Mind. In the Bhagavad Gita, Krishna said that Ahaṃkara should be subordinated to Cit, or Consciousness.

Ajna Chakra: the sixth chakra located between the eyebrows.

Akash: Space. Also the Sanskrit word meaning "ether" in both its elemental and metaphysical senses.

Anahata Chakra: the fourth chakra located in the proximity of the heart.

Ananda: Bliss arising out of Consciousness.

Ananta: the eternal nature of the soul, or lacking a self or independent nature.

Anatta: from anatman, which means "not Self" or no soul

Anitya: means impermanence. In characterizing two of the three marks of existence, anitya (impermanence) and anatman (lacking a self or independent nature), the Buddha implied that the ultimate truth is that everything is empty, for whatever is impermanent or lacks self (independent nature) is empty.

Anicca: stems from anitya, which means impermanence or conditioned existence

Angra Mainyu: as "destructive mind deduced from the Avestan-language name of Zoroastrianism's hypostasis that suggests the "destructive spirit". The Middle Persian equivalent is Ahriman.

Antaryāmin: On the whole, the inner controller, but taken from various Hindu scriptures that suggest: the human body is the temple for the Indwelling Spirit of Self, given here as the *Antaryāmin*. All the various parts of the temple structure correspond to various parts of the human body. The temple is the physical body which houses the presence of God or the Self.

Anukkampārtha: compassion that comes from Krishna's affirmation, which is guided by consciousness and not by attachment or desires on the part of beings.

Anumana: inference compared with artha-patti (presumption), upamana (analogy); also, "measuring along some other thing" or "inference") in Indian philosophy, the second of the pramanas, or the five means of knowledge. Inference occupies a central place in the Hindu school of logic (Nyaya).

Anupalabdi: negatively derived cognitive proof or non-perception, particularly so in 'non-recognition', 'non perception', where the word refers to the Pramana of Non perception, which consists in the presentative knowledge of negative facts.

Apana: in Sanskrit Apana means subtle energy that moves in abdominal area and controls elimination of waste products from the body. However, "when prana and **apana** flow together through Śusumna (the central passage of the spinal column), it becomes synonymous with life. It is also the name of the life-breath we take in with each inhalation.

Apastamba: The essence of meaning consists in the simultaneous cognition of the positive and negative sides.

Āraṇyakas. Forest dwellers; also a major body of work relating to Hindu philosophy.

Ardhanārīśvara: this is the androgynous Hindu God that is half Siva and half Parvati. It is a compound word comprising of "ardha", "nari", and 'ishvara' meaning respectively, 'half', 'woman', and 'Lord' or 'God'.

Artha-patti: presumption, compared with upamana

(analogy), or derivation from circumstances, and postulation.

Asana(s): physical exercises that follow yogic postures.

Ashrama system: four age-based stages known in Hindu cosmology as *ashramas*, based on four stages of life. The first ashrama begins with *brahmachari* or studentship, followed by *grihasta* or householder, then for the qualifying period of inner cleansing marked by retreat of forest life known as *vanaprastha. Finally, the last stage or ashrama is Saṁnyāsa* in which liberation or Moksha is sought.

Atma: Soul or Self.

Ayam Atma Brahma: Atma, or the soul, or the Self and Brahman are the same. Indeed, the Mandukya Upanishad says, "This Self is Brahman." Ayam means "this", and "thisness" refers to the 'self-luminous and non-mediate nature of the Self, which is internal to everything, from Ahaṃkara or ego down to the physical body. This Self is Brahman, which is the substance out of which all things are made.'

Bandha: When the apana energy is directed upward to meet with pranic energy through the use of the "energy lock" or bandha, it is called mula bandha.

Baudhayana: an eight century BCE Hindu mathematician who is the founder of algebra and geometry.

Bhakti: devotional unconditional love for the Divine, or from the Divine to the devotee. It also has to do with devotional service to God, with no other motivations than simply to please the Supreme Lord. It also refers to a major yoga system in the Bhagavad Gita as Bhakti Yoga that impinges on the broader philosophical understanding of Love in a much broader approach to Hindu philosophy.

Bhikshu: a Buddhist ascetic but from the Buddhist's viewpoint, a Bhikshu is one who is "above good and evil, who is chaste, who with care passes through the world"

Bijaksara: Tantric esotericism, largely because each letter, or even half letter, is a seed mantra, hence *bija (seed) and aksara,* indestructible. They represent the different acoustic vibrations of the Cosmos, in which "the fifty letters of the Sanskrit alphabet are the fifty basic vibrations that constitute the entire universe.

Brahma-dvāram: cosmic intelligence in its raw form of consciousness that is brought to Brahma's opening gate.

Brahma Jnana: divine intelligence Relative to knowledge of the Supreme Reality. Brahma Nadi: a subtle channel that is encased in the spinal cord that co-exist with Śusumn in perfect harmony.

Brahma Nadi: the tiniest of the four tubes, which is associated with pure intelligence. It is through this central canal, the Brahma Nadi, which Śabda Brahman not only passes through but it is from here where Consciousness vibrates through the entire body.

Brahmachari: the first stage of the Ashrama system, which is marked by *studentship*.

Brahman: Ultimate and Highest Reality without attributes and not regarded as a personal God. Brahman is the foundation of Advaita Vedanta and forms the central core of Hindu philosophy. See *Ayam Atma Brahma* in the above.

Brihaspati: Divine preceptor of the Gods, and one of the greatest scientist known to man in the ancient world. It is claimed by Amish in the Śiva Trilogy that Brihaspati had mastered the art of Fusion, in which he could reduce the toughest material into a gas cloud.

Buddhi: divine intelligence also known as Brahma jnana

Caitanya: human consciousness.

Chakra(s): psychic centres in the human body, known as *svadhisthana, manipura, anahata, vishudha, ajna,* and the sahasrara. Their location in the human body corresponds to, below the navel, above the navel, at the centre of the chest, at the base of the neck, and between the eyebrows.

Chaturthi: from the root *turiya*, the prefix, *char*, and the suffix, *thithi*. Turiya is a stage in meditation, char is four; thithi is a lunar day that carries certain significance. Thus, Chaturthi suggests, especially from Hindu philosophy that, Turiya is the fourth stage in in the experience of pure consciousness.

Chit or Cit: Chit, which refers to consciousness

Citrini: One of the four subtle channels associated with Kundalini yoga that runs along the spinal cord, and the safest to traverse by yogis; because its path its calmness and paleness, it is identified with Sattva guna, the purest of the pure the moon because its paleness, and identified with Sattva guna, the purest of the pure.

Dasa* or *Dasi: the perfect devotee of the Divine.

Deconstruction: an internal critique revealing that the meaning of words only occurs in relations of sameness and difference. The act of **deconstruction** takes place within the terms that have shaped the text; it does not stand outside of the text but unfolds within the position being discussed in the text itself.

Devabhasa: a reference to Sanskrit as God's language.

Devata. A divine male being.

Devi: a Goddess.

Dharma: righteousness, especially steadfastness in one's duty.

Dharmaratha: the chariot of Dharma or righteousness, which gives everlasting victory in every situation of life.

Dhvani: a synonymous extension of Nada or sound that is derived from a lower level of hearing referred elsewhere in this book as Vaikhari. Dhvani affords the listener recognition of words by virtue of the vowel-sound, considered to come from the breath of life embedded in the soul. In a manner of speaking it is a throwback to the vowel sound that emerged with first mantra known to man as Om, but which is immediately recognised by dhvani as AUM, which is the basis of all the letters of the Sanskrit alphabet, and the "soul of such refined language as poetry. In *Dhvanyaloka* of

Ānandavardhana, it is ascertained, "By the time the sentence is finished, its meaning as a unit flashes through the mind of the listener. In the same way, *dhvani,* flashes into the mind of the aesthetically sensitive listener the moment he grasps the prima facie meaning."

Dhvaniprasthāpana: gives currency to an expression. At this level sound can be analysed from being picked up from the human ear but is restricted to their context, in the same manner in which a scientist might observe certain sets of circumstances and draw conclusion just from what is observed.

Dhyan: meditation

Dukkha, The major category of Buddhist philosophy that dwells on the central belief that life in this world is characterized by suffering. Dukkha thus means suffering. In Hindu philosophy however there are three kinds of suffering that com under the concept of Taapattraya: those caused by one's own body, adhidaivika; those caused by being around others, adhibhautika; and those caused by Devas, adhidaivika.

Dvaita: duality, in which soul is seen separately from God.

Ekam: One.

Ekam evadvitiyam Brahman: there is only One, without a second.

Gana: reference to all living beings in the universe

Ganesha: Hindu Deity considered host of all divinities.

Ganesha Chaturthi: annual fourteen days celebration to mark the day "Ganesha frequencies" first reached earth

Grihasta: the second stage of the ashrama system is a householder.

Guṇas: there are three gunas, known by the names of sattva, rajas, and tamas, associated with principles of creation and the ongoing expansion of prakriti. They are referred to as tattvas or principles that have a profound effect on creation and human behavior. The last two have the potential to stifle spiritual growth, while binding one to the material world.

Hatha Yoga: a system of yoga involving mostly physical exercises.

Ida: one of the channels that straddles the Śusumn nadi

Indriyāṇi daśai: the ten senses

Ishta: Personal God

Ishvara: Highest Reality of Impersonal God

Jiva: embodied souls identify with the body rather than with the Purusha or Supreme Reality.

Jnana: Divine Knowledge or indication of truth or true principles of something. In the Bhagavad Gita there is an entire body of philosophy referred to as Jnana Yoga.

Jñānam Anantam Brahma: Truth, Knowledge, Infinity, is Brahman

Jnani: A seeker of divine knowledge: those seeking to know Krishna by studying his scriptures.

Kaala: creativity that has the power to draw the soul to pure knowledge

Kala: encyclical time.

Karma Yoga: the yoga of action.

Karuna: Buddhist's doctrine of compassion. However, the deeper meaning of Karuna is to let go and mourn our own identity and egocentric experience.

Klesha: Affliction that produce mental states, which torment, both immediately and in the long term. The five principal kleshas referred by Patañjali as poisons, are attachment, aversion, ignorance, pride, and jealousy.

Krttikā: this is the Sanskrit name of the constellation Pleiades.

Kundalini: in Sanskrit means coil serpent, spiritual power, and a subtle spiralling mass identified with the subtle body, which leads to higher consciousness; it is associated with a system of yoga nicknamed serpent power. Kundalini Yoga is both a spiritual belief system as well as a philosophical outlook on life.

Lakshana(s): This is a Sanskrit word that moves from the simple to the most profound; its most basic meaning is sign, definition, characteristic, or condition. As *Vyavartaka Lakshana*, it is distinguishing "it" from "others"; or by pointing out apparent attributes such as *Tatastha Lakshana*;

by describing its essential nature *Svarupa Lakshana*. Or, as *Lakshana vritti*, the inherent power in a sound that gives rise to a thought of certain qualities like name, form, etc., directly or indirectly associated with it.

Lasat-tanu-rupa: sub-particles that is the source of consciousness.

Linga: a variation of the lingam, linga, ling, Śiva linga, Shiv ling, which carry the meaning of "mark", "sign", or "inference", is a representation of the Hindu deity Śiva used for worship in temples. In traditional Indian society, the linga is rather seen as a symbol of the energy and potential of God, Śiva himself. Literally translated as 'phallus' but a representative catchment of the power of Śaivism.

Madhyama: is heard at an intermediate range, which is a finer quality of sound that is barely audible but experienced in the heart.

Mahabhutas: the five great elements, inclusive of akasha or space

Mahavakyas: The four great sayings that depict the Highest Reality. They are:

1. **Prajñānam Brahma** - "Prajña is Brahman" or "Brahman is Consciousness (Aitareya Upanishad) 3.3 of the Rig Veda
2. **Ayam ātmā Brahma** - "This Self is Brahman" (Mandukya Upanishad) 1.2 of the Atharva Veda.
3. **Tata tvam asi** "Thou art That" Chandogya Upanishad 6.8.7 of the Sam Veda.

4. **Aham Brahmasmi** "I am Brahman", or "I am Divine" (Brihadaranyaka Upanishad 1.4.10 of the Yajur Veda.

Maheshvara: Literally, Great God, an honorific title for Śiva.

Maitriya: an early pre-Vedic God that was a favorite of other Gods. However, Maitriya later exemplifies the Bodhisattva's virtues of kindness, fearless compassion and virya, or vigour. The name *Maitriya* is derived from the Sanskrit word maitri, meaning "kindness" or "love."

Manipura Chakra: located above the navel, close to the diaphragm.

Maruts: The shining ones, representative of the elements but individually has the power to behave like cosmic warriors and the ability to raise storms of different kinds.

Maya: Illusion, but the better definition is the lower nature of consciousness as Krishna explained in the Bhagavad Gita. In this context Maya is the efficient cause of creation and is not separate from Brahman.

Metta: The Pali word metta (maitri in Sanskrit) is related to mitta (Sanskrit: mithra), which means 'friend'. Metta can thus be translated as friendliness.

Mithra: the Hindu original of Maitriya.

Maryada Purushotama: the perfect man who rises above materialism to discover his divinity.

Yuga: Hindu epochs, such as Kritta or Treta, Dvapar, and Kali.

Mīmāṃsā: An enquiry into the nature of things; the science of philosophical logic enquiring into Vedic knowledge; two fundamental bodies of works that go by the names of Purva Mimāmsā and Uttaramimams. Also a group of logician philosophers that go by the name of "the Mīmāṃsakas.

Moksha: Liberation

Mudra: divine gestures as seen in classical dance, yoga, and even hand signs offered from divine personalities in gestures of blessings.: :

Muladhara Chakra: this very first chakra located at the base of the spine

Muni: a Hindu sage

Murthi(s) Religious carved icons representative of gods and goddesses.

Nada: Original sound from which the universe was created.

Nadi: river or channel related to the six subtle channels associated with Kundalini and psychic energies.

Nimesha: here the yogis recognize the constituent world around us that include feelings, thoughts, and the things we do; it also has to do with absorption.

Nimitta: the efficient cause, as opposed to *upādāna*, the material cause.

Nirvikalpa Samadhi: the culmination of all Spiritual practices and the achievement of the goal where one meets the Creator of all Essence, face-to-face with his own atman, the soul within which is of the same Essence as Brahman or the Creator of the cosmos.

Nityam; infinite in eternal knowledge.

Niyati: law of destiny

Nyaya: Law or philosophical category founded on logic

Pañca kleśa: the five primeval afflictions, which are sensual desire (*kāmacchanda*), anger (*byāpāda*), sloth-torpor (*thīna-middha*), restlessness-worry (*uddhacca-kukkucca*), and doubt (*vicikicchā*). These however are related more directly with Buddhist thought, but the Hindu version of the Kleshas are ancient in origin and are summarised by Patanjali in the third sloka or verse in his Yogasūtra, which is translated as ignorance, egoism, attachment, aversion, and fear of death.

Panchayatana: a form of domestic puja or worship called *panchayatana*.

Para: means "above" or the "highest" and suggests that Śabda equates with Ishvara or the highest divinity, especially for those who operate in the realm of a personal God.

Parispanda: blissful pulsation of joyful enlightenment.

Pashyanti: Śabda at this stage cannot be heard but can be "seen" by those yogis who are said to have that "inner vision".

Pingala: one of the two nadis associated with Śusumn commonly referred to as the fiery path.

ParaŚakti: Supreme Energy that pervades the universe. *Para-Śakti,* is also the Supreme Energy, existing in transcendence. Compare with *Parāpara-Śakti,* the Supreme, existing in both transcendence and imminence; and, *AparaŚakti* existing in imminence.

Pradhana: in Sanskrit language it means, "above all", "greatest among all" or "Supreme Superior 'Unmanifested one'

Prajñānam: Consciousness.

Prajñānam Brahman: Brahman is Consciousness or Supreme Knowledge.

Prakāśa: connotes "light, brightness, splendour, clearness" and also "visibly manifested".

Prakriti: Nature or Krishna's lower nature.

Prana: vital psychically charged air that transform the life force into Consciousness. In Hindu philosophy, including yoga, Indian medicine, and martial, the term refers collectively to all cosmic energies, permeating the Universe on all levels. It is the sum total of all energy that is manifest, and while prana is often referred to as the "life force" or "life energy", it also includes energies present in inanimate objects.

Pranayama: a specialised system of yogic breathing that seek to awake spiritual fortitude. However, pranayama is derived from two Sanskrit words 'Prana' and 'ayama', where 'prana' means Energy 'ayama' means elongation. So the meaning is generally understood to be the extension of the breath by regulation and restraint of breath, as instructed in the fourth limb of Patañjali's Ashtanga Yoga.

Pramana: the means by which one obtains accurate and valid knowledge, which includes proof and authority.

Pramatir: venerable sacrificers, desiring their oblation to meet regulated expectations. What is implicit in the word is the sanctity of method in approaching the need to acquire knowledge. In other words, a subject who knows the cognising consciousness, which is determined by the internal organs.

Prameya: The word *prameya* is derived from the Sanskrit word prama **meaning** "buddhi" or "cognition. Compare with *pramana*, the sources of knowledge; *prameya*, the object of knowledge; *samsaya*, doubt. The key, however is the object of proof, such as the measured or known object within the realm of Brahman or the Absolute Reality.

Prana: the Sanskrit word for "life force" or vital principle. In Hindu philosophy including yoga, Indian medicine, and martial arts, the term refers collectively to all cosmic energies, permeating the Universe on all levels. Compare with: Apana, Samana, Udana, Vyana

Pranayama: In *Pranayama*, there are two Sanskrit words combined: PRANA AYAMA. Prana means life, life force, or life element. Ayama means development or control. Pranayama, therefore, **means** development and control of the vital life force

Pratibhā: 'shining forth'.

Pratyabhijñā: derived from the Sanskrit stem, "prati", which means "something once known, now appearing as forgotten, while "abhi" relates to immediacy or immediate, and "jña" to know; hence the suggested meaning of sudden recognition of one's forgotten self. ***Pratyaksha***: inference.

Preyas: that good, which beings seek to enjoy, regardless of consequences. Compare with Shreyas, which connotes with eternal goodness associated with the Divine.

Prithvi: the Sanskrit name for the earth as well as the name of a Devi in Hinduism and Buddhism. As Prithvi Mātā "Mother Earth" she contrasts with Dyaus Pita "father sky".

Purana: Histories of creation and the lives of the Gods and Goddesses.

Purusha: Supreme Reality

Purushotama: The Ideal Man

Raga: emotions drawn from attachment

Rajas: passion

Rishi: Seer

Rita: principle of order that holds to universe together.

Śabda: Sound as testament to the evolution of consciousness in the creation of the universe.

Śabda Brahman: characteristics of Kundalini's rise, is the vibration that the yogi experiences, accompanied by a unique sound that is interpreted as Om.

Sadaśiva: the ever-auspicious materialization of the original, transcendent god, Śiva.

Sadhana: cultivated discipline of enquiry into the nature of Reality.

Sadhak: student of divinity

Sadhu(s). *Holymen.*

Saguna: means "with attributes". The term "Saguna Brahman" implies that God has a name and form and other attributes.

Sahaja: Once Self-realization has been attained, there is full and lasting knowledge of the Self. "sahaja" means "state" but this stage of samadhi is not a state - it is our true nature. It is permanent compared with nirvikalpa, samadhi, savikalpa, vikalpa.

Sahasrara Chakra: the top-most chakra located at the crown of the head.

Sākṣi-caitanya: to become the witness that transcends the changing states of the mind.

Śakti or Śakti

Samadhi: one of the higher states in meditation likened to a death-like experience similar to dreamless sleep but where a different kind of consciousness is experienced.

Samana: one of the five "vital airs," concerned with the digestive system. More generally, relates to assimilation and integration of perceptions with existing knowledge.

Śankara: another name for Śiva, the doer of "good", which emanates from *Śreyas* the principle of the greatest good, as opposed to *Preyas*, that good, which beings seek to enjoy, regardless of consequences.

Sāṃkhya: One who has right understanding; also, one of the six systems of Indian Philosophy.

Saṁnyāsa: Saṁnyāsin is one who has reached the state of renunciation within the Hindu philosophy of four age-based stages known in Hindu cosmology as *ashramas*, whereupon the aspirant is heretofore a bona fide saṁnyāsa

Saptarishis: the seven seers responsible for the roots of Hindu philosophy and the Hindu religion.

Śāstrayonitvāt: the source of knowing from the highest authority, which requires no other references, or footnotes, not that which comes from inference or even perception. ***Sat and Satya:*** Sat is the root of many Sanskrit words and concepts such as sattva "pure, truthful" and satya "truth". As a prefix, in some context it means true and genuine; for example, sat-śastra means true doctrine, sat-van means one devoted to the true.

Sat-cit- ānanda: connotes existence, consciousness, and bliss

Sattva: Pure or Truthful Existence

Shanti: Peace.

Shastra: the scriptural texts that make up the Hindu Religion and offer insights into Hindu philosophy.

Śiva Samhita: a Sanskrit text of ancient origins on yoga, which predates the Vedic period written by an unknown author. The text is addressed by the Hindu god Śiva to his consort Parvati: consort of Śiva and mother of Ganesha.

Sphota: connotes "bursting forth" and has an element of light attached to it that inversely alludes to Śabda Brahman

Śreyas: the principle of the greatest good, as opposed to **Preyas**, that good, which beings seek to enjoy, regardless of consequences.

Shuddha Vidya: considered as pure knowledge

Sva-bhāvā: generally it means ones true nature

Svadhisthana Chakra: the second chakra located at the navel

Smarta: a unified system of worship that is inclusive of the major sects in Hinduism.

Spanda or Spandana: deals with vibration and it impact with creation: whenever there is stress or Divine action there is vibration', which gives rise to sound. However, this is not ordinary sound; it is a movement, which has a will of its own that invariably connects to Consciousness.

Śrutis: that which the ancient Rishis and Sages heard that became designated scriptures. Reveal knowledge or scriptures

Śuddha-bodha-svābhāvā: sub-particles that is the source of consciousness.

Śunya: emptiness, void, zero. Buddhi concept of Nothingness.

Śusumna: a place to experience bliss, which is testimony that yogic fire has been risen sufficiently, through the grace of Kundalini.

*Sushupt*i - dreamless sleep

Sutras: an aphorism or a collection of aphorisms in the form of a manual or, more broadly, a text in Hinduism or Buddhism. Literally it means a thread or line that holds things together and is derived from the verbal root siv-, meaning to sew.

Tabular rasa: in Hindu aesthetics, the word "rasa" originates from Sanskrit that meant "sap", "fluid", or "essence", but which came to mean flavor, sentiment, or emotion: regarded as one of the fundamental qualities of classical music, dance, and poetry. However, **Tabula rasa** is a made up Latin phrase borrowed from Sanskriti culture, and translated as "blank slate" in English and originates from the Roman tabula or wax tablet used for notes, which was blanked by heating the wax and then smoothing it.

Tamas: ignorance or low in consciousness. Tamas, rajas, and sattwa, correspond to ignorance, passion, truthful existence

Tanha - thirst or craving

Tanmatras: subtle sensory qualities like colour, taste, smell, sound, and touch

Tantra: One of the oldest system of mystical practices in Hinduism that upholds indivisibility of Kundalini Yoga.

Tattva: indicates a true or real state, truth or reality, or a true principle indicative of a category.

Tat Tvam Asi: That is what you are.

Trishul: Lord Siva's three pronged trident. It is recognized as His ubiquitous symbol. He is depicted as holding a Trishul and it is also found alongside Siva's saguna (with attributes) Linga form. Trishul symbolizes three fundamental powers or Śakti of iccha, kriyas and jnana – will, action and knowledge. Through progressive expansion of three Śaktis, the Unmanifest impinges into universal experience.

Turiyavastha: a state in yoga that is beyond the states of waking (*jagruti*), dream (*svapna*), or deep sleep (*sushupti*).

Upādāna, the material cause. It is also a type of breath called, the spiritual breath, which is referred to by the great Masters as responsible for opening the gate to Samadhi.

<u>***Upamana***</u>: analogy.

Upanishad: Commentaries at the end of each of the Vedas that form the logos of Hindu philosophy.

Vac: speech.

Vac Devi: Goddess of Speech; an appellation of Sarasvati.

Vaikhari: the grossest of sound energy, first heard among divine beings during creation.

Vaisheshika: The Vaisheshik system was developed by Rishi Kanad, from whose name the particles got the name "Kan"; they are indestructible, and eternal particles that are neither created nor destroyed.

Vaishnava: followers of Vishnu, Rama, and Krishna.

Vajrini: One of the four nadis encased in a tube within another tube that is associated with Citrini and Brahma Nadi, which traverses the spinal cord from the Muladhara to the Sahasrara. Vajrini is considered the path of the sun in Kundalini Yoga, which is only attempted by the most skilful of yogis.

Vakya-sphoṭa: where the entire sentence is thought of (by the speaker), and grasped (by the listener) as a whole.

Vanaprastha: the third stage of the spiritual aspirant becomes a forest dweller to pursue internal and spiritual cleansing.

Vasanas: latent subconscious tendencies that express as unconscious forward movement, ad infinitum from previous lives until liberation or Moksha is attained.

Vedangas: several leaned works that literally means, limbs of the Vedas.

Vedanta: literally means the end of the Vedas because most of the commentaries that form the gist of Hindu philosophy are fond here: at the end of each of the Vedas.

Videshvara or Shuddha *Vidya*, which is considered as pure knowledge

Vidya: limited knowledge. *Raga* or emotions drawn from attachment

Vijananam: dispassionate knowledge of the self

Viparīta Buddhi: perverted intellect as "a great hindrance"; it keeps one far away from the truth

Vimarśa: is the monitoring agent that is part of the Self, or from the point of view of Śaivism, the power endowed in Śakti.

Vishudha Chakra: the fifth chakra located in the throat.

Vishvadev: All the Gods who are said to be the 'Preservers of Men' and 'Bestowals of Rewards', sons of Vishva.

Vishvakarma: The Architect of the Gods.

Virat Purusha: the one who sets Śabda in motion in the grossest form in order to be understood by all.

Vivartavāda: superimposition

Vrat: religious observance.

Vyana: literally means "outward moving air" and moves from the centre of the body out to the periphery. This vayu pervades the *whole* body, and is a coordinating, connecting force. It has no specific seat, but rather coordinates all the powers such as sensory awareness, and runs through the whole network of the 72,000 nadis or passageways of prana in the body, connecting the functions of the nerves, veins, muscles and joints and circulates nutrients and energy

Yantra: the Sanskrit word for a mystical geometric diagram, especially diagrams or amulets supposed to possess occult powers in astrological or magical benefits in the Tantric traditions of the Indian religions.

Yogamaya: Krishna's lower nature which deals with prakriti or Nature

Yogah karmasu kauśalam: yoga as expertness in action.

Yoni: physically, the vulva; spiritually and philosophically, the source of creation

Yuga: Hindu epochs of different time duration lasting for thousands of years.

About the Author

While Balkrishna Naipaul is eminently and widely known as an internationally aclaimed novelist and poet, he is nevertheless no stranger to the euridite world of philosophy. He has lectured and presented scholarly papers at major philosophical forums in Canada, the United States, and Britain. Indeed, while studying at London, he was a close friend of British philosopher, Bertand Russell, who no doubt sparked in him a kindred interest in philosophy, even though the major thrust of his studies had to do with history, international relations, and economics.

In his nine novels and poems Balkrishna is often identified as a quiet but deep social thinker, for which he has captured the title of Saahitya Mani (Gem of Literature) for his fiction, and Saahitya Shiromany (Crest Jewel) for his poetry. Both are from the Shikshayatan Institute of America. Prior to this, in 2006, Balkrishna received from the World

Business Forum their most lucrative award for his contribution to World Literature. In 2012, he was selected by the Shabdakantih Awards Academy for the Order of Literature. Besides being recognised by the Indo Caribbean communities in both Canada and the U.S "for his numerous distinctive works of literature …for the edification of humanity", in 2012 the Government of Trinidad and Tobago honoured him with a gold medal and Lifetime Literary Achievement Award for his contribution to the nation's 50 years of Literature in Commemoration of the country's Golden Independence Anniversary.

Praise for Balkrishna Naipaul's Fiction

Praise for *SANGAM:* A masterpiece of storytelling... a Noble piece of Literature ...the first and best book to tell the true story about the background of the so-called indentured workers from the Indian subcontinent –Gita Dubay in The West Indian.

Reading Sangam *was no less than meditating. Just felt being on the other side of the world... a powerful storyline and a thought-provoking theme, this book has a soul* – Sunita Pahuja, Former **Second Secretary, Indian High Commission, Trinidad and Tobago**

Sangam is an exploration of a new form of secularism where religion is practiced in the heart, not in market places. It is a spiritual journey where the writer transcends the barriers of time and space with remarkable ease. *Manoj Barpujari, Journalist, literary and art critic, India*

Dancing Moon Under The Peepal Tree, A panegyric reflection of what is real. A literary watershed. *Malay Mishra, former Indian High Commissioner to Trinidad & Tobago* in Yatra.

Praise for The Mansion: The Mansion is a brilliant book introducing a fresh genre and style into the art form of the novel. *Churaumanie Bissundyal, Sanskrit Scholar, Literary Critic, Playwright and Novelist.*

Praise for The Other Side of The House
"A rare Literary Gem...' *Caribbean New Yorker*

Praise for *Suwan and The Circle of Seven*
Balkrishna Naipaul's skill in seeing the world through the eyes of child abuse is the most impressive pieces of writing I have come across
– *Prof.Kevin McCabe, Poet and Literary Critic*

Praise for *The Yoga of Love*:
The Yoga of Love is the crème de la crème of Mr. Naipaul's Trilogy: where story line enmeshes with social philosophy and where, Meena, a child from the crèche develops into the most radiant of women – and where the yoga of love is brought to life. *G-Times Literary Supplement*

Praise for *Legends of The Emperor's Ring*: The language of the book is reminiscent of D.H. Lawrence's *Women in Love* and Scott Fitzgerald's *The Great Gatsby*. His lyricism sweeps and enwraps the reader in a sweet suspension between realism and surrealism. *Churaumanie Bissundyal, Literary Critic and Playwright.*

Praise for *Arc Of The Horizon*
Balkrishna Naipaul has shown, in Arc Of The Horizon, to be a present day Shakespeare, in so far as his mastery of the English language and understanding of the human spirit are concerned. *Eugene A. Bronson, author, Spiritual Dawn: A Spiritual Autobiography*

www.ingramcontent.com/pod-product-compliance
Lightning Source LLC
Chambersburg PA
CBHW072001150426
43194CB00008B/959